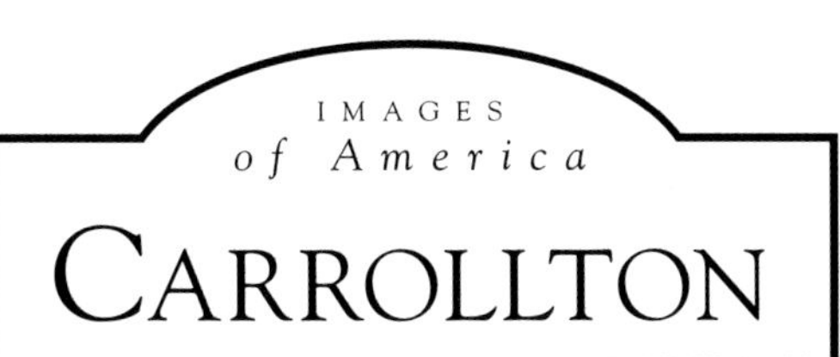

CARROLLTON

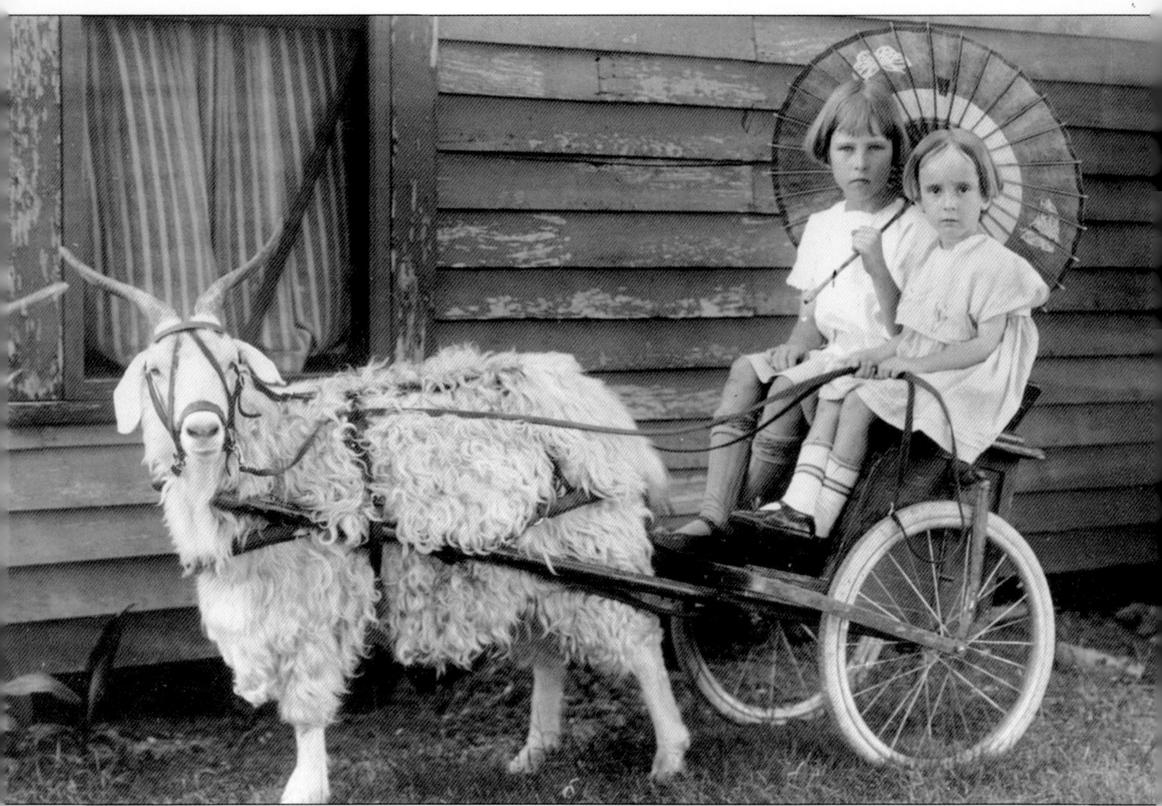

MAUREEN AND MARY FRANCES DAVIS. This nostalgic photograph of two little girls sitting in a cart pulled by a goat in front of the family's weathered homestead is of two great-granddaughters of the Reverend David Myers, who was one of Carrollton's earliest settlers and a community leader. (Courtesy of Hal Simon, Nix family collection.)

ON THE COVER: **CARROLLTON DEPOT.** Three railroad lines intersected at the Carrollton depot. The Cotton Belt line ran east and west; the Dallas and Wichita, which later became the Missouri, Kansas, and Texas line (MKT or "Katy"), ran north and south; the St. Louis and San Francisco ("Frisco") ran from the south to Carrollton and then northeast. The railroads provided both passenger and freight services, establishing Carrollton as a major shipping point for cotton, cattle, and bricks by the early 1900s. In 1924, a portion of the Katy track was electrified to accommodate the passenger cars of the Dallas-to-Denton line of the Texas Interurban Railway. The last passenger train service through Carrollton was on August 17, 1935, when the Cotton Belt train from Addison to Fort Worth was discontinued. (Courtesy of Fancy Oliver Tanner.)

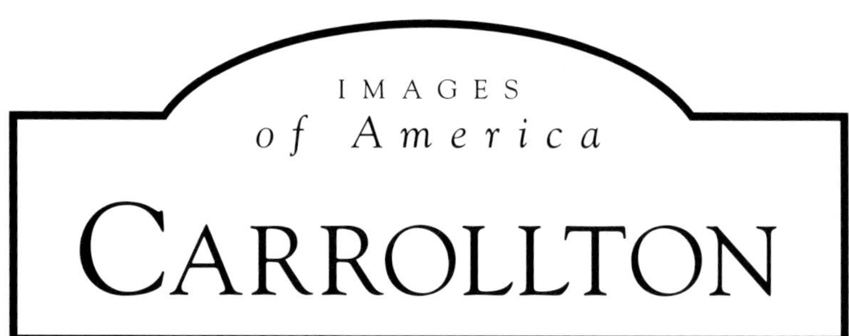

Toyia Pointer

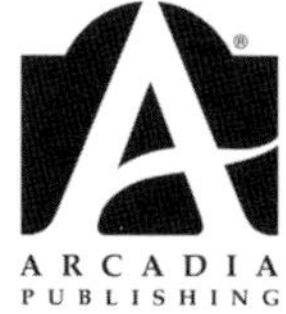

Published by Arcadia Publishing
Charleston SC, Chicago IL, Portsmouth NH, San Francisco CA

Printed in the United States of America

Library of Congress Catalog Card Number: 2008920085

For all general information contact Arcadia Publishing at:
Telephone 843-853-2070
Fax 843-853-0044
E-mail sales@arcadiapublishing.com
For customer service and orders:
Toll-Free 1-888-313-2665

Visit us on the Internet at www.arcadiapublishing.com

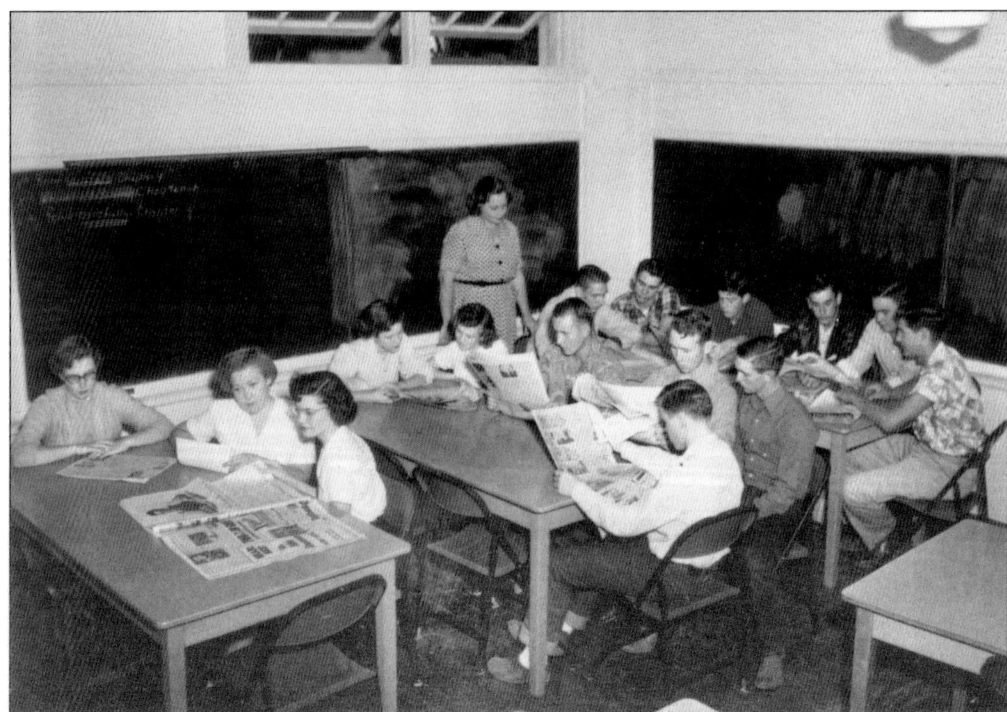

GEORGIA MYERS OGLE'S JOURNALISM CLASS, 1952–1953. A native of Carrollton and a descendant of pioneer families, Georgia Myers Ogle worked in the Carrollton school system until her retirement. She taught courses in English and journalism and encouraged and guided her students. Ogle was a dedicated local historian and a charter member of the Peters Colony Historical Society, as well as its first president. Ogle later researched, wrote, and published the book *Elm Fork Settlements: Farmers Branch and Carrollton*. The book is an invaluable source of historical information on the early development of these two cities. (Courtesy of the A. W. Perry Homestead Museum, Ogle Collection.)

CONTENTS

ACKNOWLEDGMENTS

The intent of *Carrollton* is to present photographs that will be interesting to the casual reader and to share little-known facts about Carrollton and its development, as well as to spotlight the collection of photographs held by the A. W. Perry Homestead Museum. There are many more individuals, families, and events that made important impacts on Carrollton but who are not represented within these pages due to space limitations. Photographs were obtained from known and available sources, particularly the collections compiled by Georgia Myers Ogle, which were donated to the A. W. Perry Homestead Museum, and the collection compiled by Peggy Perry Oliver and made available by her family. Both of these women were dedicated local historians and preservationists who diligently collected, preserved, and identified these photographs.

The collection of photographs presented in this book would not have been possible without the contributions of many other people as well. The book relied on the large number of photographs in the collection of the A. W. Perry Homestead Museum, and I would like to thank the City of Carrollton and the Parks and Recreation Department for focusing on preservation. Individual contributors include Fancy Oliver Tanner, Howard J. Cox, Hal Simon, Willie Rainwater, Linda Sollinger, and Ed Williams. A special acknowledgement goes to the members of the Peters Colony Historical Society, who enthusiastically celebrate and preserve the area's history through their publications so they can be shared with future generations. I am grateful for the assistance of Lynette Jones in the Carrollton Public Library and Christopher Barton in the City of Carrollton's Urban Development Department. I also want to thank Hal Simon, a descendant of two of Carrollton's earliest residents, the Nix and Myers families. He is a colleague in the museum field who has mentored and guided me since my arrival in Carrollton and graciously assisted in editing this book.

Last but not least, I want to thank my patient and understanding family, especially my daughters, Sylvie and Emma, who offered me sweet encouragement, and Paula Pointer for assisting me while I spent many late nights and entire weekends sorting through images and writing.

INTRODUCTION

Carrollton grew from a small group of settlers that came to this area beginning in the 1840s from places like Illinois, Kentucky, Tennessee, Indiana, and Missouri and from as far away as England and Ireland. These early settlers planted the first seeds of community by building homes, schools, churches, and businesses in the late 1800s and early 1900s. From this first group, Carrollton grew to 150 people in 1885 and continued developing into a thriving Dallas suburb, with its largest population growth taking place between 1970 and 1980 when it increased by 193 percent. Carrollton's historic past is evident in the remaining structures that surround its old downtown square, including the train depot and the homes of the Carrollton Heights Historic District.

William and Mary Larner were the first to come to the area in 1842. The Larners and other families came in response to the advertising of the Peters Colony Company, which sought to attract families to Texas with the promise of free land and a chance for prosperity. The Peters Colony Company was comprised of 20 businessmen, 11 of which resided in London, England. The company was led by William S. Peters and was headquartered out of the Louisville, Kentucky, music store of his son William C. Peters. They petitioned the Republic of Texas and were granted the first of four contracts on February 4, 1841, to settle a large portion of North Central Texas extending all the way to the Red River. Under the first contract, they were responsible for attracting 200 families. Each family would receive a section of land that equaled 640 acres. A single man qualified for half a section or 320 acres. In return, the company would get 10 sections of land for every 100 families it successfully settled. The last of the contracts expired in 1848, and because of the various contracts and because interests in the company changed hands often, there was much confusion over the actual ownership of the land. This confusion went unresolved until the 1850s.

Many of Carrollton's early residents came from Carrollton, Illinois. Among those were the Myers, Nix, Witt, Lee, and Perry families, who all arrived in the 1840s and took advantage of the offer of free land through the Peters Colony contract. Texas became a part of the United States in 1845. Other families emigrated from England, beginning with John and Mary Jackson and their eight children, who made the trip by boat across the Atlantic Ocean and then by wagon to Dallas County, Texas, in 1848. John Jackson, while still in England, purchased 640 acres of unseen land at the rate of 50¢ per acre. They were followed by the Morgan, Furneaux, and Rowe families, who made up what was known as the English Colony in the northeastern part of the area, extending into southern Denton County. These families were wealthy landowners who built elaborate homes on large estates. They displayed their European sensibility by giving graceful names to their elegant homes like Tor Hill, Hampstead, and Barton Hall.

Carrollton was fortunate to be at the intersection of three rail lines. The Dallas and Wichita was the first to lay down tracks and establish a depot in 1878. It later became the Missouri, Kansas and Texas, also known as the MK&T or "Katy." The Cotton Belt arrived in 1888, and the St. Louis and San Francisco, or "Frisco," intersected with the Katy by 1903. The railroads made it possible for Carrollton to become a vibrant place for both businesses and community. Carrollton was a center for shipping lumber, livestock, grain, cotton, and cottonseed. The manufacturing of bricks and the gravel industry developed in the early 20th century. Today these same rail lines are making it possible for Carrollton to become a hub of activity once again with the expansion of the Dallas Area Rapid Transit's light-rail commuter lines. The north/south line that will connect Carrollton to downtown Dallas is currently under construction.

After the city's official incorporation in 1913, private water and electrical utilities became available to residents living within city limits, which at that time measured about 1 square mile. The 1920s saw a volunteer fire department form, and a gazebo became the center of an active business district. Civic engagement and community sports began to play an important role. In the 1930s, Dallas oilman "Colonel" C. W. Josey purchased 70 acres in Carrollton and built a home on the site that came to be known as Josey Rancho, which eventually consisted of more than 1,000 acres on which they held rodeos and buffalo and Texas longhorn cattle were raised. A police department was added, and city services and infrastructure were expanded in the 1940s and 1950s. In 1963, Carrollton's schools were the first schools in Dallas County to be integrated. Carrollton grew rapidly in the 1970s as it transitioned from a rural community to a prosperous Dallas suburb. In 1976, the city participated in many U.S. Bicentennial–related celebrations, and volunteers restored and opened the A. W. Perry Homestead Museum to honor Carrollton's rural beginnings and courageous settlers.

Carrollton's population is now 120,000, and the landscape has changed considerably since its rural beginning. This is a perfect time to revisit Carrollton's history, and new residents and visitors alike will be pleased to discover the community's historic past.

One

COURAGEOUS SETTLEMENT
PETERS COLONY

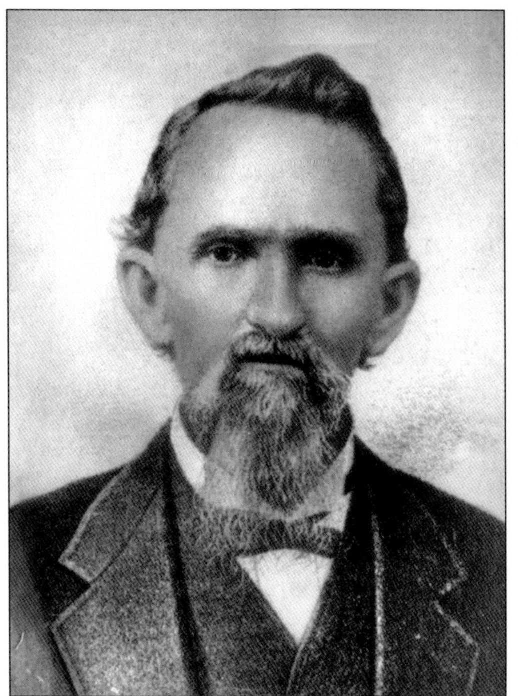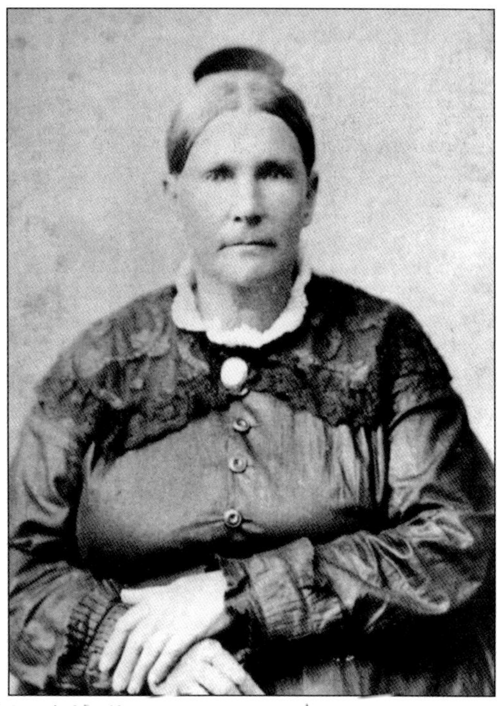

A. W. AND SARAH PERRY. Alexander Wilson and Sarah Huffman Perry married in 1840 in Greene County, Illinois. Along with their three young children and $30 cash, the young couple set off on their journey to the Republic of Texas in 1844 to claim one of the 640-acre sections of land that was being promised to immigrants willing to settle there by building a cabin and farming at least 10 acres. A. W.'s older brother Middleton Perry was already living in Texas near Lancaster at the time and was surely an influence on A. W.'s decision to come to the area. The Perrys' original "headright" property was located near I-35 and Trinity Mills. Later they would sell this property and acquire many more acres. (Both courtesy of A. W. Perry Homestead Museum.)

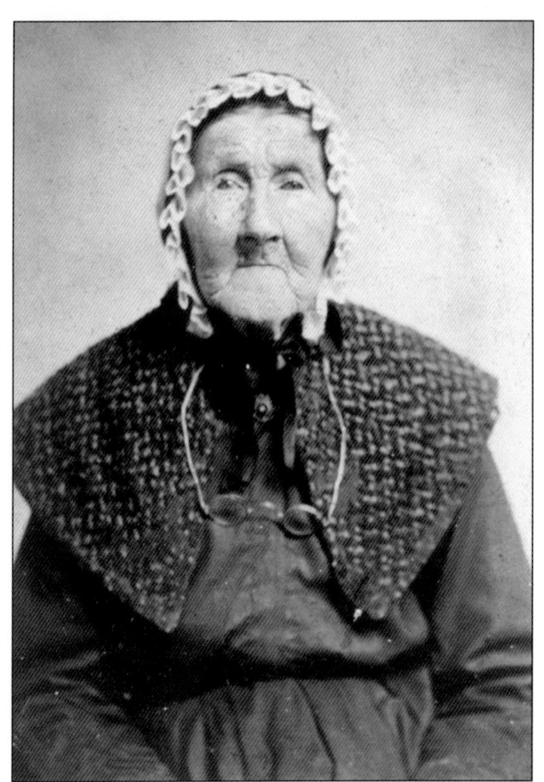

LETITIA REDDISH MYERS. David and Letitia Myers met and married in Kentucky and moved to Indiana and later to Illinois before beginning their immigration to Texas in the fall of 1845. They traveled with seven young children and at least three grown children and their families. Along the way, Letitia gave birth to the youngest of her 14 children, and the family did not reach Dallas County until March 1846. David Myers was a Baptist minister, and soon after their arrival, he established Union Baptist Church. Letitia's husband died in 1856, and she struggled to support her young children in the following years and during the Civil War. She later went to live with a son in Jack County and passed away in 1885. (Courtesy of Hal Simon, Nix family collection.)

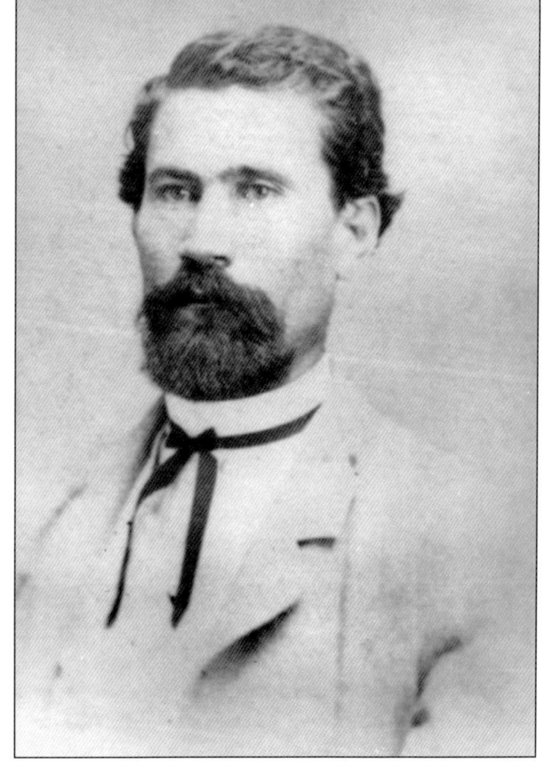

WADE HAMPTON WITT. Wade Hampton Witt was one of the original owners of the mill at Trinity Mills. By 1850, Witt was living in the Carrollton area. In the winter of 1861, he led a group of 100 men to defend against Native Americans raiding in Denton County and later served as a captain in the 18th Texas Calvary in the Confederate Army during the Civil War. (Courtesy of A. W. Perry Homestead Museum, Ogle Collection.)

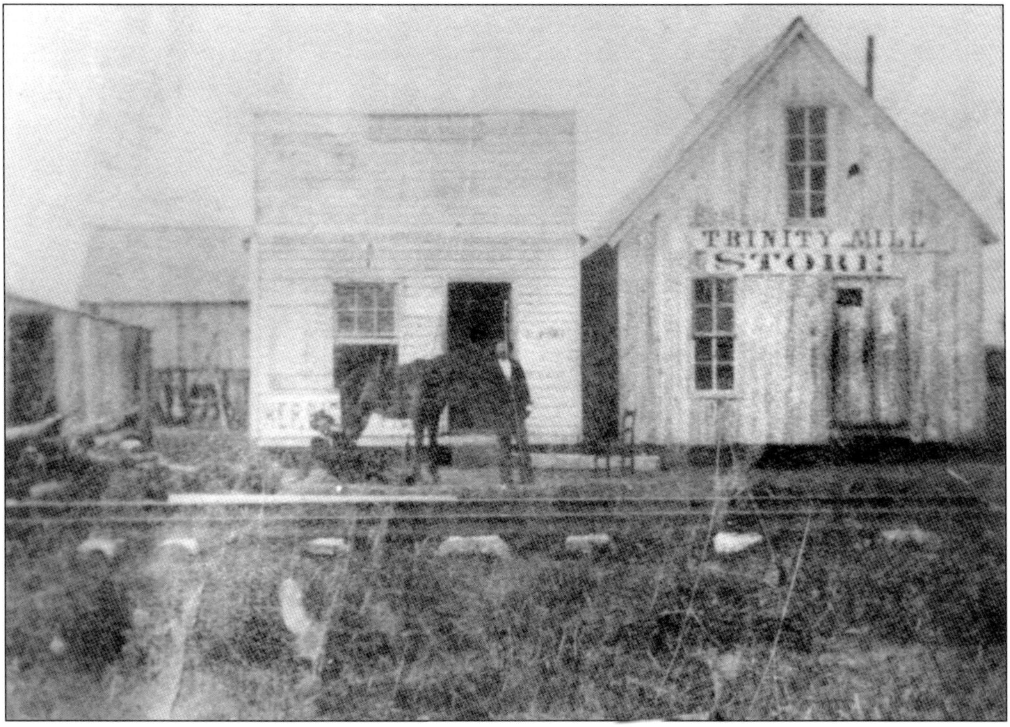

TRINITY MILL STORE AND BARN, C. 1860. Twin brothers Preston and Pleasant Witt came to the area in 1842 and established a mill east of Addison on White Rock Creek. Following them to the area were four other brothers, including Wade Hampton Witt. Around 1853, Wade Hampton and Preston Witt entered into a business relationship with A. W. Perry and built a two-story rock steam mill on his land in the area that later became known as Trinity Mills. In 1855, Perry sold his interest in the mill and the land to the Witts. The Trinity Mills Store and barn milled flour and timber. People came from miles around for the mill's services and to purchase supplies from the store. (Above, courtesy of Fancy Oliver Tanner; below, A. W. Perry Homestead Museum, Ogle Collection.)

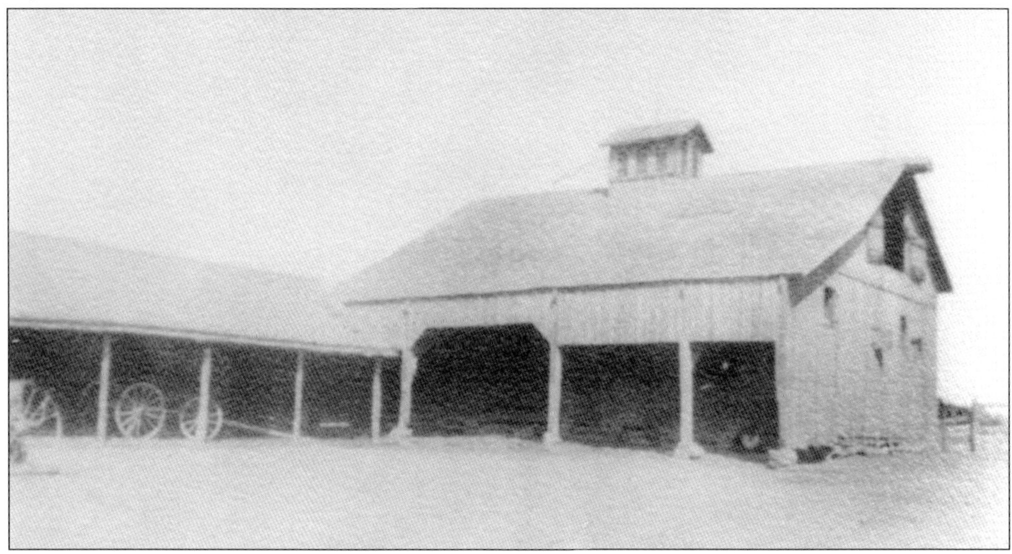

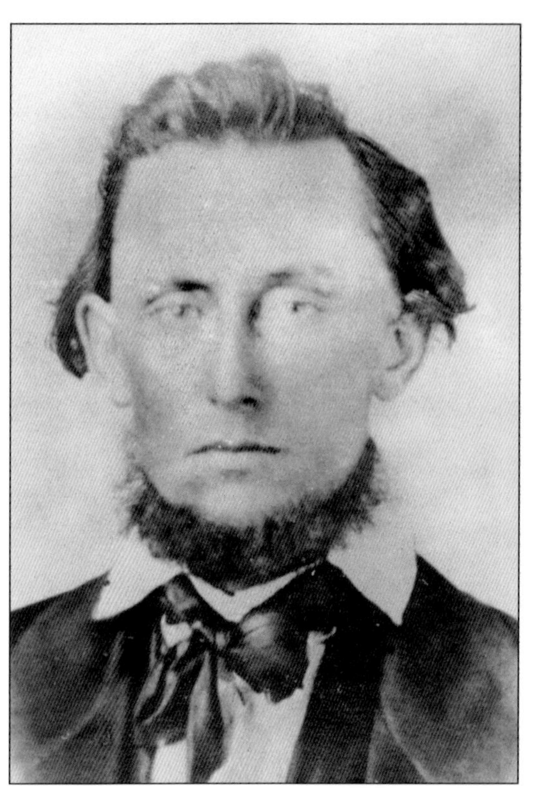

WESTERN AND SARAH NOBLE PERRY. Western Perry, the oldest of the Perry brothers, was influenced by the successful moves of two of his younger brothers, Middleton and Alexander, who had both settled in Dallas County. Middleton Perry was the first to emigrate and settled in the area that later became Lancaster. Western Perry immigrated to Carrollton in 1846 along with his wife Sarah Noble Perry and their nine children. Four more children were added to the family after the move to Texas. He was dedicated to and active in the Union Baptist Church. Church records show that he helped to build a school near his home in the Trinity Mills area. Western died in 1870, and both he and wife Sarah are buried in Farmers Branch's Keenan Cemetery. (Both courtesy of A. W. Perry Homestead Museum, Ogle Collection.)

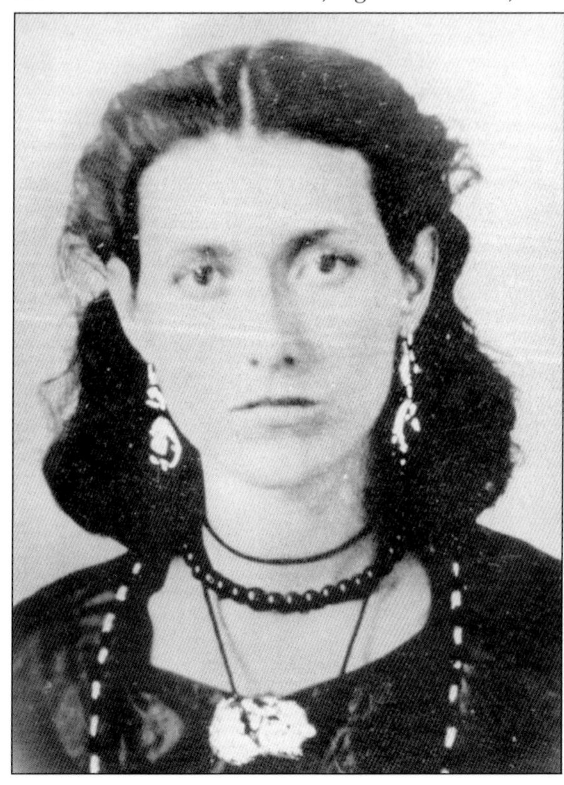

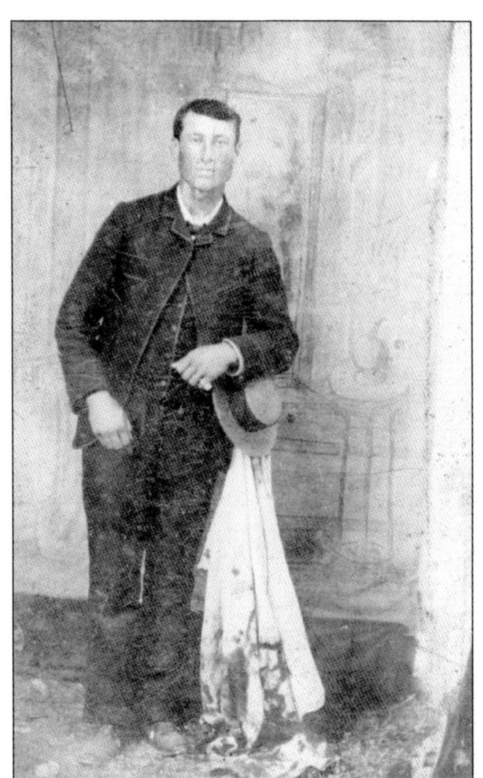

DAVID HARRISON AND MARY MYERS NIX.
As the oldest child of John and Sarah Nix, David Harrison Nix emigrated from Carrollton, Illinois, in the 1840s along with his parents and was issued his own section of land to cultivate. David married Mary Myers in 1857. Mary was the daughter of Rev. David Myers, who also came from Illinois in the 1840s. So many families migrated from Carrollton, Illinois, including the Perrys, Larners, Lees, Myers, Nix, and others, that many historians believe this is where Carrollton, Texas, got its name. (Both courtesy of Hal Simon, Nix family collection.)

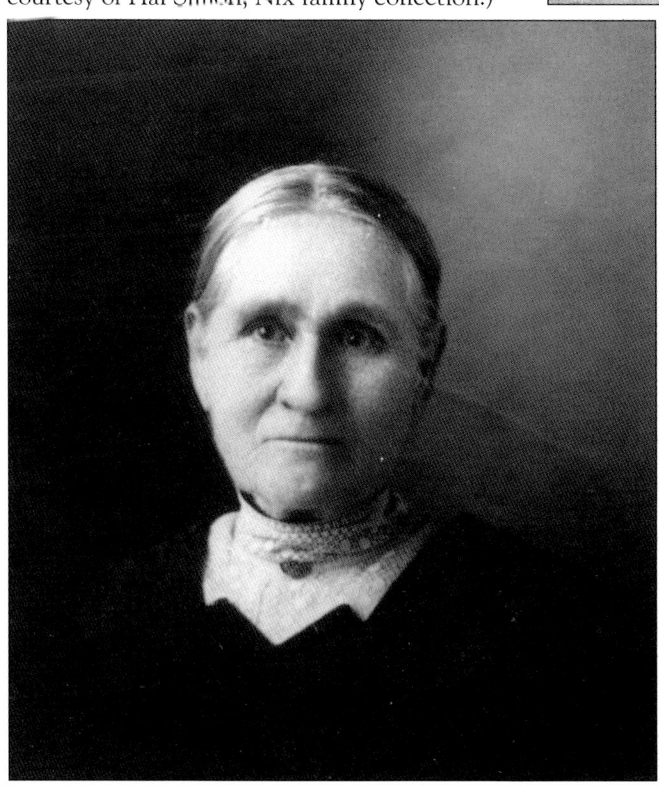

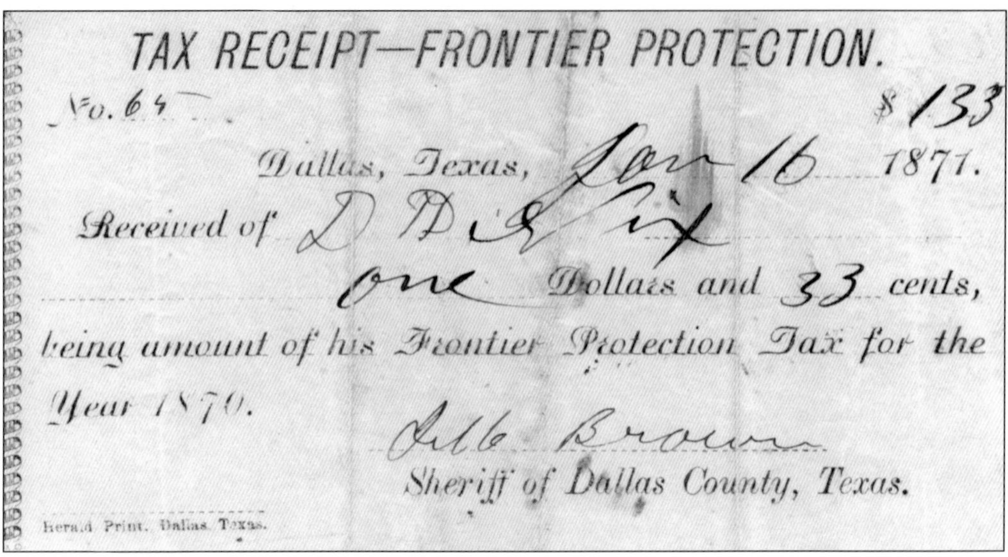

TAX RECEIPT—FRONTIER PROTECTION.

No. 64 . $ 133

Dallas, Texas, Jan 16 1871.

Received of D D Nix

One Dollars and 33 cents,

being amount of his Frontier Protection Tax for the

Year 1870.

Sheriff of Dallas County, Texas.

Herald Print. Dallas, Texas.

FRONTIER PROTECTION TAX RECEIPT, 1871. This tax receipt was issued to David Harrison Nix in 1871 by the Dallas County sheriff for frontier protection. In the early years of the Peters Colony settlement, groups of men would have relied upon each other to defend their homes and farms. (Courtesy of A. W. Perry Homestead Museum, Ogle Collection.)

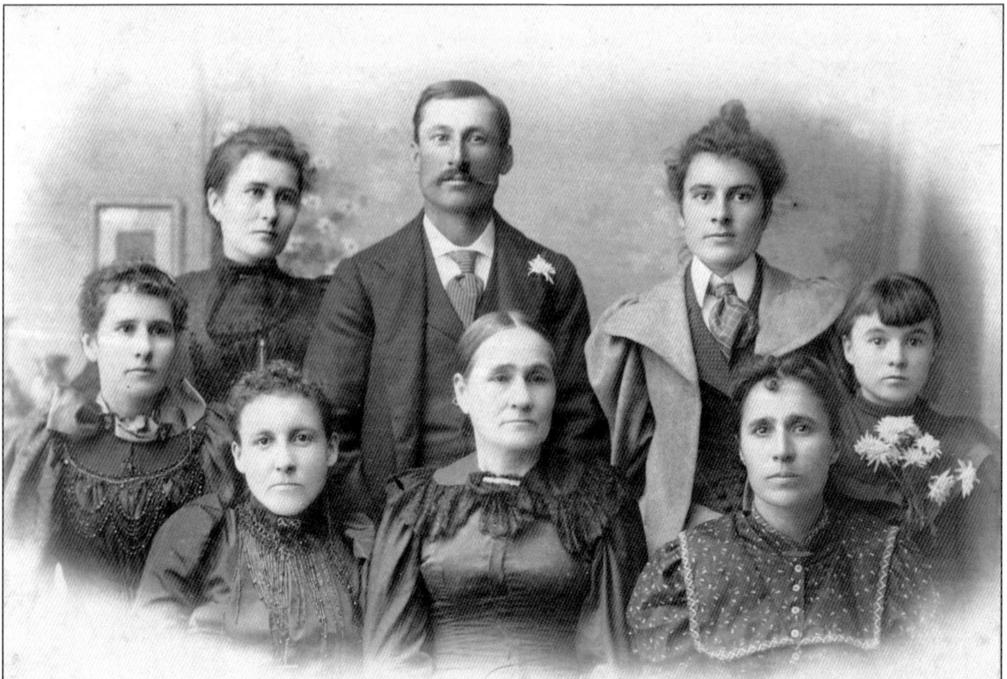

MARY MYERS NIX AND CHILDREN. Mary Myers was a daughter of the Reverend David Myers and his wife, Letitia Myers. She married David Harrison Nix in 1857, and they had seven children. Pictured here from left to right are (seated) Myrtle, Mary, and Ethel; (standing) Julia, Delia, Harrison, Ida, and Minnie. (Courtesy of Hal Simon, Nix family collection.)

14

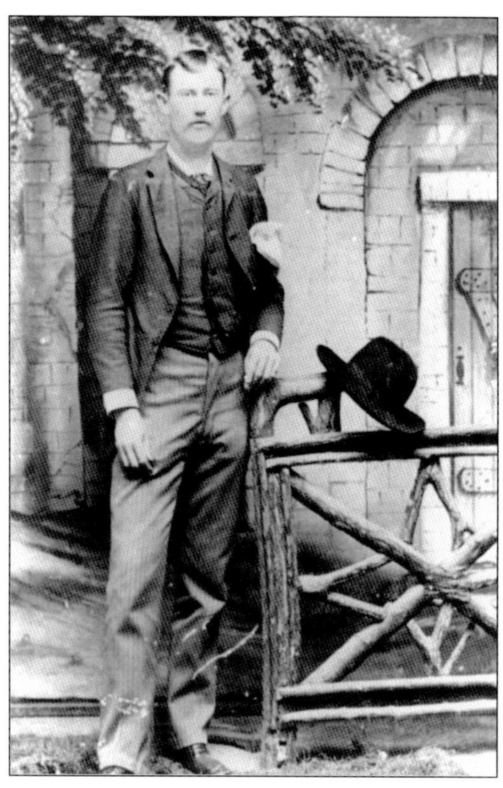

REV. ELI WITT. Born in 1816, these two portraits show Eli Witt as a young man and later near the age of 99. Eli Witt and five other Witt brothers came to Dallas County from Green County, Illinois, between 1842 and 1850. A Baptist minister, he served as the pastor of Union Baptist Church in 1856. He was also one of the charter members of the area's Masonic Lodge, which was established in 1858. The lodge building, or "hall," was located at Frankford Cemetery. The second floor was reserved for lodge meetings, and school and religious services took place on the first floor. (Both courtesy of A. W. Perry Homestead Museum, Ogle Collection.)

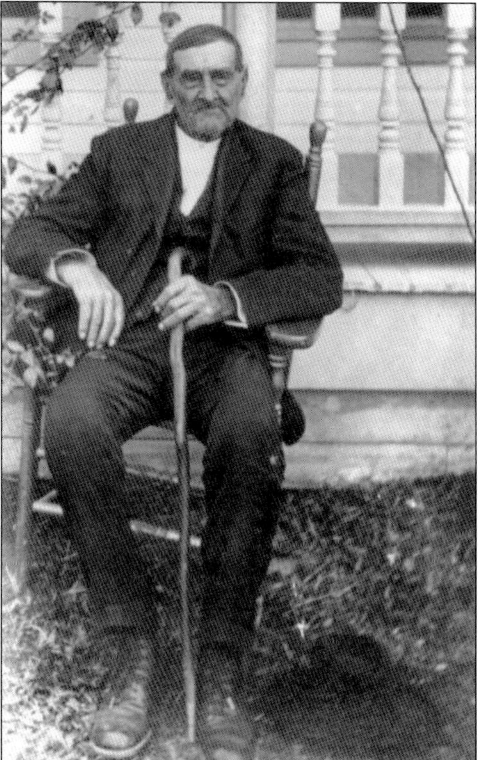

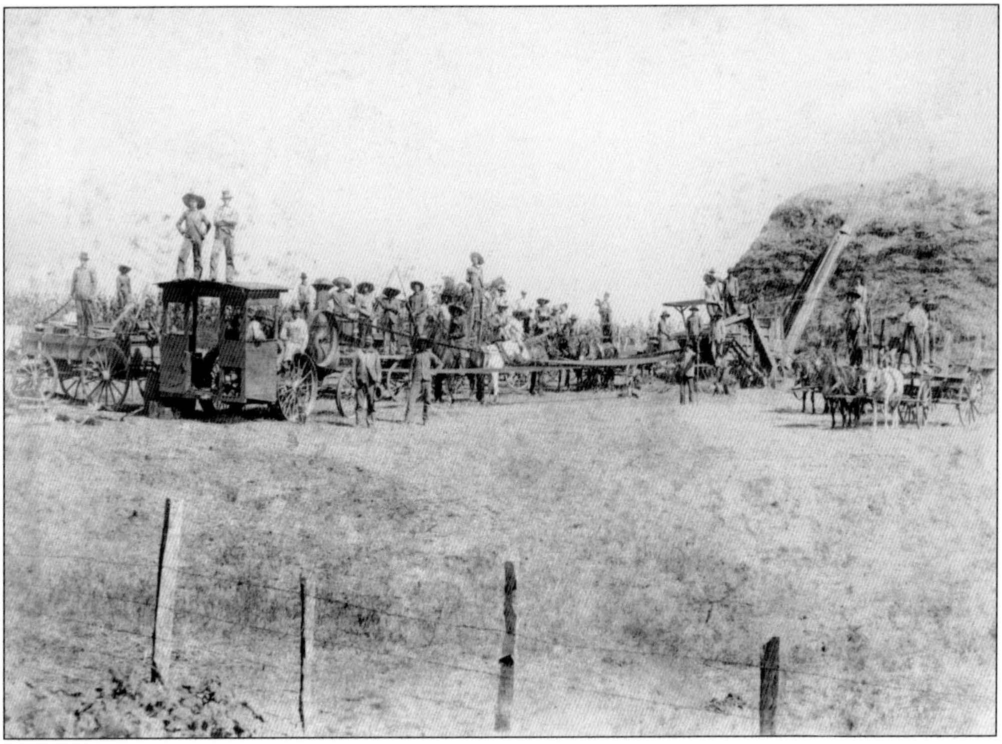

MORGAN FAMILY FARM, TOR HILL. Methodist minister John Henley Morgan came to Carrollton from Torquay, England, in the early 1850s. He married a Scottish woman, Margaret Oliver, who immigrated to Texas around 1858. A brother named Joseph Morgan joined them in 1860. Their farm, also known as Tor Hill, was located near the present-day community of Hebron in southeast Denton County. The couple constituted part of what was referred to as the "English Colony" because of the number of English families who immigrated around the same time to the area, which also included the Furneaux and Jackson families. These photographs depict a threshing crew at the Morgan farm around 1915. Threshing is the process of separating seeds or grain from straw after harvesting. (Above, courtesy of the City of Carrollton; below, A. W. Perry Homestead Museum, Ogle Collection.)

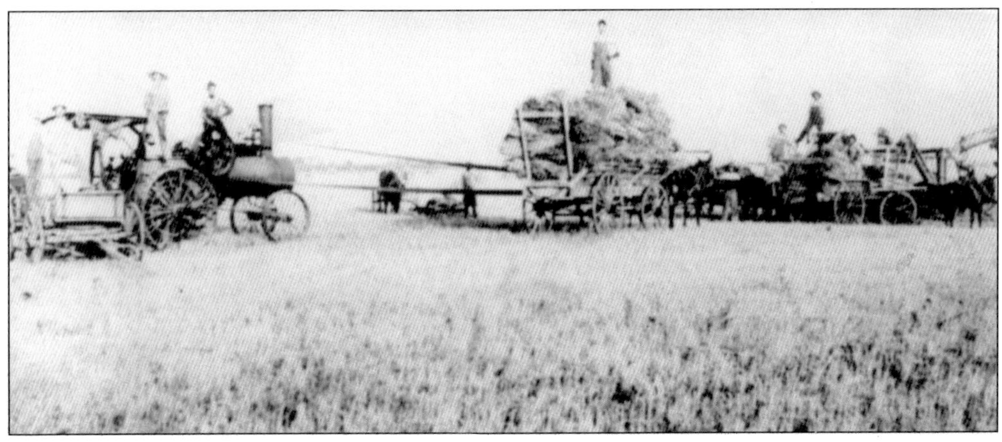

CARRIE MURPHY FURNEAUX. William Furneaux, who immigrated to Texas from Devonshire, England, in 1857, married Fanny Jackson, the daughter of John and Mary Jackson. The Jacksons emigrated from England in 1848 with their children. William was a successful farmer and businessman, and he owned a large estate in the southwest portion of Denton County that is now located within Carrollton's city limits. The Furneaux estate had a large, elaborate two-story home. (Courtesy of A. W. Perry Homestead Museum, Ogle Collection.)

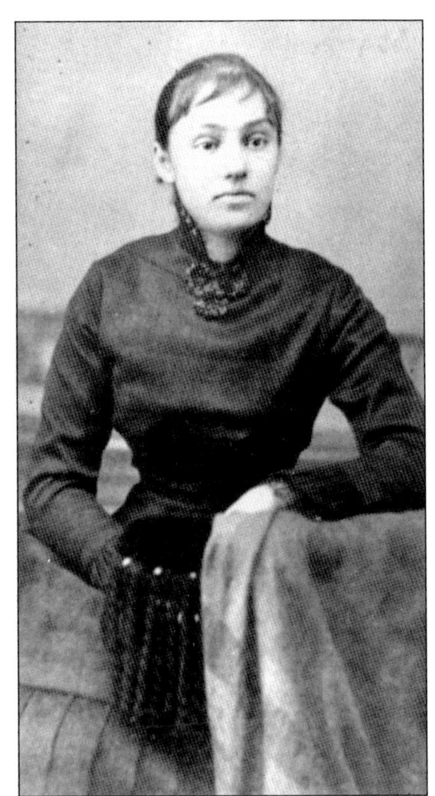

FRANK PERRY HOME. This stone home has been identified as the home of Frank Perry, which stood on present-day Crosby Road near Josey Lane. The woman in the photograph has been identified as Eula Warner Perry. Eula was the daughter of Judge John Warner, who emigrated with his family from Ireland in the 1850s. She married William W. Perry, a grandson of A. W. Perry. She is pictured with five of her eight children. One of her daughters, Vera Perry Lowrey, owned and operated the Carrollton's Plaza movie theater. (Courtesy of A. W. Perry Homestead Museum, Ogle Collection.)

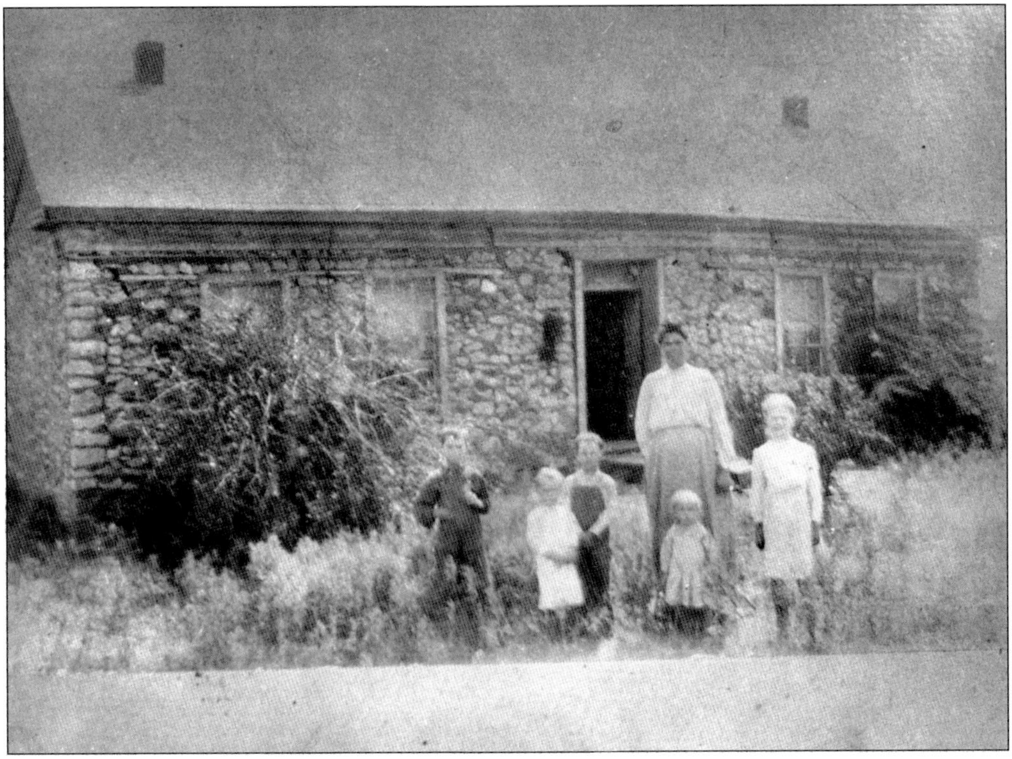

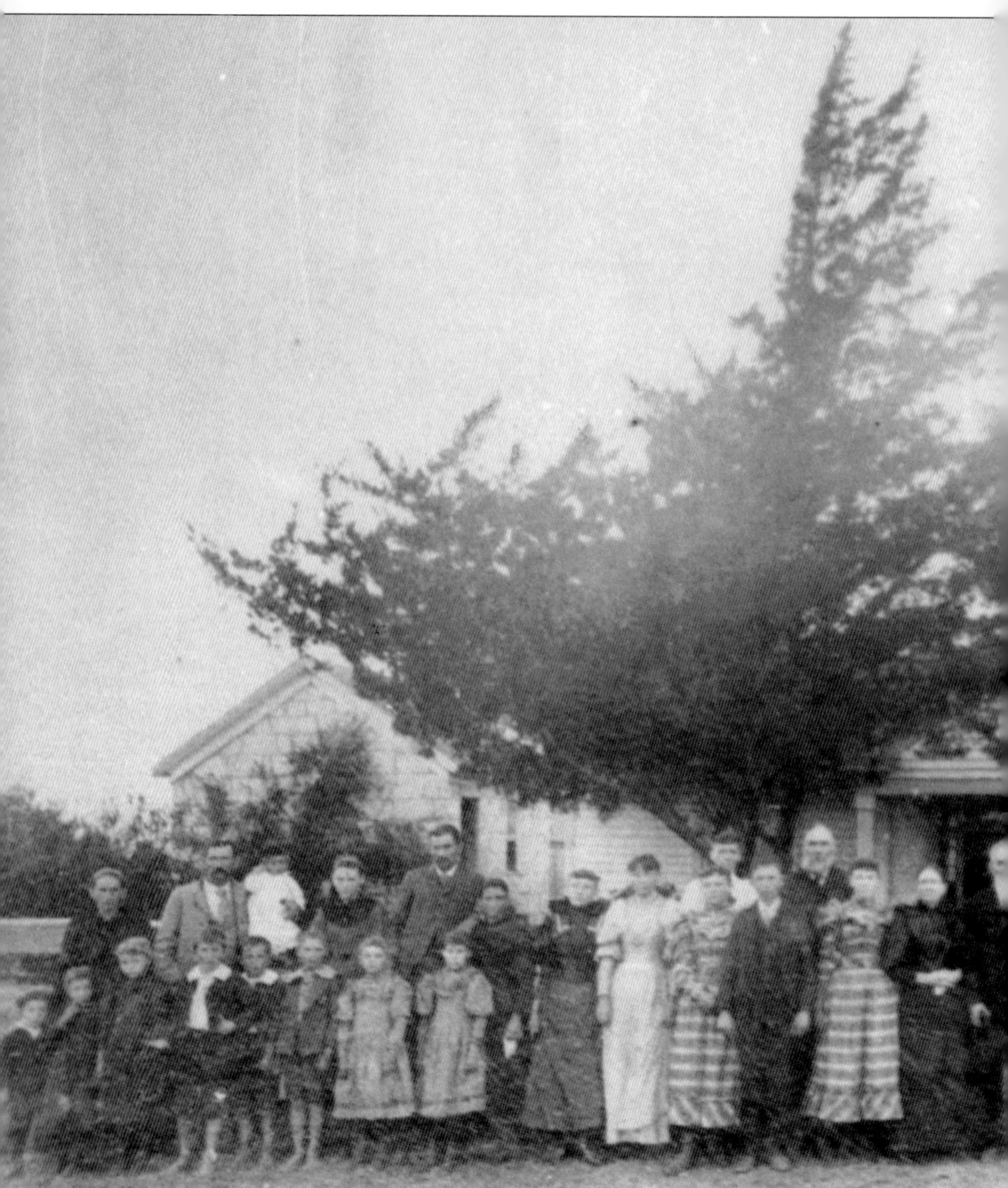

ALEXANDER WILSON PERRY FAMILY, 1895. This photograph was taken of the Perry family at a gathering in front of A. W. and Sarah's home, a simple wood-framed structure with a separate kitchen built of stone (left). Like many families of the time, the Perry family was large; Sarah gave birth to 14 children and all but four survived to adulthood. A. W. and Sarah are in the center, the couple's sons and their families are on the right, and the daughters and their families are to the left. A. W. was a farmer and rancher; a stockman who bred horses and mules, as well

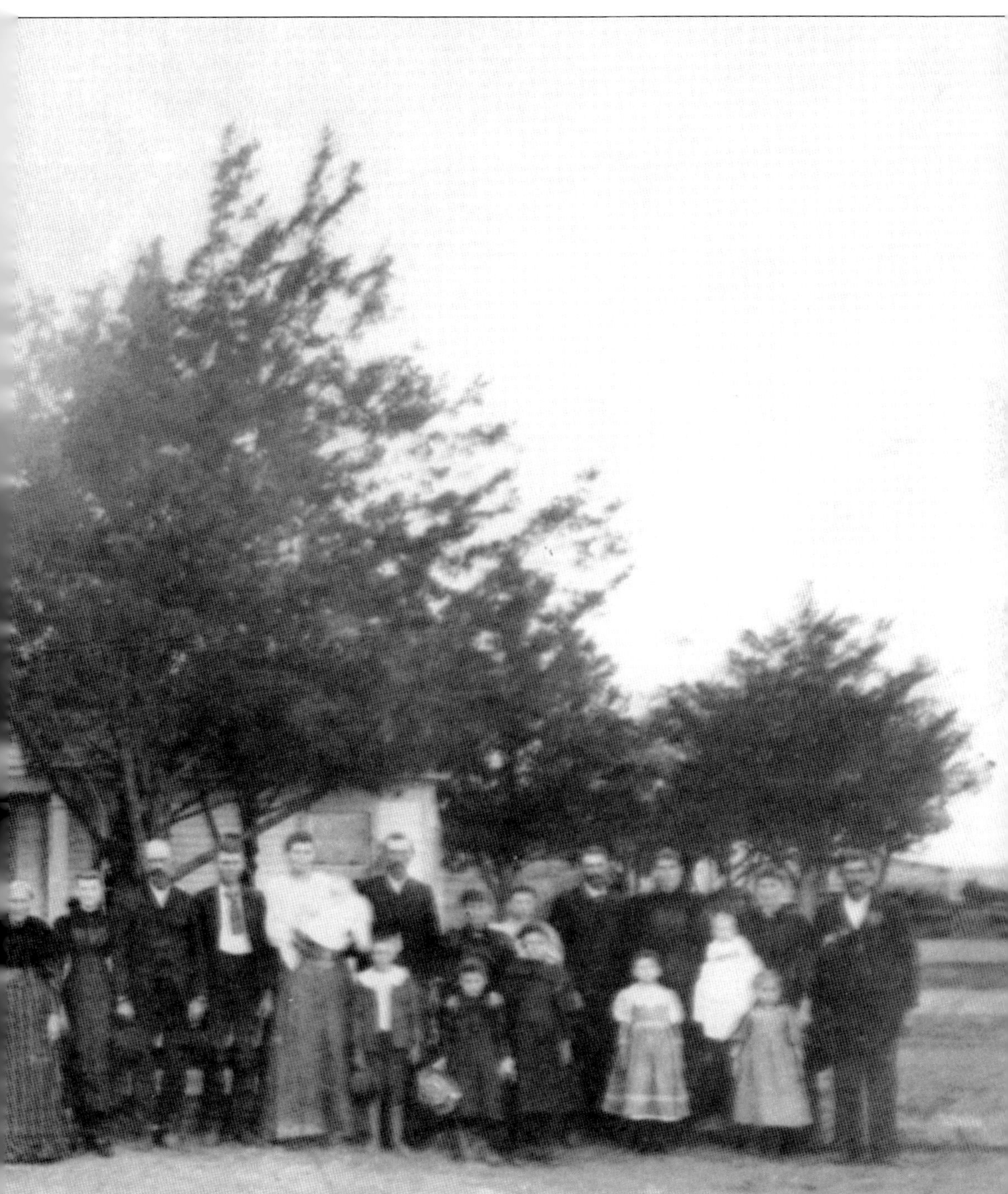

as raising cattle. He has been called the founder of Carrollton because he donated land for railroad rights-of-way and platted town lots. He also donated land for a train depot, schools, churches, and the first public cemetery. During his lifetime, he came to be known as one of Dallas County's most prominent citizens. Sarah died in 1896, and upon the death of A. W. in 1904, his property was divided between their surviving children. (Courtesy of A. W. Perry Homestead Museum, Ogle Collection.)

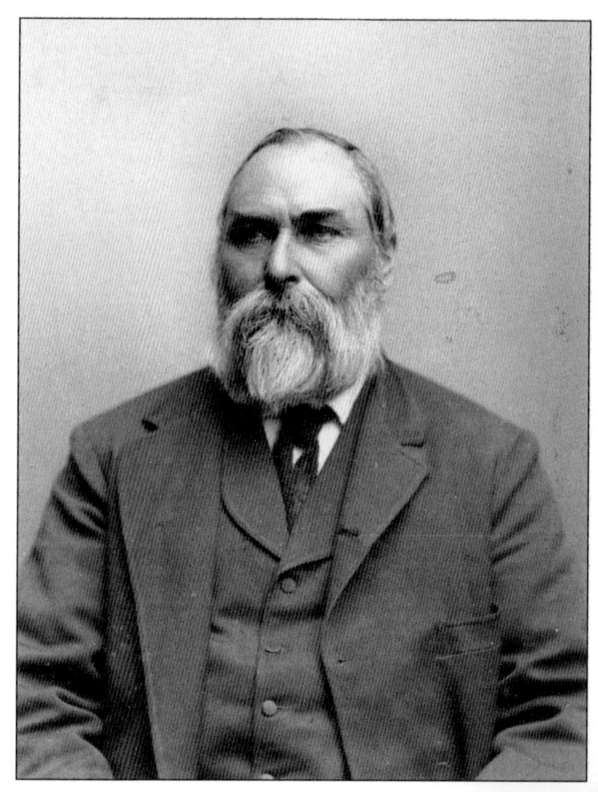

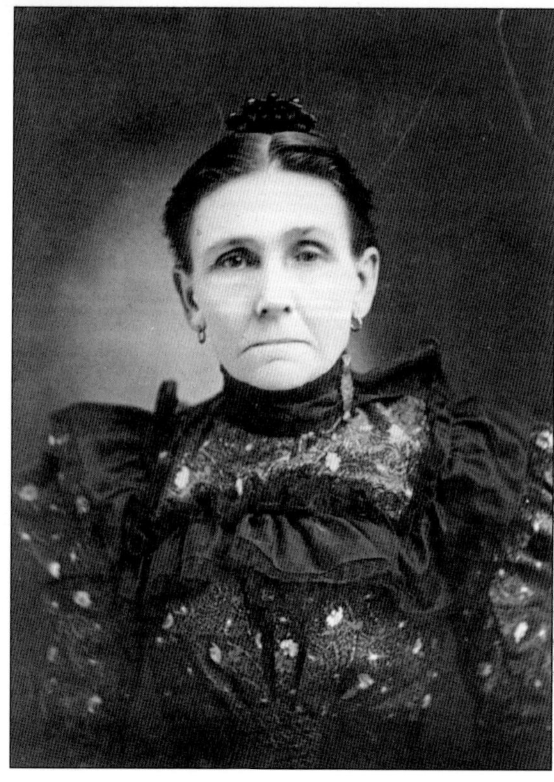

THOMAS AND HARRIET PERRY WARNER, 1880S. Thomas Warner's family immigrated to Texas from Cork County, Ireland, in 1852. Thomas traveled by ship with his parents and four brothers. Several of Carrollton's early families were from England and Ireland. They had been attracted by advertisements from the Peters Colony Company and the offer of free land. Thomas married Harriet Malinda Perry on January 27, 1870. The fifth child of A. W. and Sarah Perry, Harriet was born in 1848 in the area that later came to be known as Carrollton. (Both courtesy of A. W. Perry Homestead Museum.)

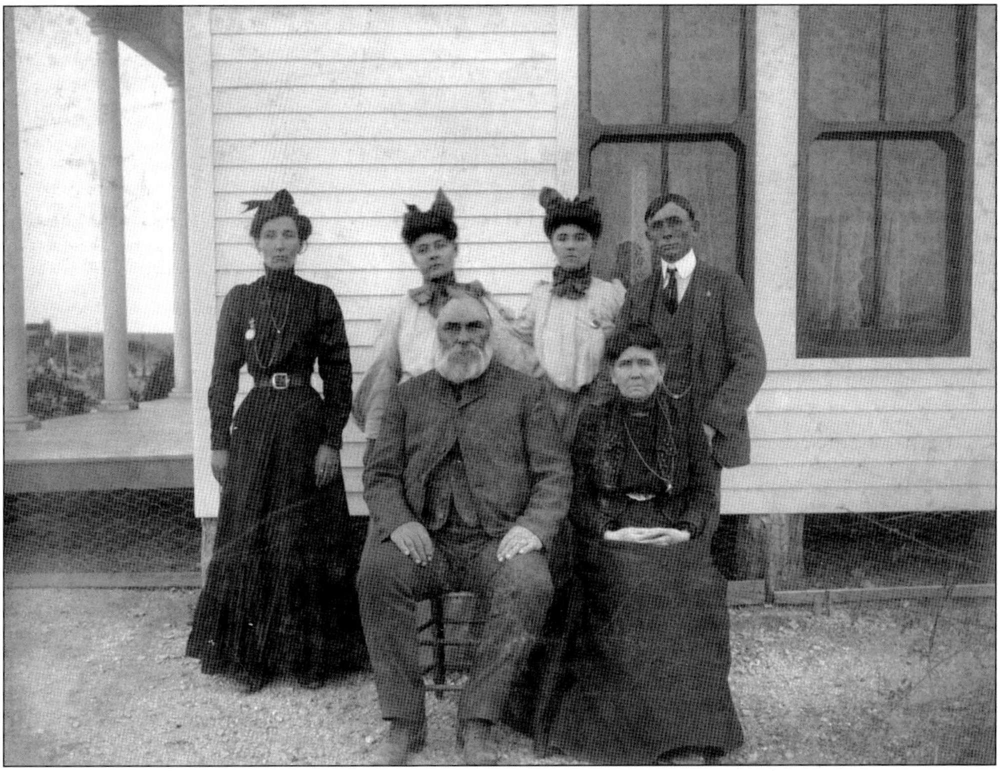

THOMAS WARNER FAMILY, 1904.
Thomas Warner and his wife, Harriet
Perry Warner, are shown with their
four children in front of their home,
which was known as Fair View Farm.
Pictured from left to right are Sue,
Kate, Lou, and Tom Warner. Their
two-story family home can be seen
in the background and featured a full
balcony extending over the porch
below. (Courtesy of A. W. Perry
Homestead Museum, Ogle Collection.)

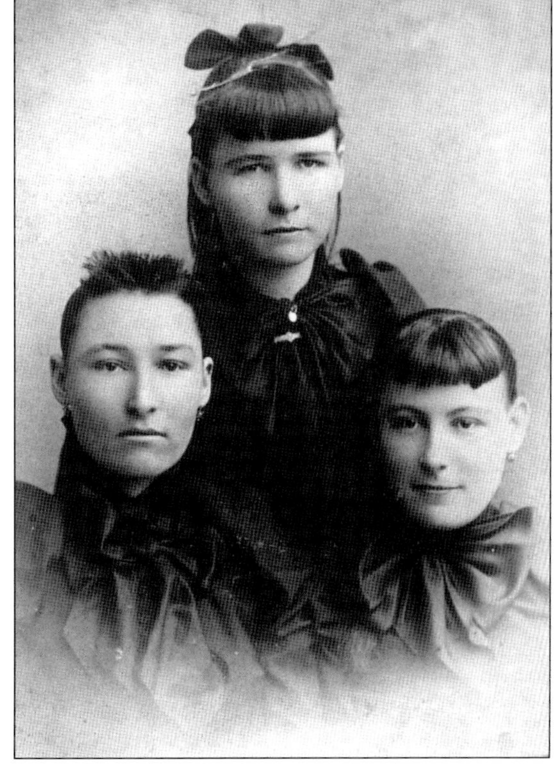

WARNER GIRLS, 1880s. Thomas and
Harriet Warner's three daughters, Kate,
Sue, and Lou, are shown from left to
right in this portrait as teenagers. A
"crayon portrait," a large, hand-colored
photograph, of this same image hangs on
display in the A. W. Perry Homestead
Museum. The larger version of this
portrait was donated by the Perry-Oliver
family on behalf of their cousin Fannidella
Webb Meadows, whose mother was Sue
Warner Webb. (Courtesy of A. W. Perry
Homestead Museum, Ogle Collection.)

21

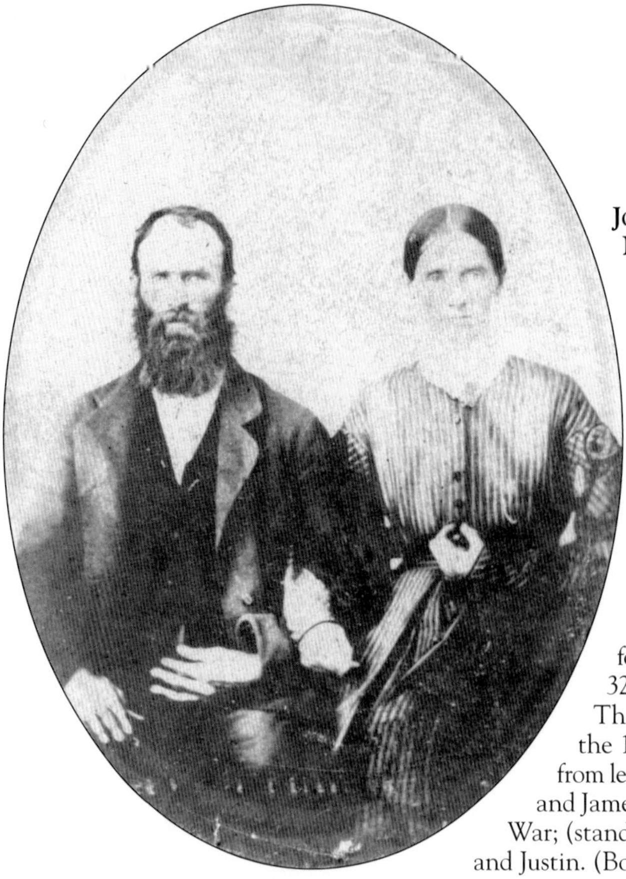

Joseph Harrison and Margaret Noland Cox and Sons. Joseph Harrison and Margaret Noland Cox are pictured in the small portrait (left). He was born in Virginia and she in Kentucky, where they married. The couple later immigrated to Missouri in 1843. In 1857, along with eight of their unmarried children, they moved to Texas after much of the land disputes between the Peters Colony, the settlers, and the state had been resolved. They purchased land in Carrollton from John Myers for $1,600 and later purchased another 320 acres from Joshua B. Lee for $600. The second portrait (below) shows 5 of the 11 Cox children, who are identified from left to right as (seated) Howard, Joseph, and James, each of whom served in the Civil War; (standing) two younger brothers Thomas and Justin. (Both courtesy of Howard J. Cox.)

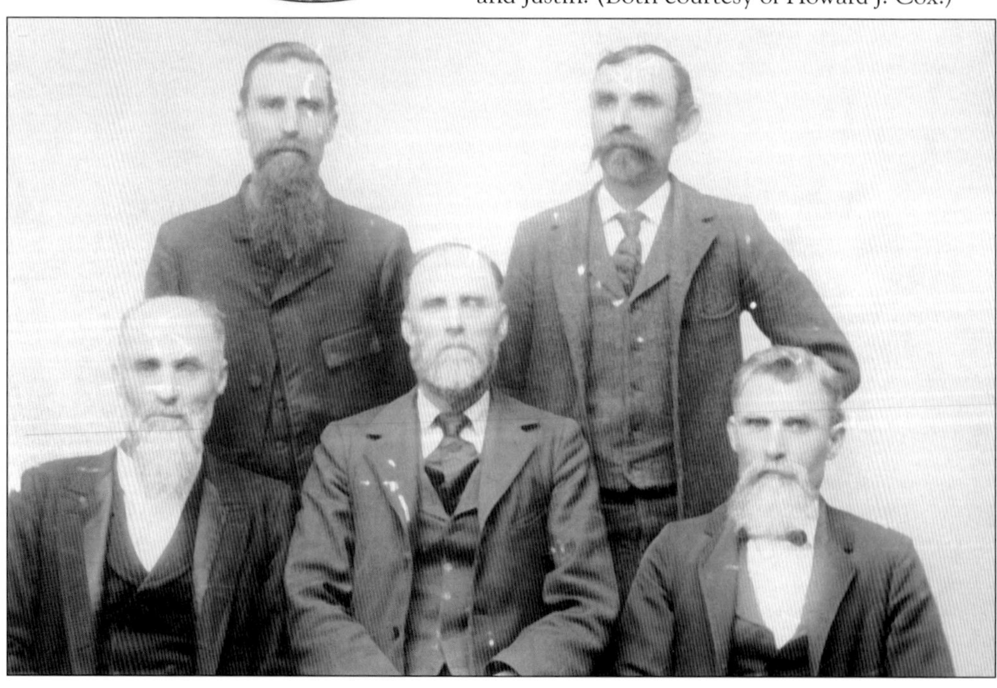

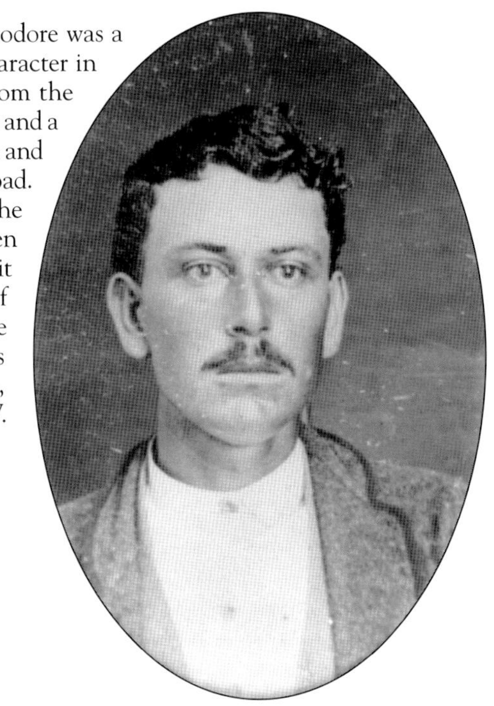

SANFORD COMMODORE PERRY. Sanford Commodore was a son of A. W. Perry and figures as the central character in one of the most tragic and notorious stories from the period. A small settlement, which included a store and a blacksmith's shop, was located between Carrollton and Trinity Mills just off present-day Old Denton Road. It was known as "Poor Town" after the owner of the store, George Poor. It was a place where local men and travelers could stop for a drink as well as visit the blacksmith. In a tragic event in the winter of 1875, Sanford was shot and killed while visiting the store. A grieving A. W. Perry issued a reward for his son's killer, but the accused relocated to California, and justice was never served. (Courtesy of A. W. Perry Homestead Museum, Ogle Collection.)

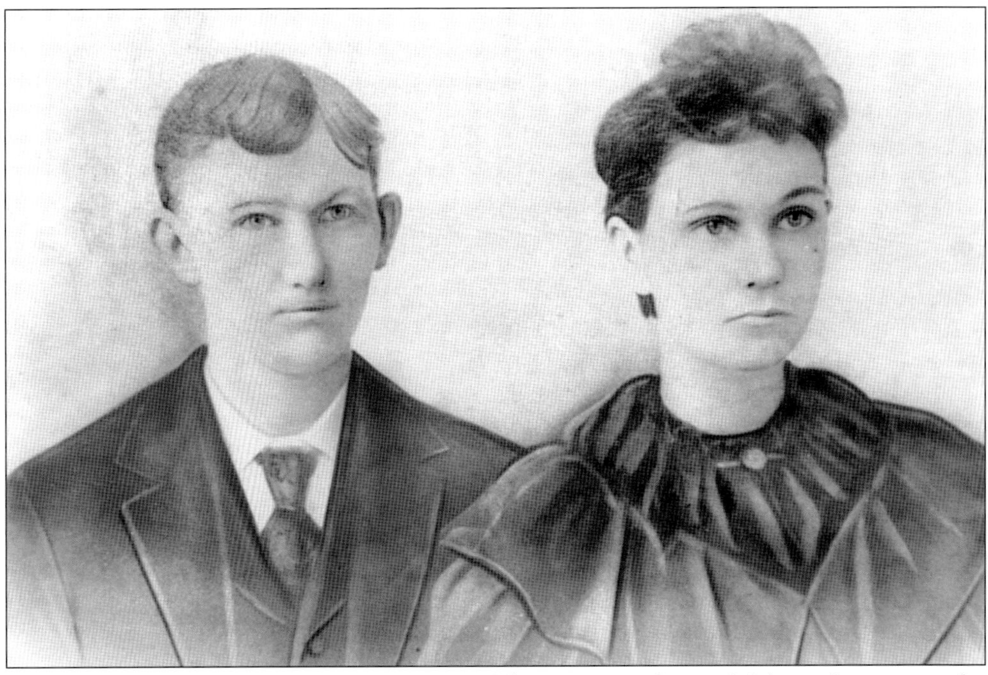

JAMES BOOKER BRYAN AND MAGGIE PERRY. This portrait of a youthful couple presents the grandchildren of two of Dallas County's earliest residents and community leaders. James Booker Bryan, a grandson of the founder of Dallas, John Neely Bryan, and Maggie Perry, the granddaughter of A. W. Perry. Bryan's father, John Neely Bryan Jr., moved to Carrollton with his family and his widowed mother, Margaret Beeman Bryan, and lived in the area of the present-day Josey Ranch property. (Courtesy of A. W. Perry Homestead Museum, Ogle Collection.)

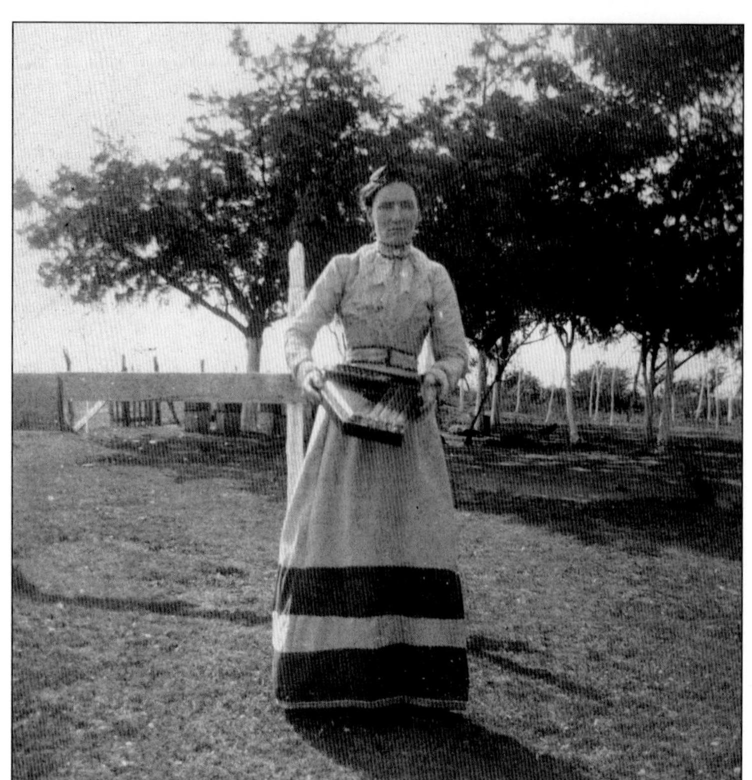

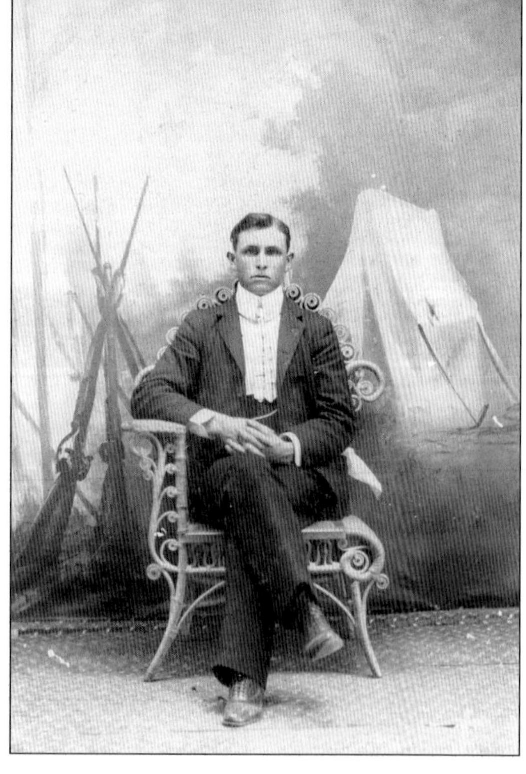

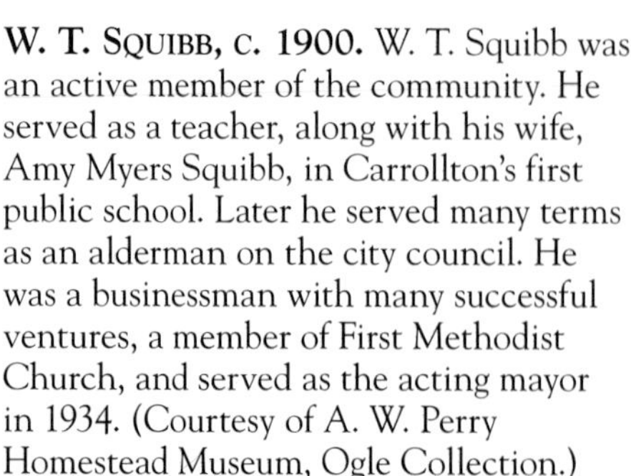

W. T. Squibb, c. 1900. W. T. Squibb was an active member of the community. He served as a teacher, along with his wife, Amy Myers Squibb, in Carrollton's first public school. Later he served many terms as an alderman on the city council. He was a businessman with many successful ventures, a member of First Methodist Church, and served as the acting mayor in 1934. (Courtesy of A. W. Perry Homestead Museum, Ogle Collection.)

Two

PRIDE AND PROSPERITY
SUCCEEDING GENERATIONS

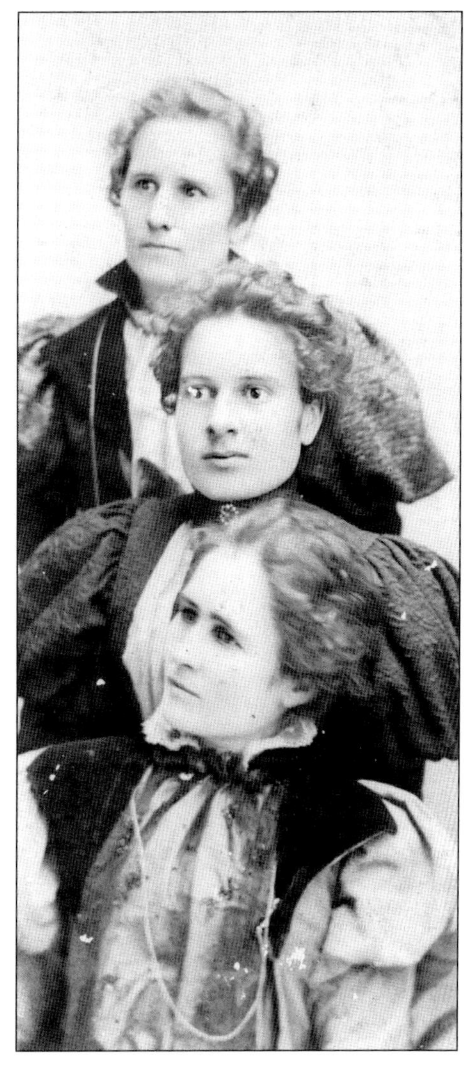

IDA, MYRTLE, AND MINNIE NIX. This photograph of three daughters of Mary Myers and David Harrison Nix illustrates the prosperity that succeeding generations of the original Peters Colony settlers experienced. At the time it was taken, Carrollton was well established as a hub of railroad activity and a central shipping point for cotton and cattle. While still primarily an agricultural community, its citizens had access to the luxuries and fashions of the day, as evidenced by the stylish clothing of the Nix sisters. (Courtesy of Hal Simon, Nix family collection.)

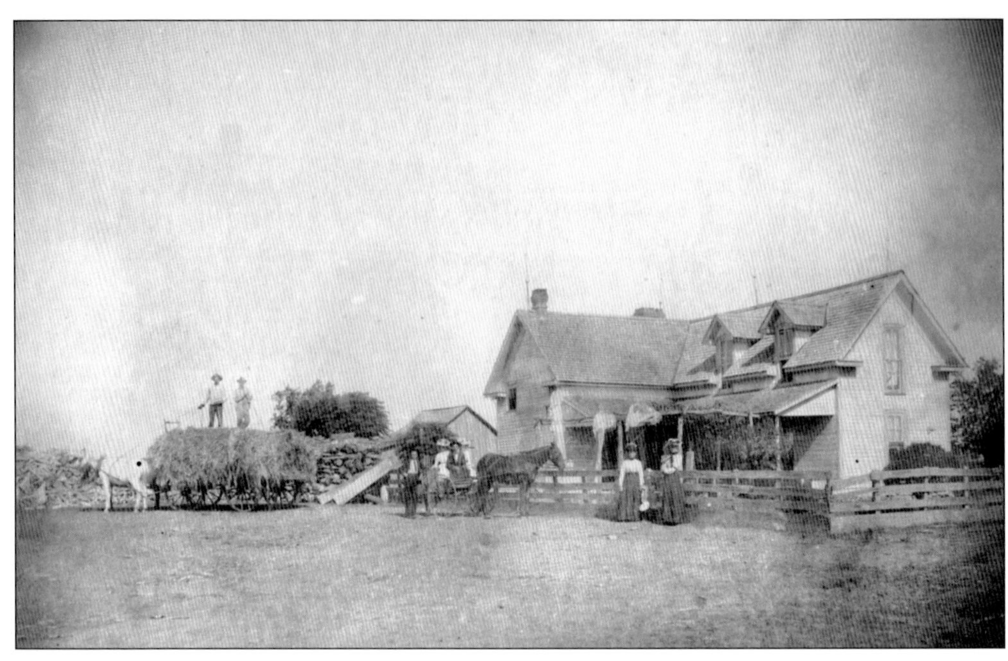

W. D. Fyke Home, c. 1915. This is the home and farm of William D. Fyke prior to 1916. W. D. was born in the Carrollton area in 1858 to pioneer parents Archer and Jemima Myers Fyke. He married Lura Dale Perry, daughter of A. W. Perry (also an original Peters Colony settler), in 1880 and the couple had four children. W. D. was a farmer and is credited as an excellent beekeeper and one of the largest producers of honey in the area. (Above, courtesy of A. W. Perry Homestead Museum, Ogle Collection; below, City of Carrollton.)

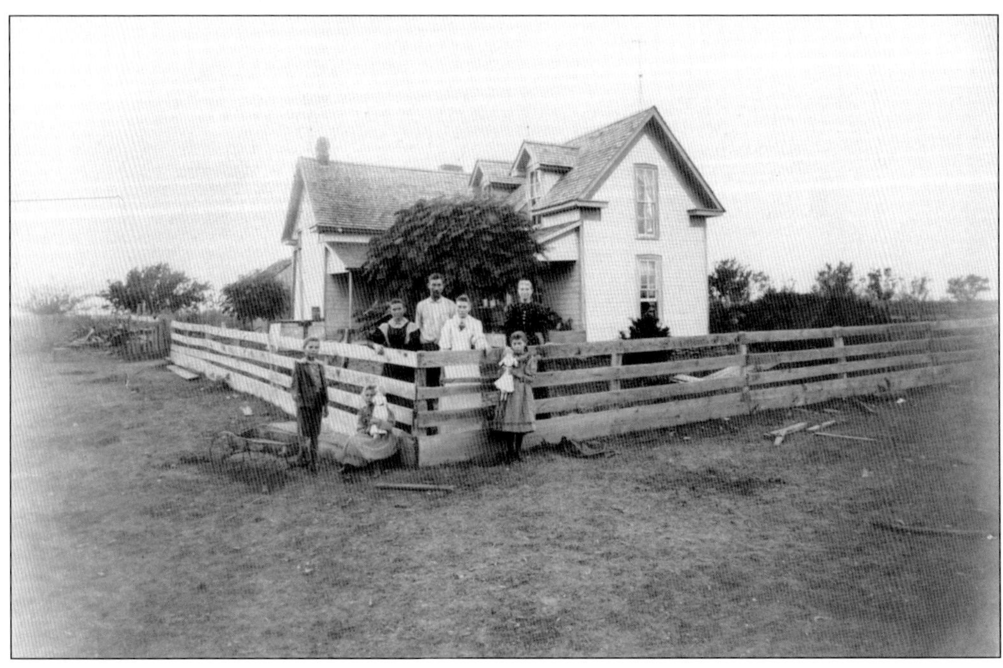

WILLIE D. AND HERBERT DARRELL MYERS.
Darrell Myers poses with his younger sister Willie
and a goat. These grandchildren of W. D. and
Lura Dale Fyke are representative of the first full
generation of Carrollton residents whose parents
had also been born in Carrollton. (Courtesy of A.
W. Perry Homestead Museum, Ogle Collection.)

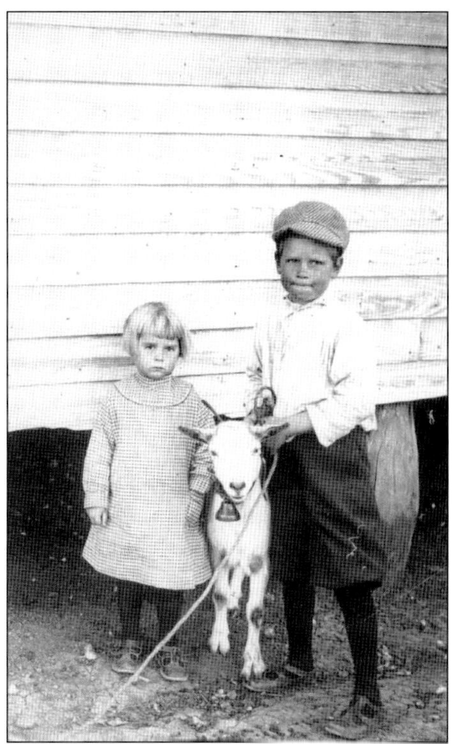

BRAKE CHILDREN AND DARRELL MYERS.
Grandchildren of Lura Dale Perry and W. D. Fyke
are shown in the yard of the family farm. Sisters
Averil, back left, and Emabel, far right, look on
as their much younger brother Fyke Brake poses
with a gun. Their infant cousin Darrell Myers is
seated second to the right. (Courtesy of A. W.
Perry Homestead Museum, Ogle Collection.)

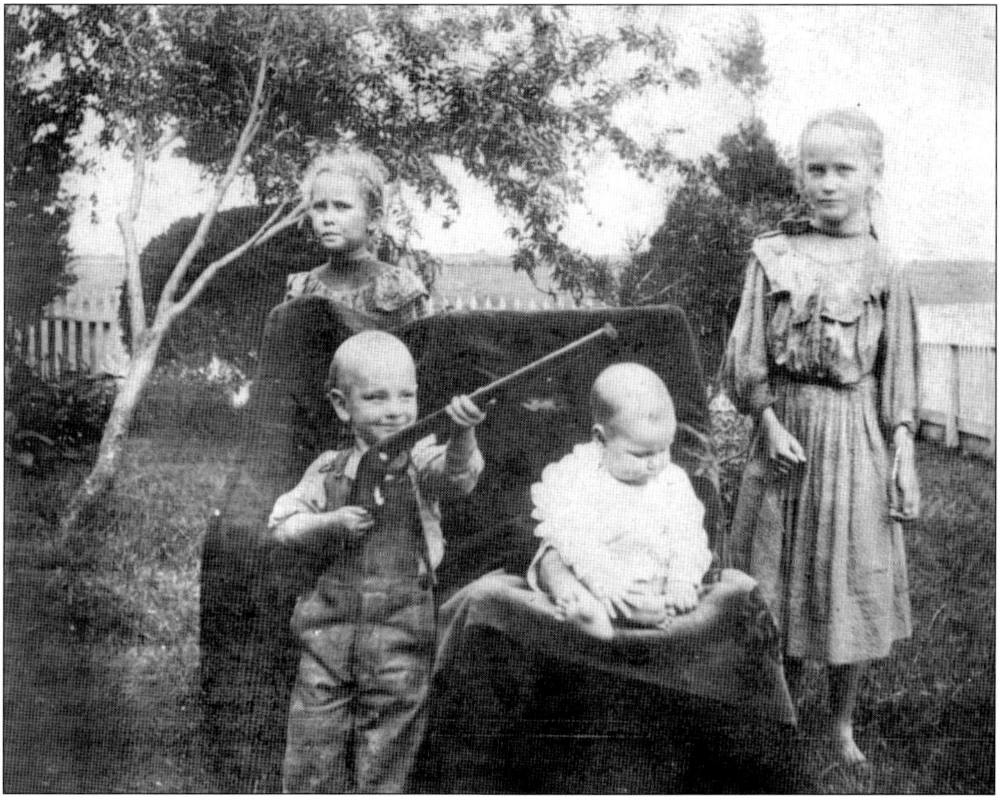

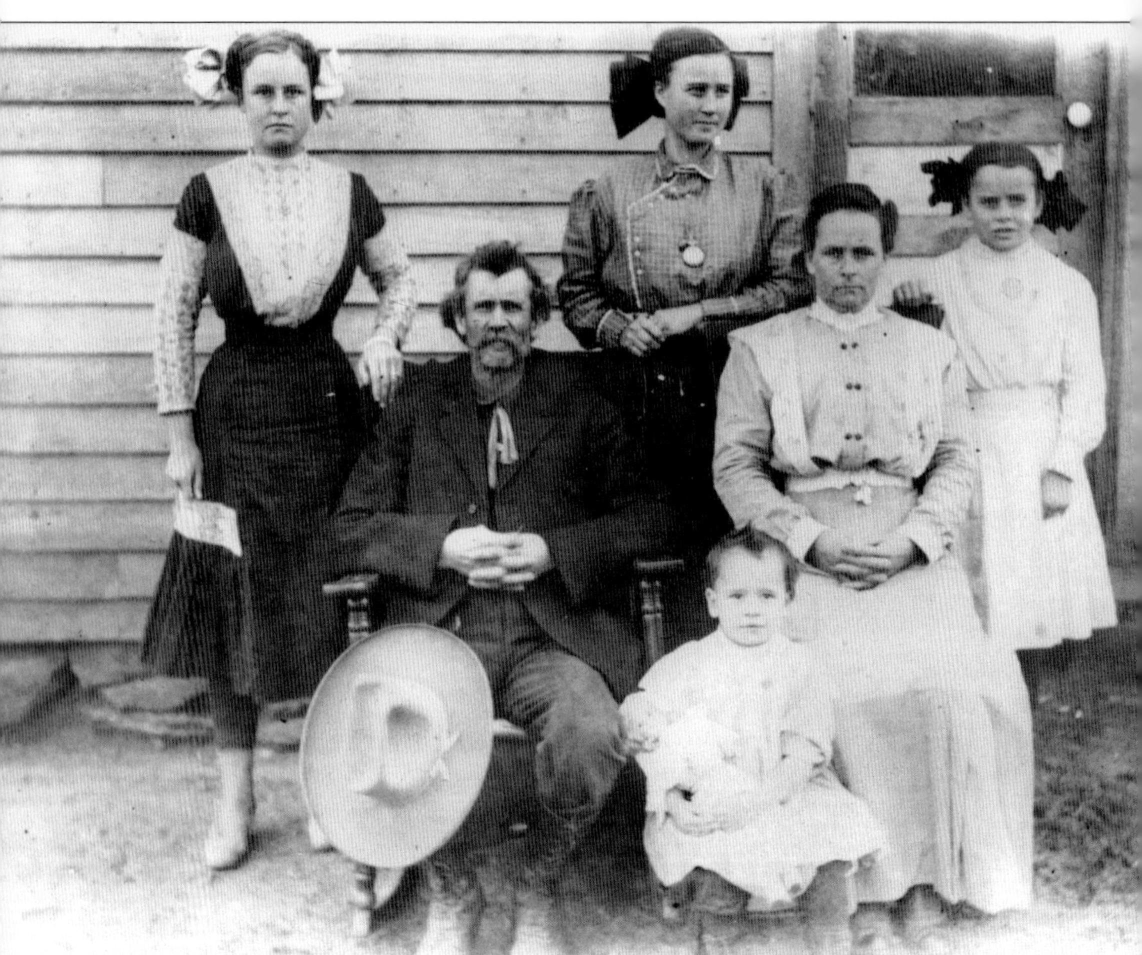

G. W. FYKE AND FAMILY. George Washington Fyke, a brother of W. D. Fyke, is shown here with his family. Pictured with him are his wife, Laura Brake, and their daughters, from left to right, (standing) Georgia, Jemima Pearl, and Elva; (seated) and Dale. In the background there is evidence of the common practice of using locally collected stones for home foundations. Using the wood of the indigenous "Bois d'Arc" tree, also known as Osage Orange, for foundation supports was also common. Wood from this tree was used because of its strength and availability. (Courtesy of A. W. Perry Homestead Museum, Ogle Collection.)

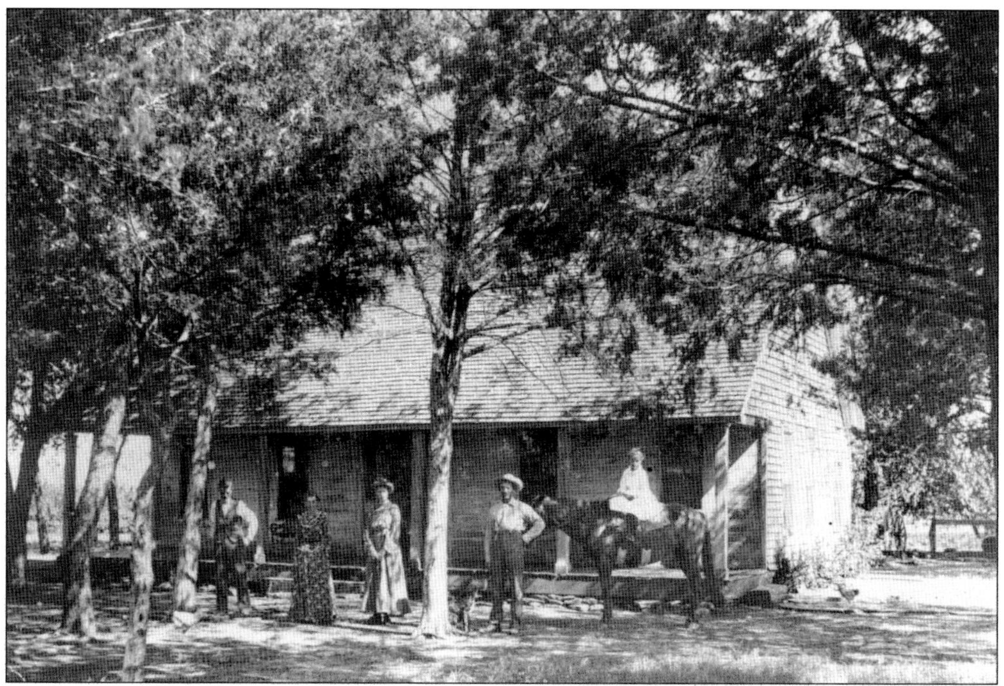

Nix Family Homestead, c. 1900 and 1955. The home and farm of Harrison and Minnie Miller Nix was located near modern-day Webb Chapel and Fyke Road. Cedar trees that graced the front of the home, which no longer stands, can still be seen in this area and mark the location of the home. In the photograph from 1900 above, the subjects are identified from left to right as James Miller, Minnie's father; Minnie Miller Nix; unidentified; Harrison Arthur Nix; the horse named Butterfly; and Fannie Nix Davis. The photograph below shows the same home around 50 years later. (Both courtesy of Hal Simon, Nix family collection.)

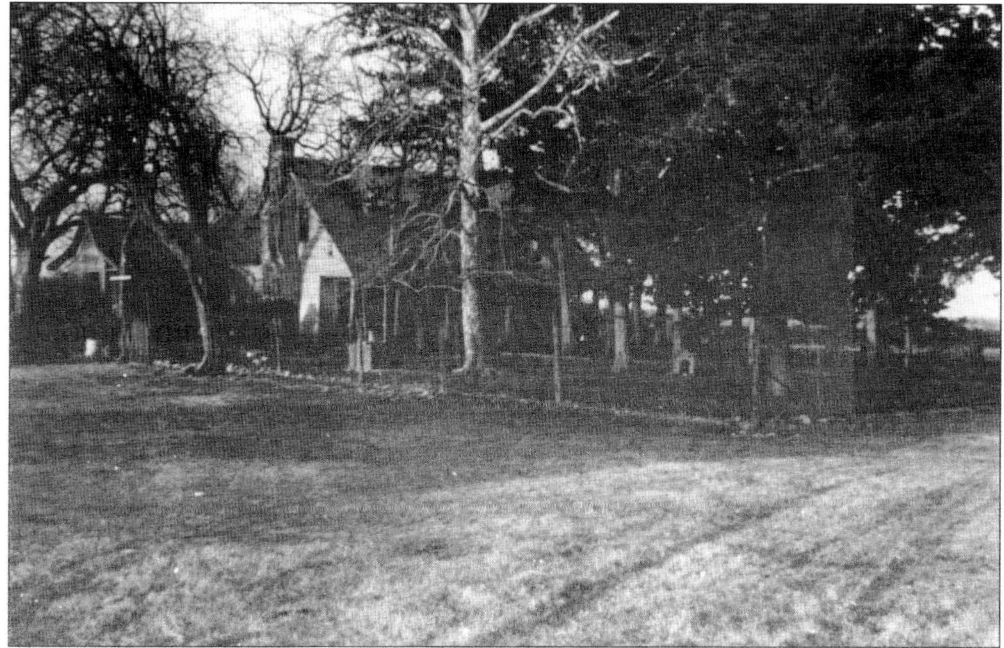

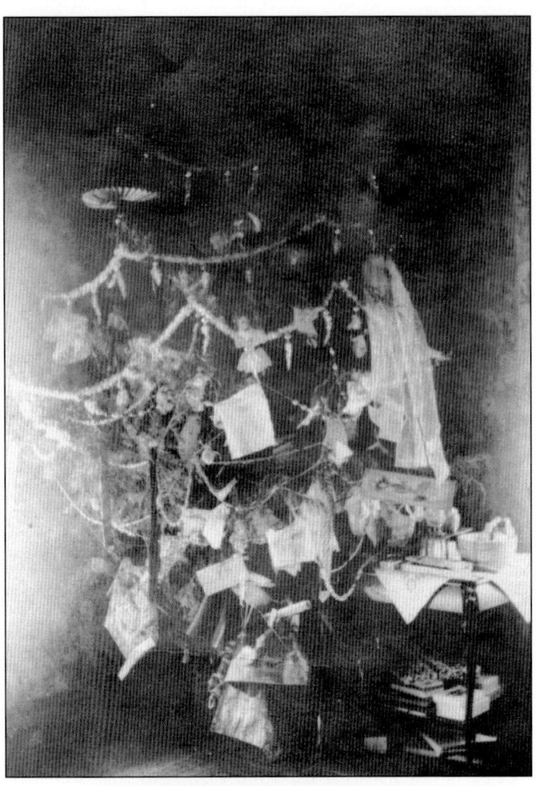

CHRISTMAS TREE ON NIX FARM, 1900. This is a typical Christmas tree at the turn of the 20th century. It shows the differences between the fashion of the time and today's tastes. The Nix family festively decorated their tree with dolls, ornaments, paper fans, and garlands. (Courtesy of Hal Simon, Nix family collection.)

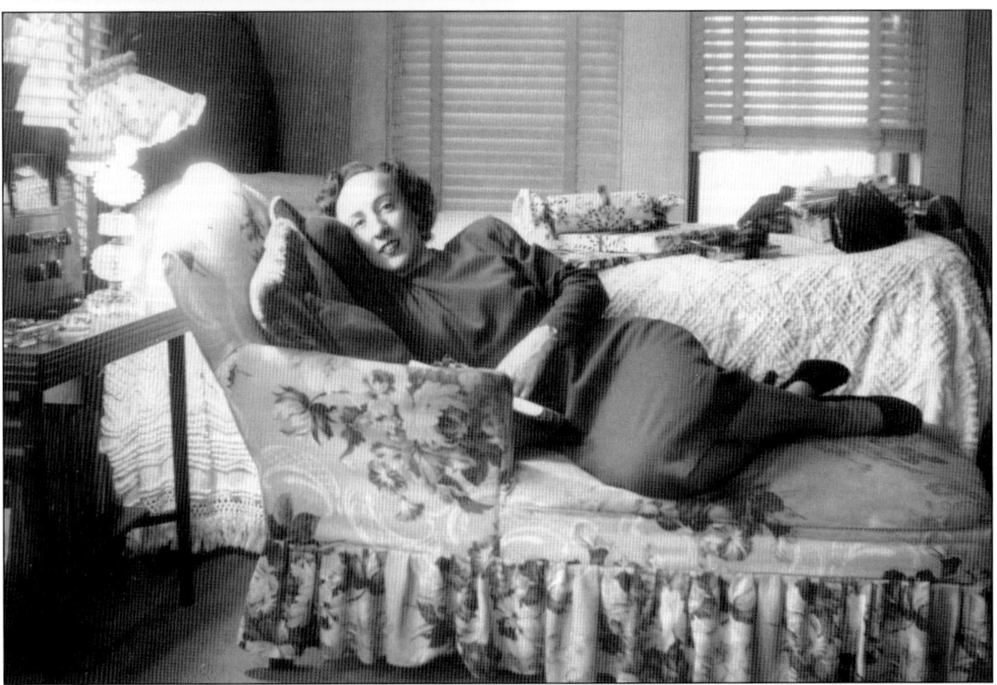

MAUREEN DAVIS SIMON, 1950s. A daughter of Fannie Mae Nix Davis, Maureen Davis Simon reclines on a chaise lounge during the Christmas holiday season. Wrapped packages can be seen on the bed behind her. (Courtesy of Hal Simon, Nix family collection.)

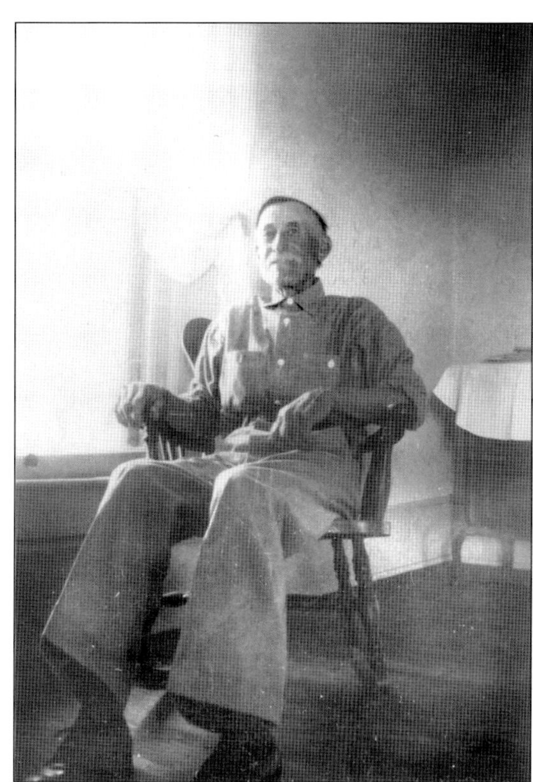

HARRISON AND MINNIE MILLER NIX.
Son of David and Mary Myers Nix,
Harrison Nix married Minnie Miller
and had three children. Their daughter,
Fannie Mae, and one son, David, both
survived to adulthood, while they lost
another son in infancy. (Both courtesy
of Hal Simon, Nix family collection.)

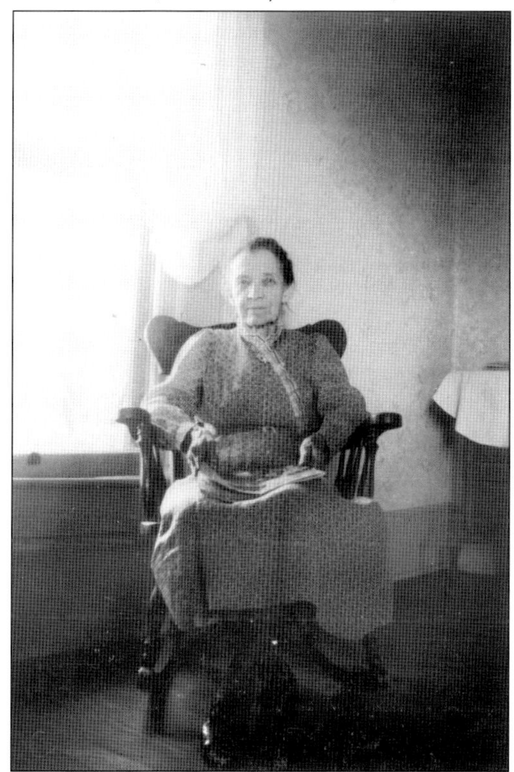

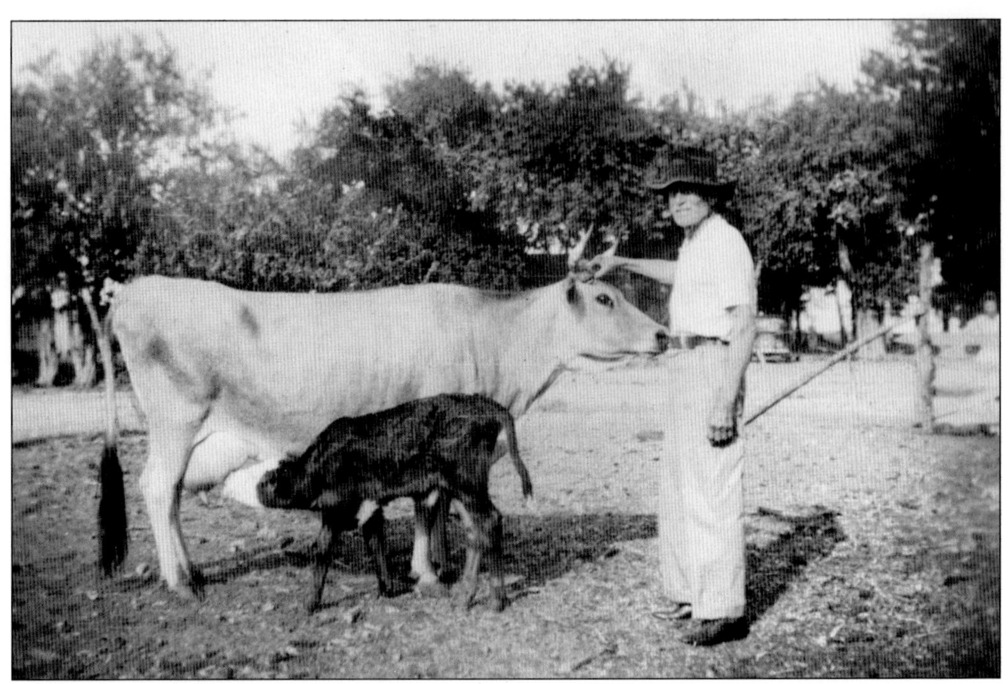

HARRISON NIX AND HIS PRIZE-WINNING JERSEY.
Harrison Nix raised Jersey milking cows on his farm
in Carrollton near Webb Chapel and Fyke Road. This
image shows one of his most prized milking cows and a
calf. Carrollton was primarily a rural area up until the
early 1970s when it experienced a residential building
boom. (Courtesy of Hal Simon, Nix family collection.)

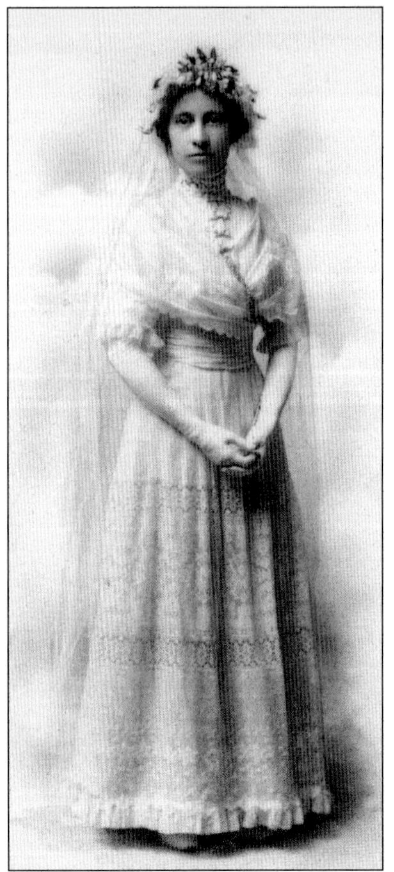

FANNIE MAE NIX DAVIS. The wedding gown of Fannie
Mae Nix of Carrollton, who married Ray Davis on
December 12, 1912, survives as a family treasure today.
The wedding ensemble is still complete, and each piece
has been preserved. It has been featured in a number
of museum exhibits in the Dallas and Carrollton
areas because of its condition and representative value
as an example of a local wedding dress of the time.
(Courtesy of Hal Simon, Nix family collection.)

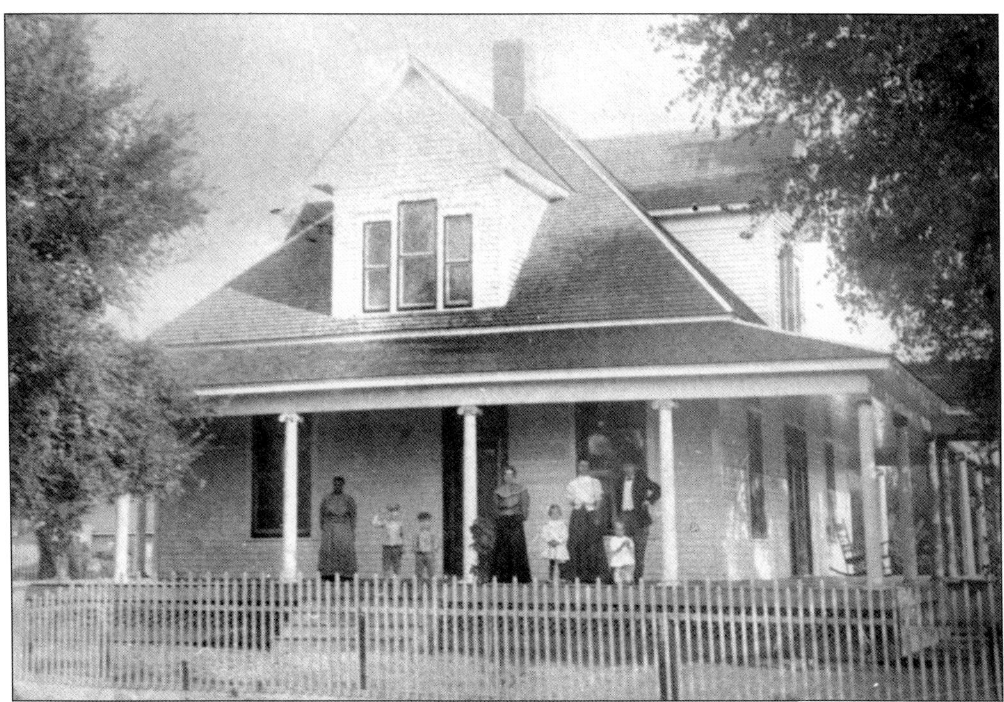

J. C. DAVIS HOME, 1907. In 1895, J. C. Davis came to Texas from Georgia and set up business ventures in Plano, Garland, and later Farmers Branch and Carrollton. He built three brick structures on the Carrollton Square, including the Carrollton Mercantile Company and the First State Bank of Carrollton in 1903. He was an active community member and served as mayor of the city in the 1940s. The adults standing in this photograph from left to right are identified as Davis's cook, Liza Trulove; J. C. Davis's mother; and Mr. and Mrs. J. C. Davis. The couple's children standing with them are unidentified. (Courtesy of A. W. Perry Homestead Museum, Ogle Collection.)

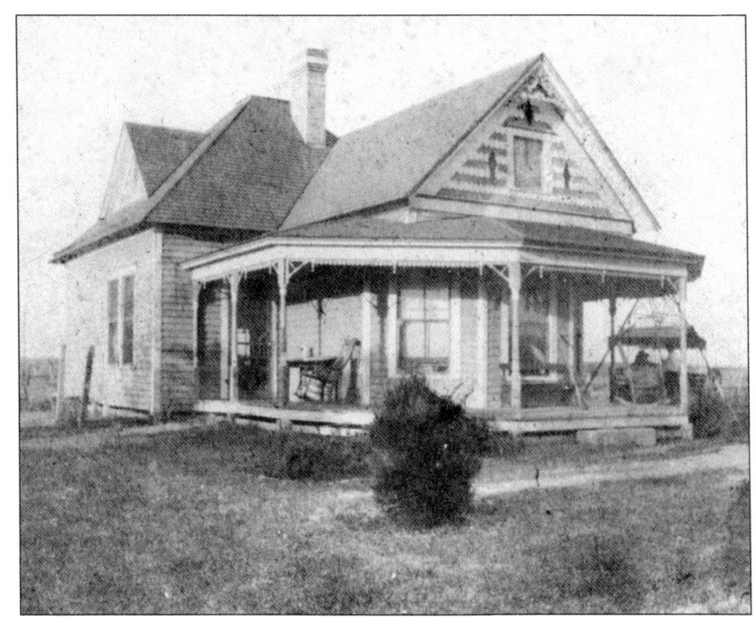

JAMES M. KENNEDY HOME. The home of James M. Kennedy was near the modern-day site of Columbian Club, a country club built and opened in the 1950s. His mother, Mary Kennedy, immigrated to Texas from Arkansas as a widow with two sons in the early 1840s. (Courtesy of A. W. Perry Homestead Museum, Ogle Collection.)

33

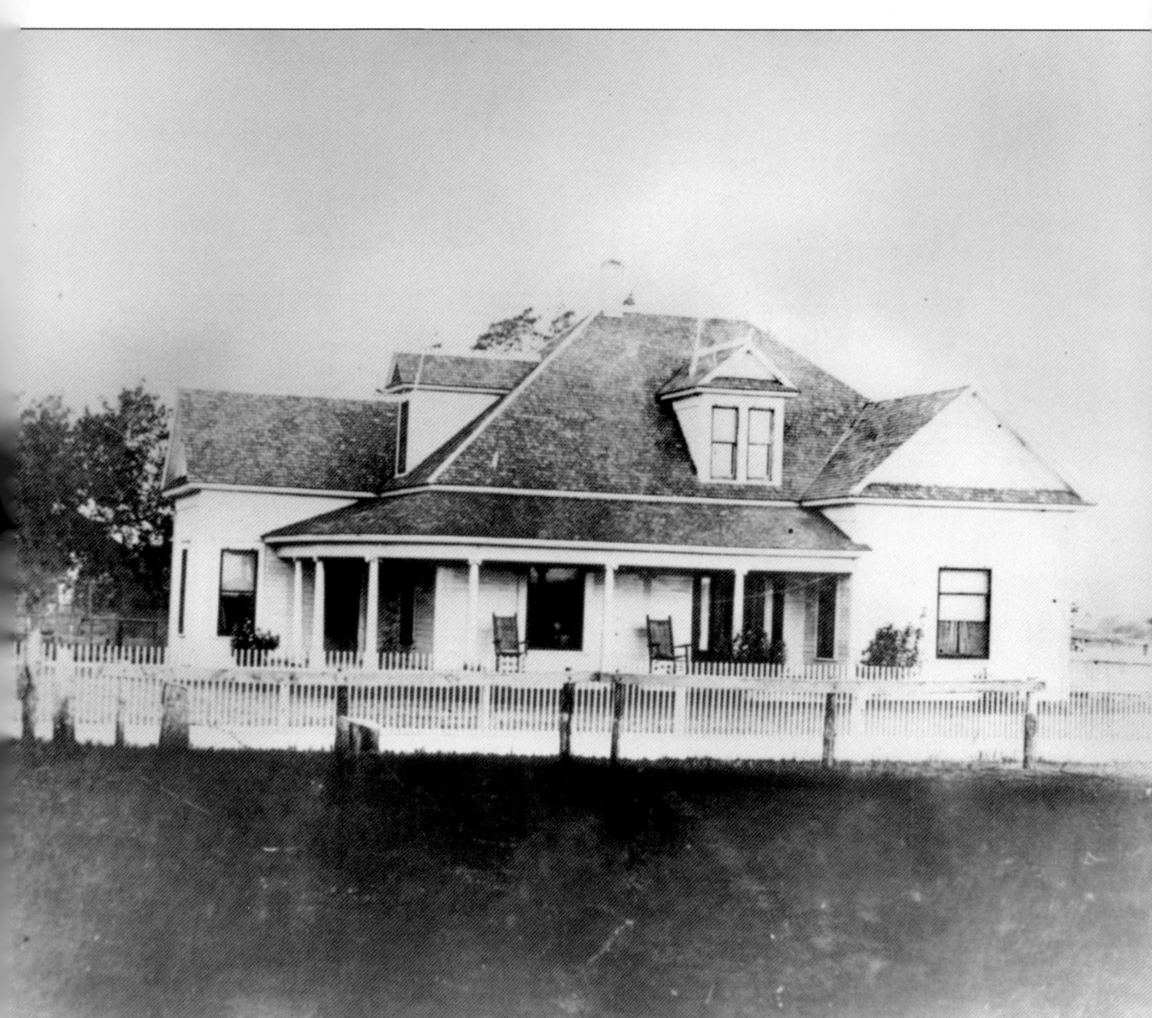

DeWitt Clinton Perry Home, 1909. This photograph depicts the home of DeWitt and Francis Grimes Perry in 1909 shortly after it was built. When DeWitt's father, A. W. Perry, passed away in 1904, he inherited the property that contained the family home, which was built in 1857. DeWitt and his family lived in the original home built by A. W. until constructing this larger, more modern home in 1909. DeWitt, Francis, their daughter Pearl and her husband, Arthur Gravley, moved out of the earlier home and into a tent on the property while they salvaged materials to be reused in the new home. Sheep were raised on the property until the passing of DeWitt Perry in 1933. Horses grazed in the meadow of the property until Francis Perry passed away in 1967—just before her 101st birthday. In 1976, after being donated to the City of Carrollton by Pearl Perry Gravley, the home became the A. W. Perry Homestead Museum and opened to the public. The rocking chairs visible on the front porch were preserved and are on display at the museum, which is located at 1509 North Perry Road. (Courtesy of A. W. Perry Homestead Museum, Ogle Collection.)

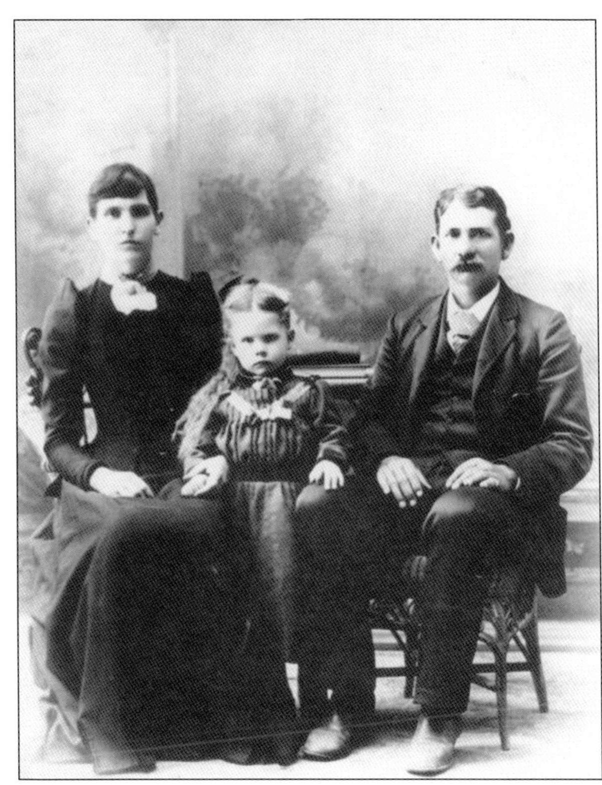

DeWitt Perry Family. DeWitt Clinton Perry, Francis Grimes Perry, and their only child, daughter Pearl Perry, are pictured in these photographs. Pearl was married and had one child of her own by the time her parents' home was built in 1909. She and her husband, Arthur Gravley, lived with her parents until they constructed their own home, which was located near present-day Spring and Perry Roads. Following in the philanthropic tracks of her father and grandfather, who both donated land for schools and churches, Pearl also donated property to the First United Methodist Church and eventually donated 12 acres of land, including her family home, for a museum and park to honor the pioneer settlers of Carrollton. (Both courtesy of A. W. Perry Homestead Museum, Ogle Collection.)

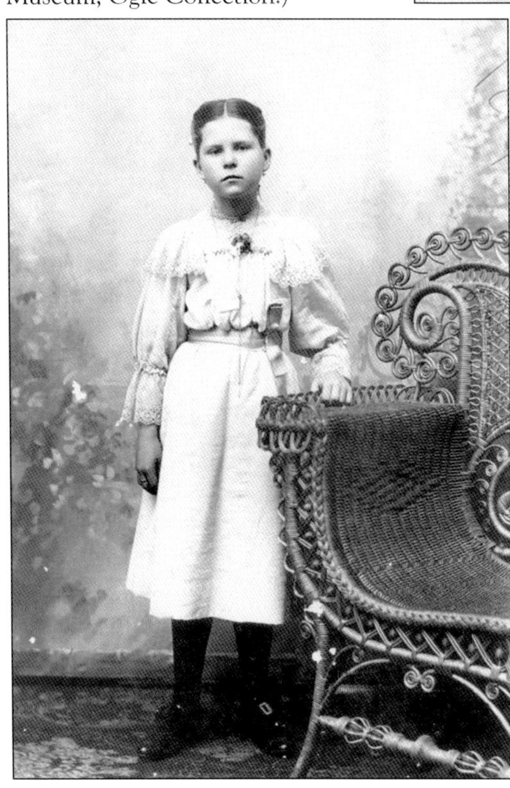

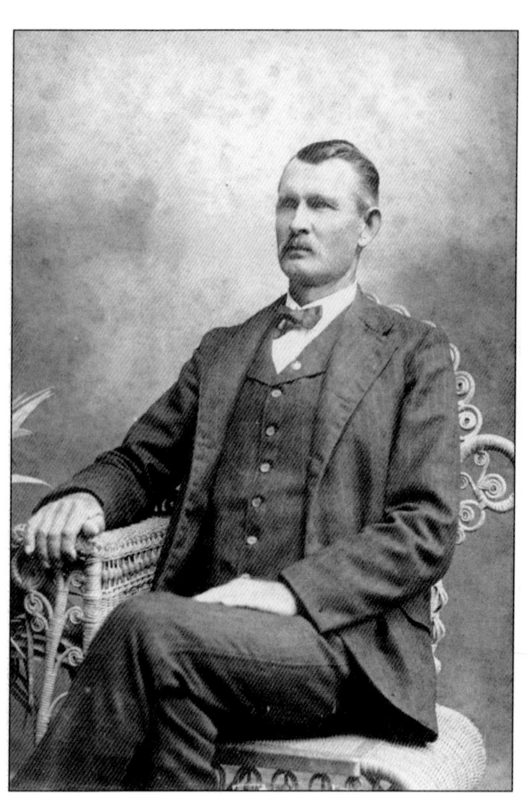

ELISHA AND ELISHA FYKE AND FAMILY.
Elisha Fyke's father, Archer Fyke, came to Texas and met and married Jemima Myers, one of the daughters of local preacher David Myers. Elisha married Lillie Nix, and they had five children. The family portrait includes mother Lillie and children, from left to right, (standing) Mae, Oscar, and Lottie; (seated) Ray and Irene. Elisha died in 1896. (Both courtesy of A. W. Perry Homestead Museum, Ogle Collection.)

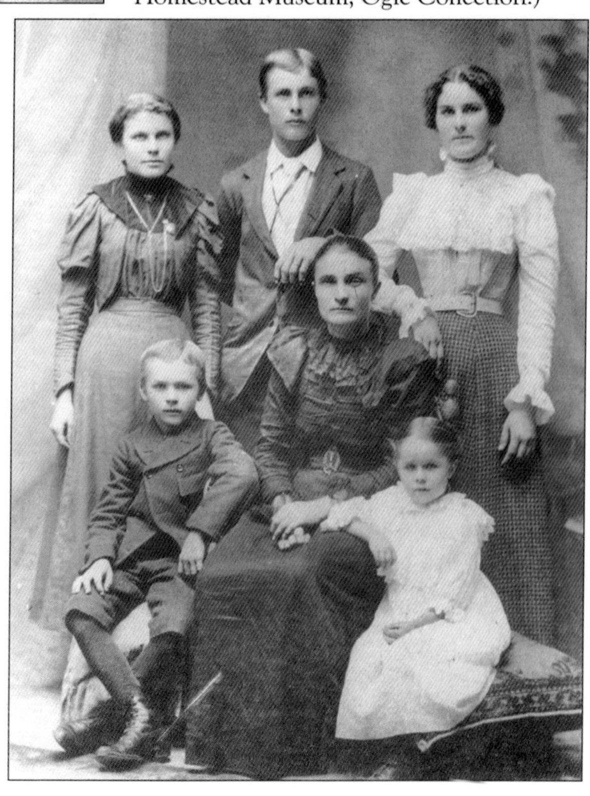

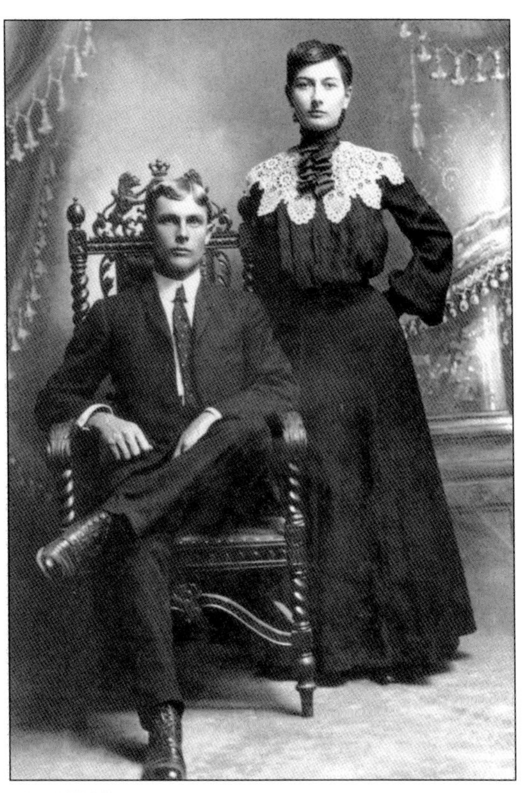

CLAUDIA NEELY AND OSCAR FYKE. Oscar Fyke, son of Elisha Fyke, married Claudia Neely in 1904. She had come to Texas from Tennessee with her family in 1900. The couple first lived in Farmers Branch until the flood of 1908 forced them to relocate to the Fyke farm in Carrollton. Later Oscar opened Carrollton Café on the square in the 1920s. (Courtesy of A. W. Perry Homestead Museum, Ogle Collection.)

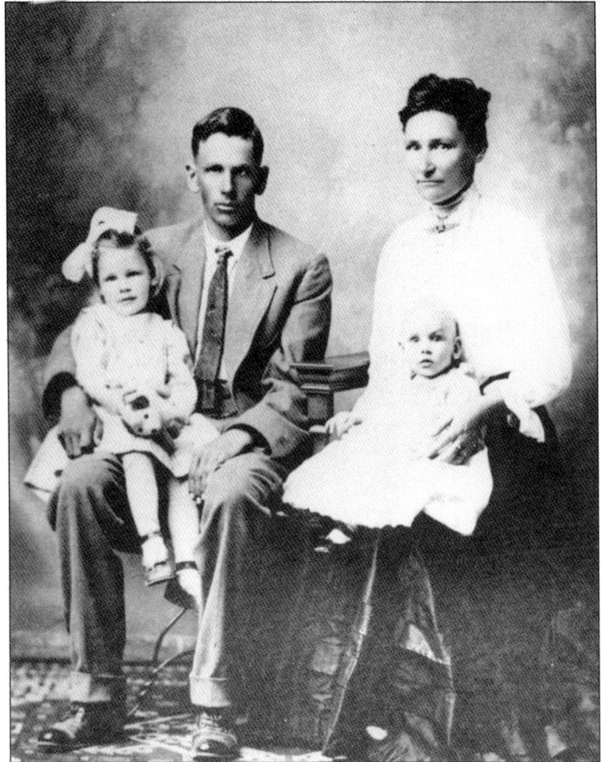

ASHLEY AND SUE WARNER WEBB FAMILY. Pictured here are Ashley Webb and his wife, Sue Warner Webb, and their children Fannidella and Thomas Warner Webb. Sue Warner was a daughter of Thomas Warner, who had emigrated from Ireland, and Harriet Perry. The Webbs donated land for the first public park in 1924, Webb Park, which was located south of present-day Crosby Road near the Katy railroad tracks. The Women's Civic Study Club donated the playground equipment. (Courtesy of A. W. Perry Homestead Museum, Ogle Collection.)

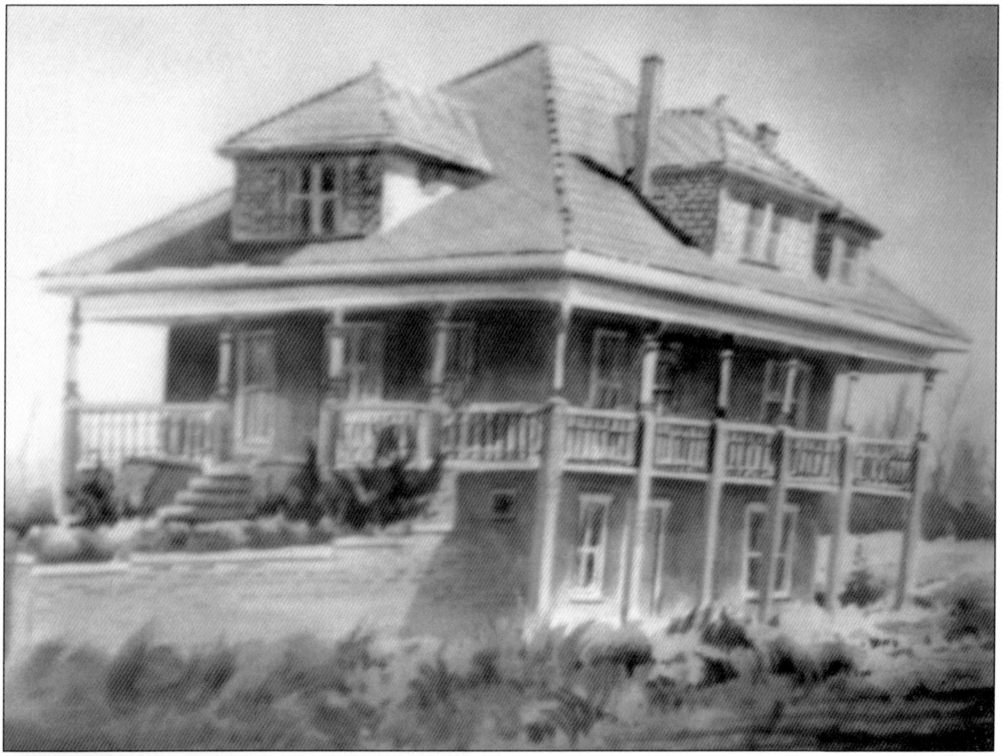

BELL ALLEN HOME, 1910. This three-story, prairie-style home was built in 1910 with Carrollton brick. It is located on Clint Street in the historic Carrollton Heights neighborhood and was occupied by civic leader Belle Allen for 46 years. (Courtesy of City of Carrollton.)

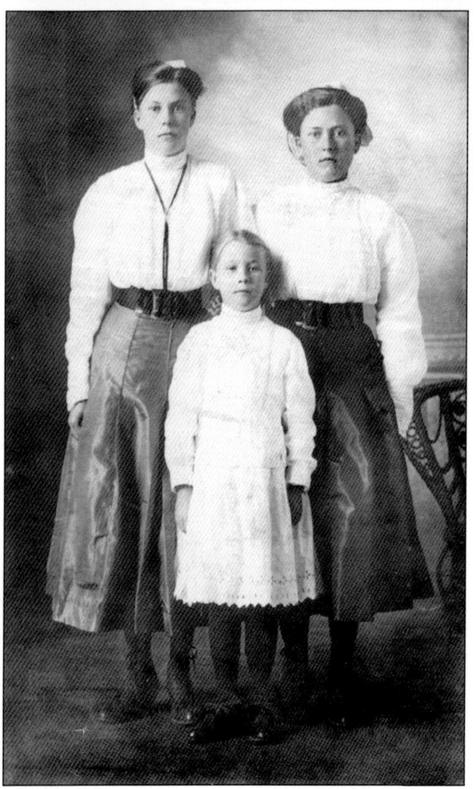

REAL-PHOTO POSTCARD, C. 1900. The girls in this image are unidentified. The photograph is printed onto a postcard. Postcards were often made with portraits of individuals or town landmarks and were sent to friends and family. (Courtesy of A. W. Perry Homestead Museum, Ogle Collection.)

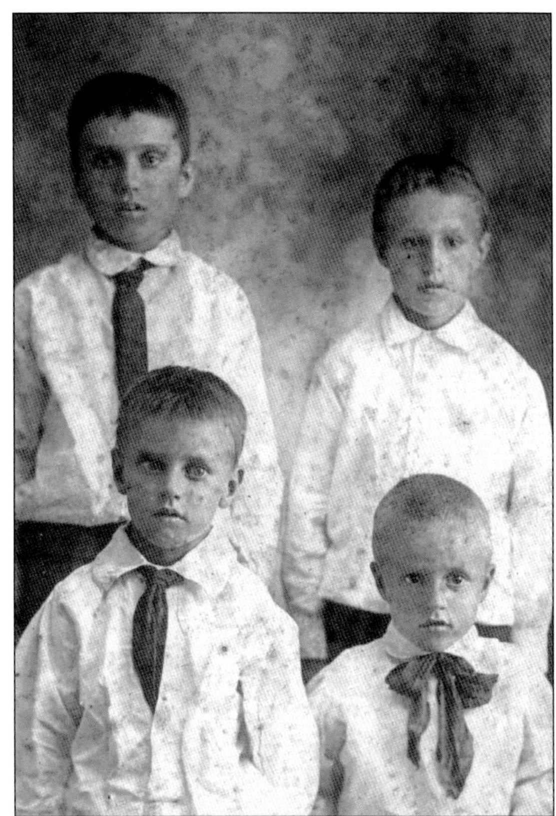

THE GOOD BOYS. This group is identified as brothers Clarence, Rex, Arthur, and Allen Good in the photograph to the right and Clarence, Rex, and Arthur Good in the photograph below as young men. They were descendants of John and Sara Nix, who emigrated from Illinois in 1846. Their granddaughter, Adelia, married Marion Good, and the couple had nine children, including these four. (Both courtesy of Hal Simon, Nix family collection.)

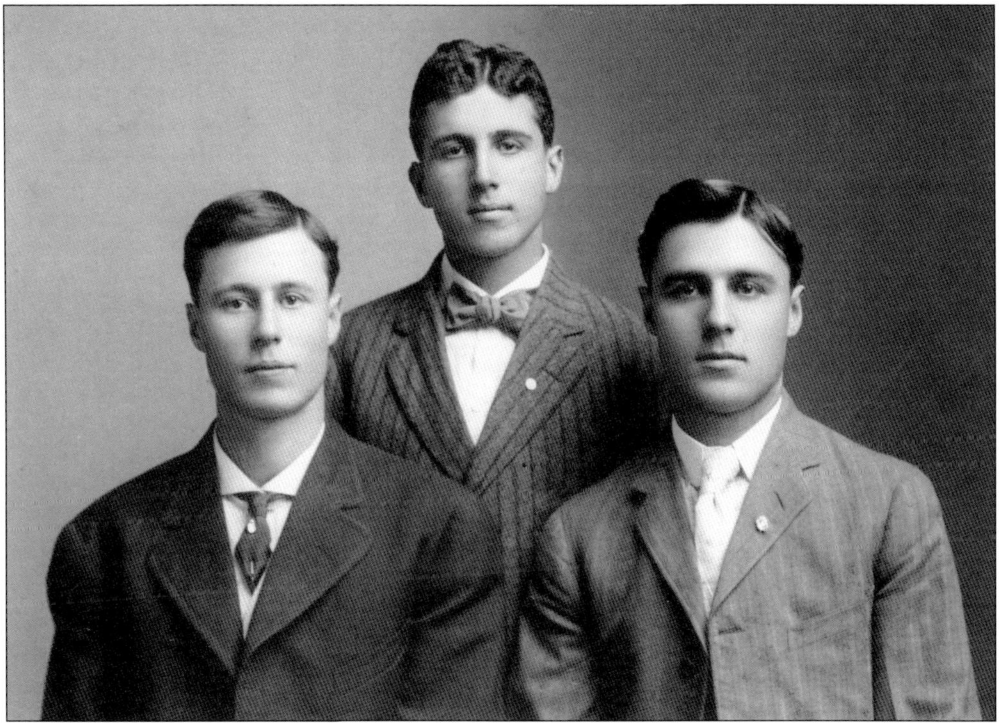

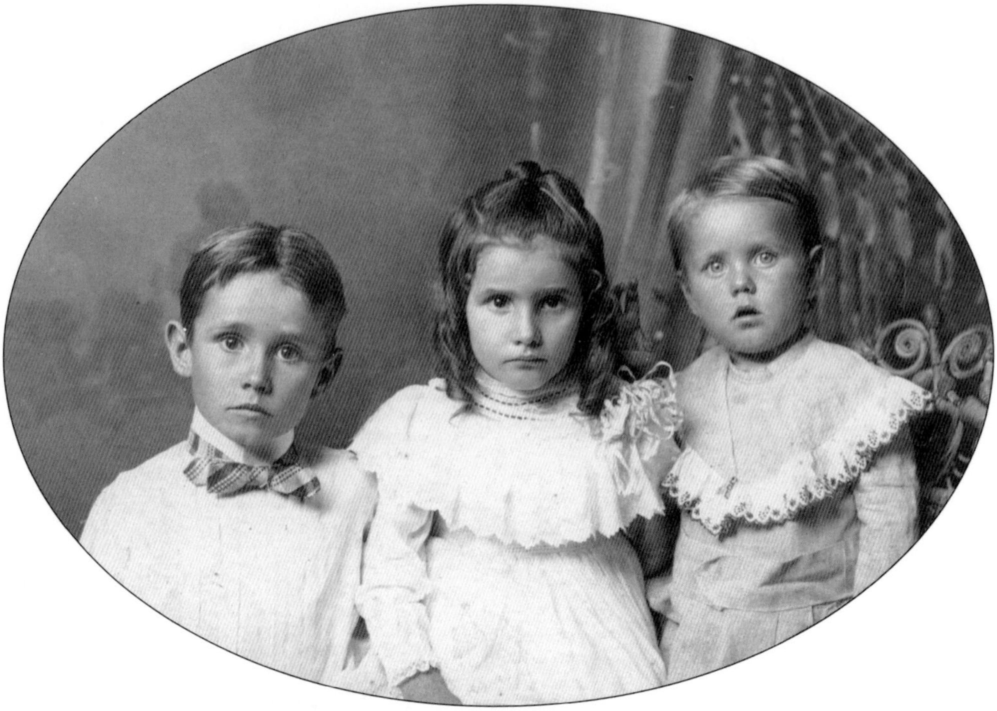

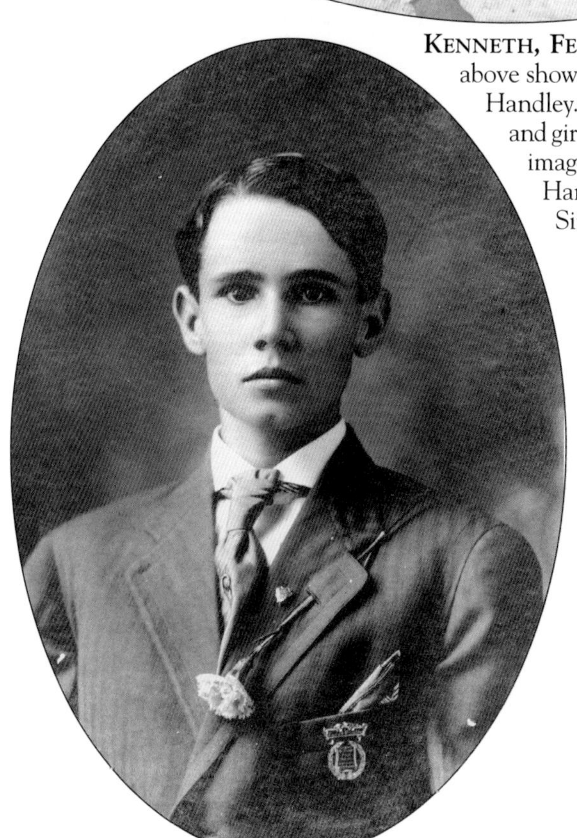

KENNETH, FERN, AND PETE HANDLEY. The portrait above shows three children of Ida May Nix and Peter Handley. The delicate clothes of the younger boy and girl were typical of the early 20th century. The image to the left shows a still-elegant Kenneth Handley as a teenager. (Both courtesy of Hal Simon, Nix family collection.)

CLOSE TIES. Similar to most other small towns, Carrollton was a tight-knit community. Many of the residents were related in some way or another to each other and the early settlers of Peters Colony. The children and grandchildren of those early residents grew up together, attended the same churches and schools, and mingled in town at businesses forming around the square. These photographs show the close ties of families and friends with these young men having their portraits taken together. The three men in the photograph to the right are identified as Oscar Fyke, Nathan Butler, and Fred Mingle. The subjects in the image below are cousins Oscar Fyke and Willie Nix. (Both courtesy of A. W. Perry Homestead Museum, Ogle Collection.)

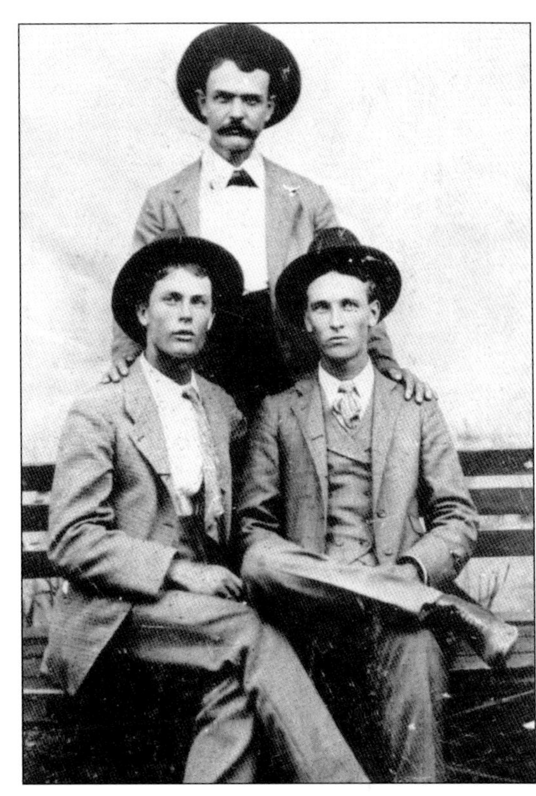

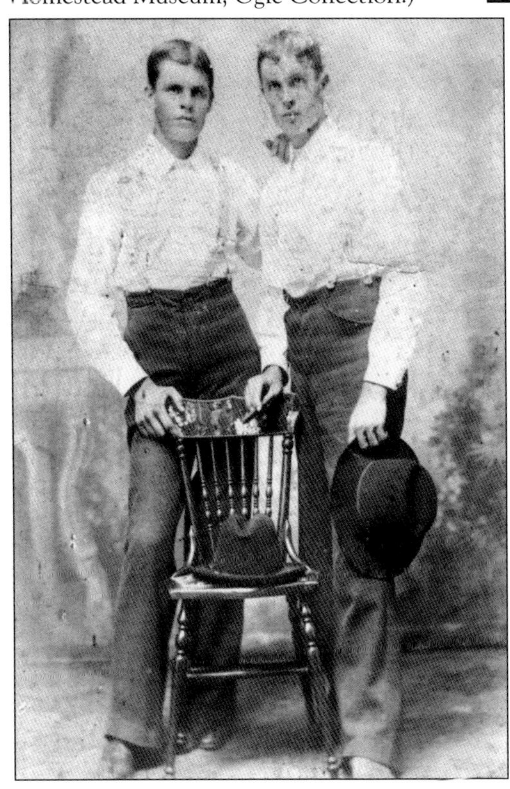

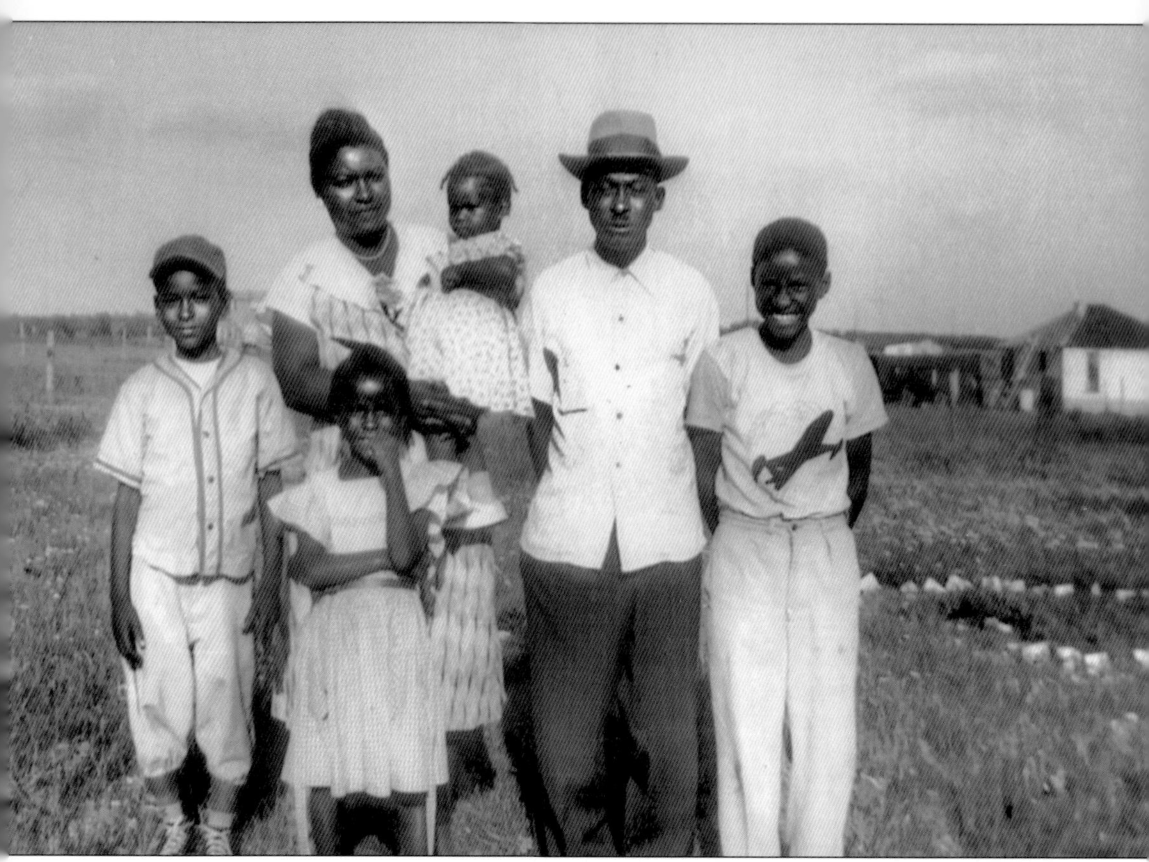

RAINWATER FAMILY, KELLER SPRINGS COMMUNITY, AND HEADS LANE, C. 1955. Charlie "Wash" Rainwater married Annie Heads in 1932, and they had eight children, two of whom died in infancy. This photograph was taken on the family's 90-acre farm located north of Keller Springs Road that Annie's grandfather Rufus Heads had owned. Rufus was a reverend and farmer who taught many in his community how to read and write. Her father, Walter Heads, owned 219 acres of land north of old downtown Carrollton and also owned property on the west side of town near the Elm Fork of the Trinity River, which was known as Heads Park. The park was a popular gathering place for African American residents to enjoy dances and picnics. Heads Park later became Sandy Lake Amusement Park. Like many rural towns in Texas at the time, black and white citizens lived separately, attending their own churches and schools. In 1948, the population of Carrollton was 1,140 people, including 294 white families and 33 black families. (Courtesy of Willie Rainwater.)

Three

CENTER OF COMMUNITY
TOWN SQUARE

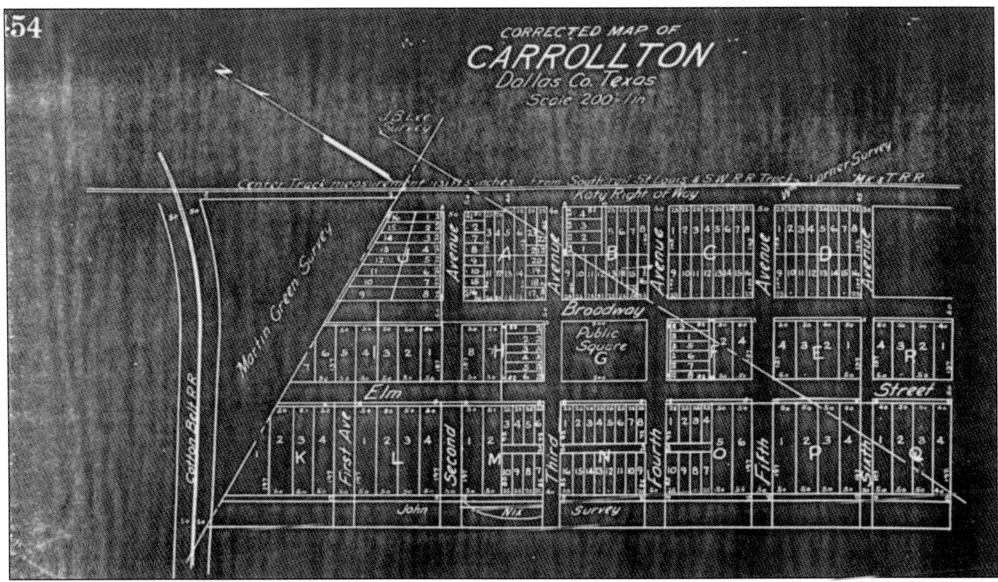

1913 CARROLLTON MAP. Carrollton officially became a city in 1913 when it was incorporated. This corrected map of the business district was submitted by George F. Myers at that time. It shows the center of the town square and the locations of the Cotton Belt and Katy rail lines. It also references the original surveys of land on which the town was built, which includes portions of the Lee, Larner, Nix, and Green surveys. (Courtesy of A. W. Perry Homestead Museum, Ogle Collection.)

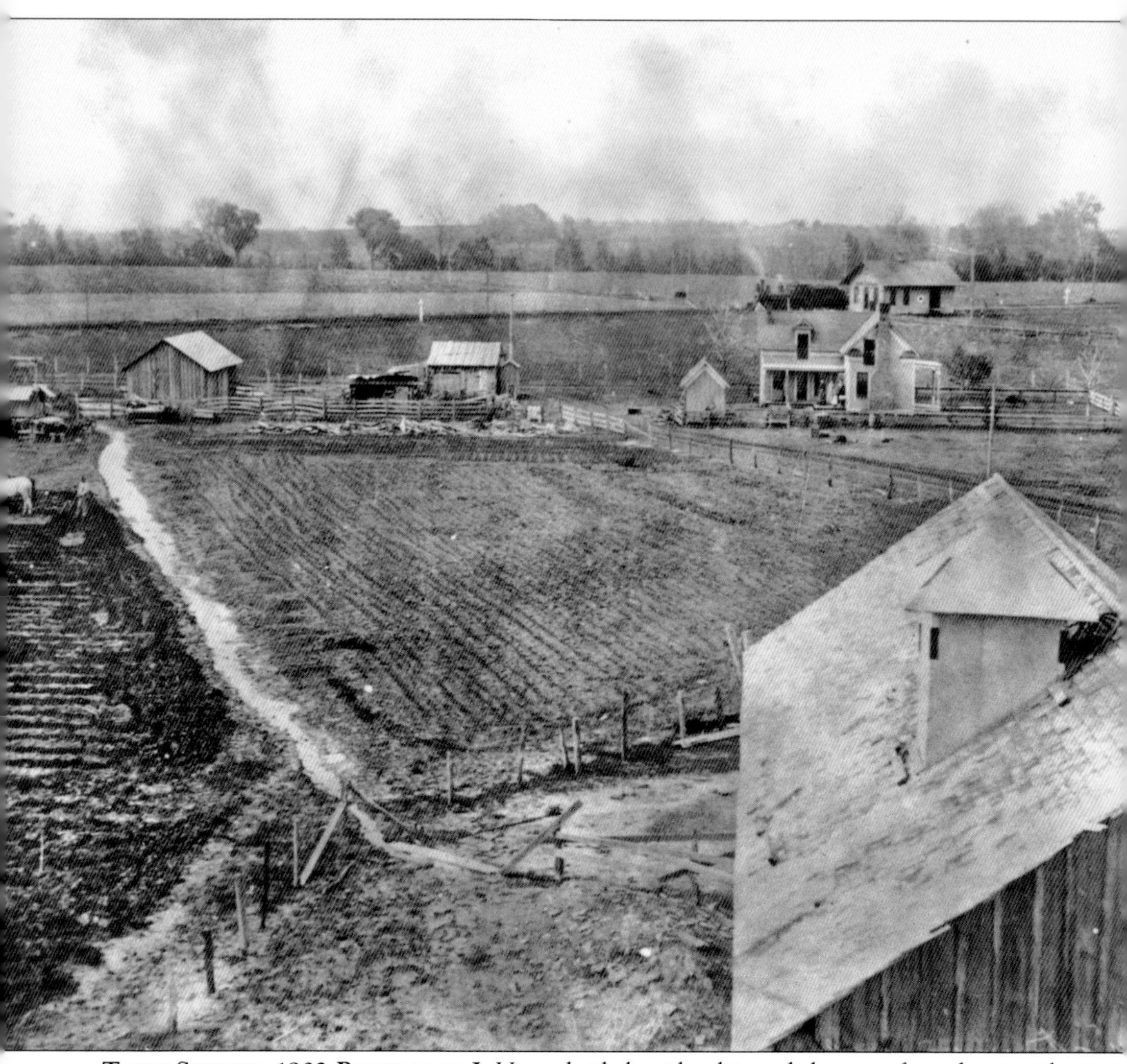

TOWN SQUARE, 1902 PANORAMIC I. Viewed side-by-side, this and the next four photographs provide a panoramic view of Carrollton in 1902. This series was taken near the location that would later be known as the town square. Businesses and homes were established around the center of the square and were supported by the three railroad lines that cross here. The photographer climbed onto the roof of a building on the south end of town and photographed from west to east. The train depot with a train engine waiting can be seen in the top right of the image. Just below, a family has stepped onto the porch of the farmhouse to have their photograph taken too. Also note the man steering the plow as the horse pulls him along, making neat rows in the field on the left. Gray smoke billows from the smokestack located on top of the building to the right of where the photographer was perched. (Courtesy of A. W. Perry Homestead Museum.)

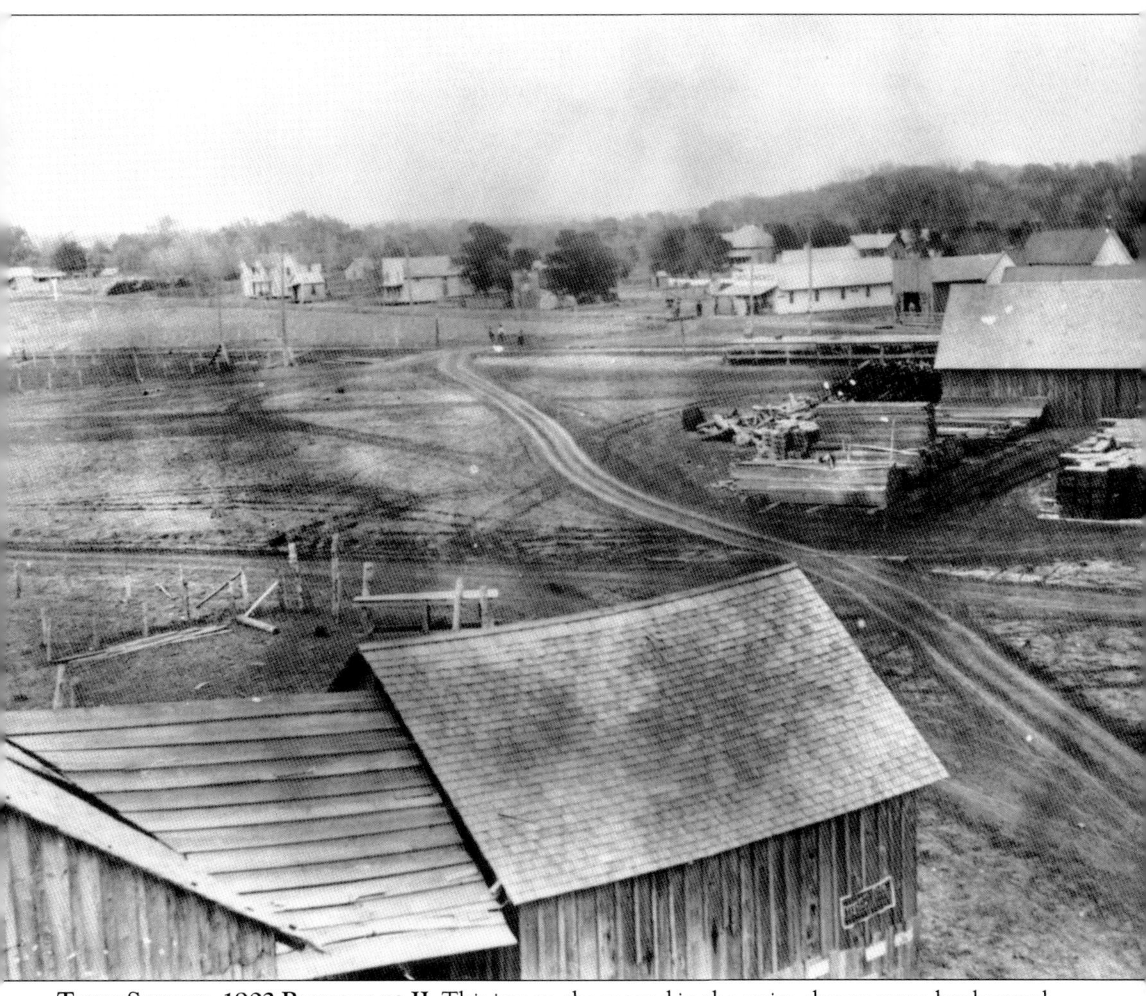

TOWN SQUARE, 1902 PANORAMIC II. This image, the second in the series, documents a lumberyard and a farm-implements store among the various businesses captured by the photographer's lens. Telephone poles and lines are also evident. The telephone was first available in Carrollton in 1890. Lines extended from the town square to area homes and businesses. To make a telephone call, the caller would ring the operator located on the square and tell her the name of the person he or she would like to be speak with, and the operator would manually connect the lines through a switchboard. (Courtesy of A. W. Perry Homestead Museum.)

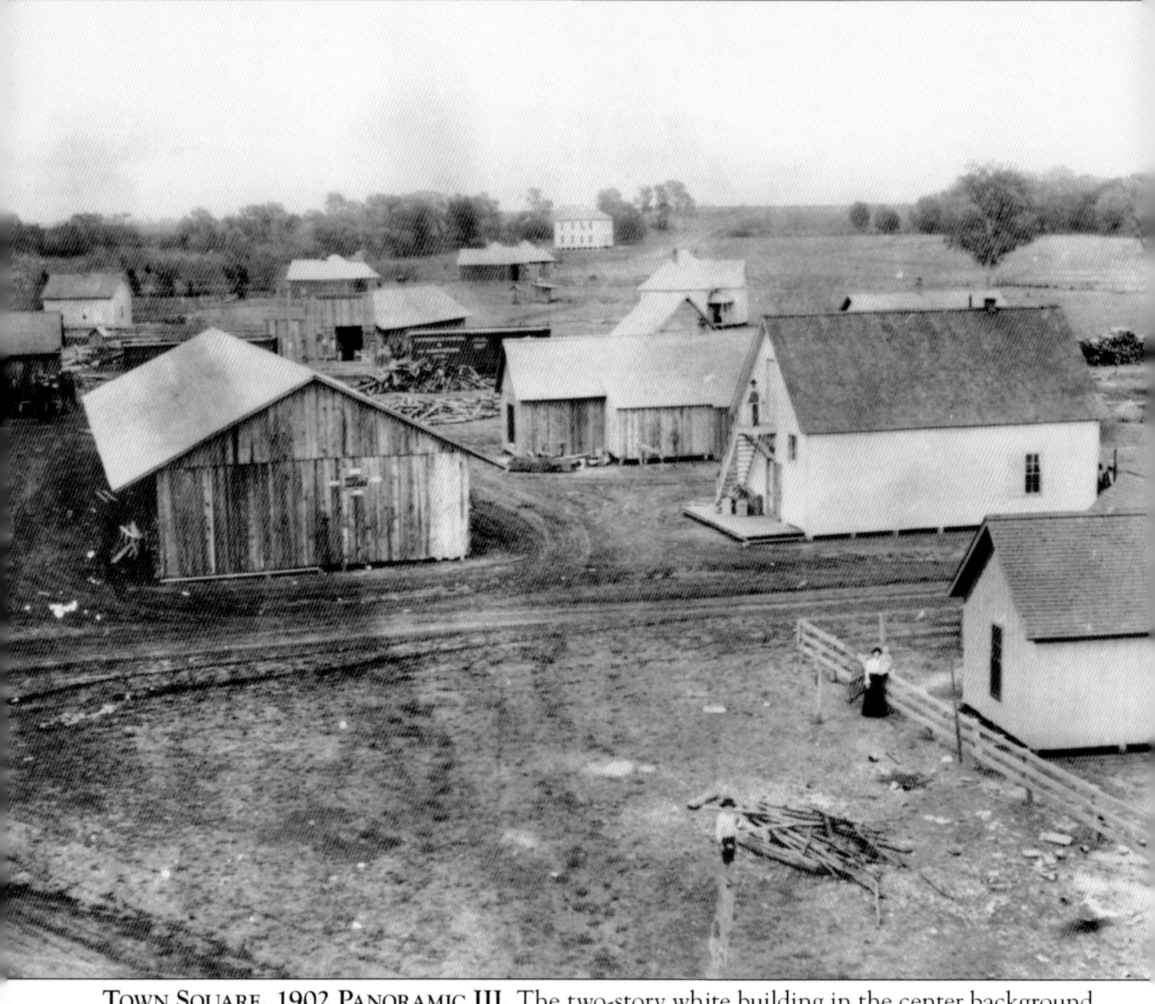

TOWN SQUARE, 1902 PANORAMIC III. The two-story white building in the center background of this image was the town's newly opened schoolhouse. This building was located at what is now the intersection of Belt Line Road and Erie Street east of the town center. A woman with an infant poses against a wooden fence, while a young boy stands in short pants and a hat next to a woodpile. A man stands at the top of the stairs at a second-story, rear entrance to a building. Stacks of wood and crude lumber dot the scene, reminding the viewer how important this resource was for construction, cooking, and heating homes and businesses. (Courtesy of A. W. Perry Homestead Museum.)

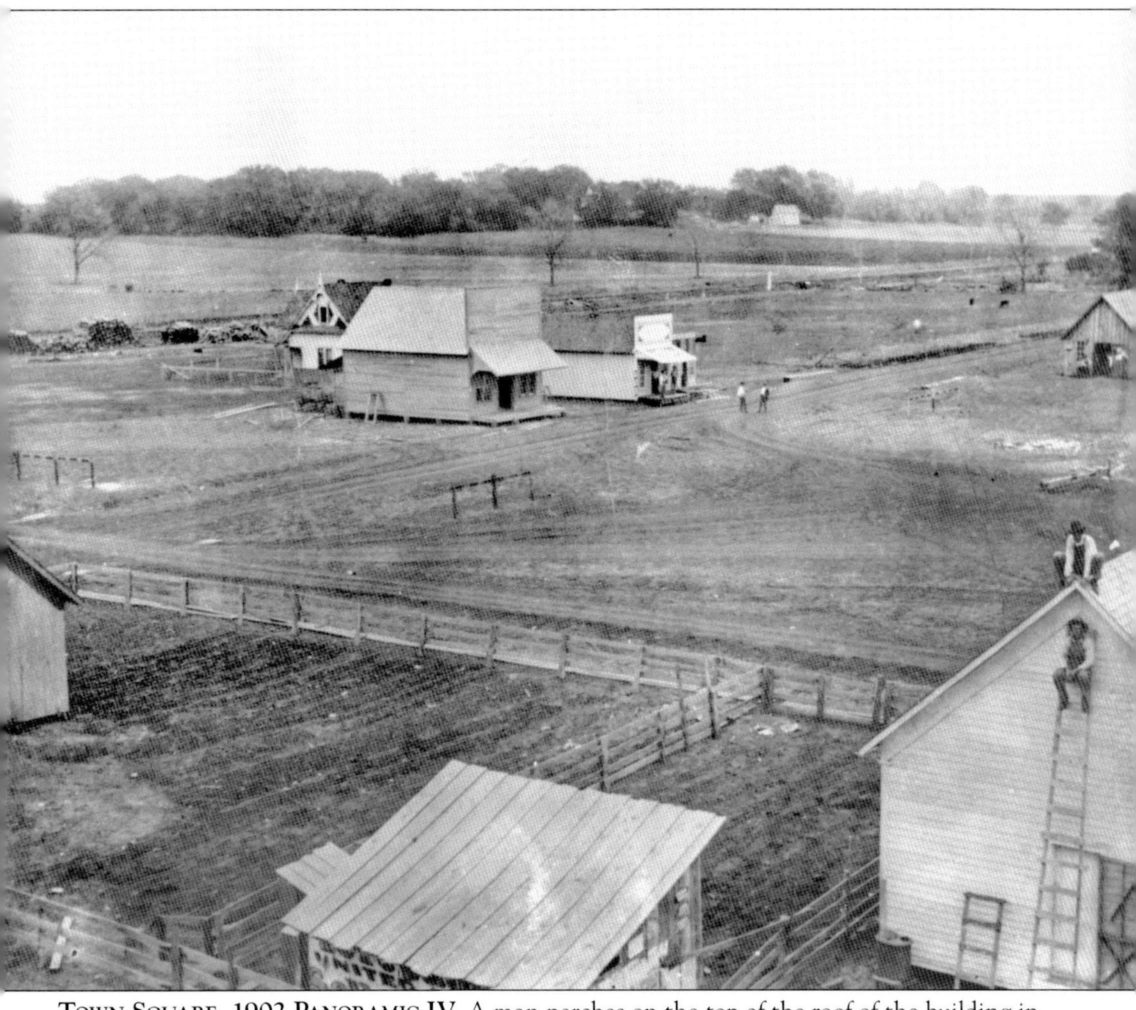

Town Square, 1902 Panoramic IV. A man perches on the top of the roof of the building in the lower right, and another sits atop the ladder leaning against the structure. Businesses and an ornately decorated home sit in the center of the image. Hitching posts for horses are located outside of each home and business. Clearly worn roads are visible in the dirt. With heavy rain and bad weather, these unpaved, dirt roads would have been hard to navigate with horse-drawn vehicles. (Courtesy of A. W. Perry Homestead Museum.)

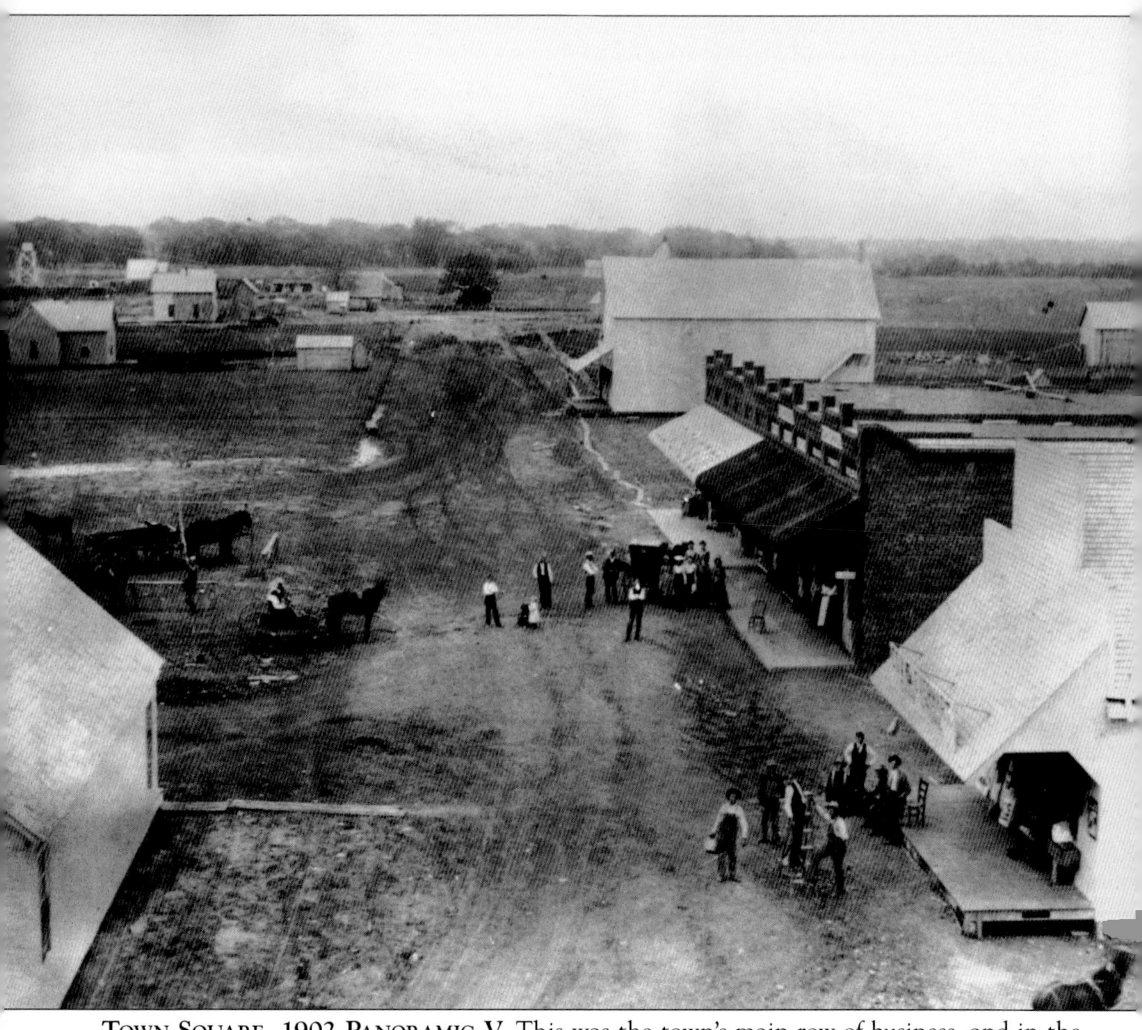

TOWN SQUARE, 1902 PANORAMIC V. This was the town's main row of business, and in the foreground is the Cox and Everhart general store with some of its wares stationed out front on its entry porch. Gentlemen have come out to position themselves for the camera. Ladies can be seen standing in the street in their best dresses and looking up toward the photographer to be included in the town portrait. Horses rest from pulling their wagons and buggies in the area surrounding the well. The location of the well later became the location of the gazebo and the focal point of the business district. (Courtesy of A. W. Perry Homestead Museum.)

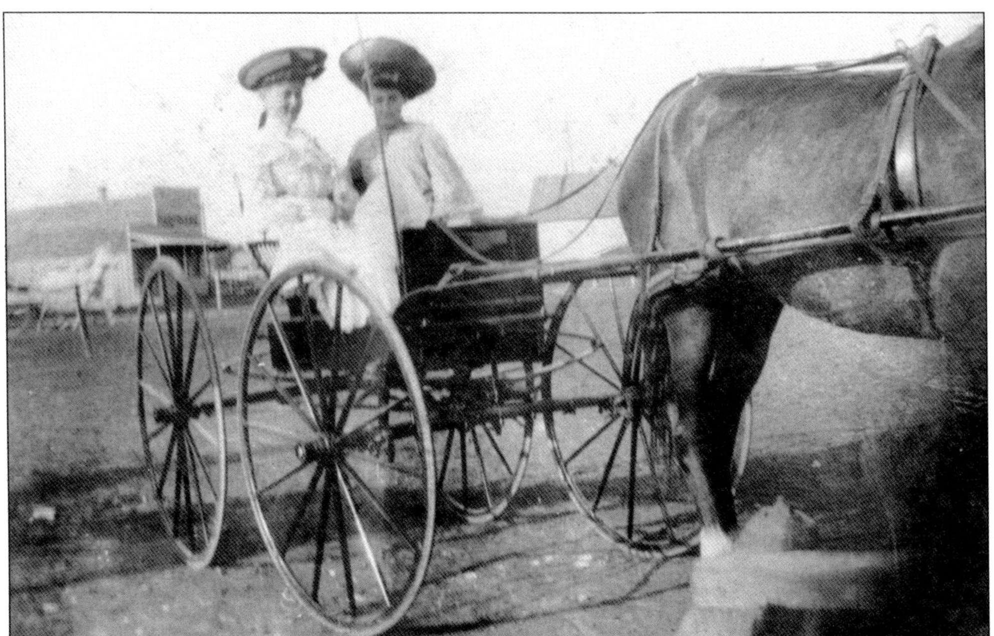

GOING TO TOWN. Before automobiles, people relied upon horses and horse-drawn carriages and wagons to get from one location to another. On regular trips to the general stores in town, to go to church, or to go out visiting friends and family, buggies like these would be used. The buildings on the square can be seen behind the girls seated in the buggy. The women in these photographs are unidentified. (Both courtesy of A. W. Perry Homestead Museum, Ogle Collection.)

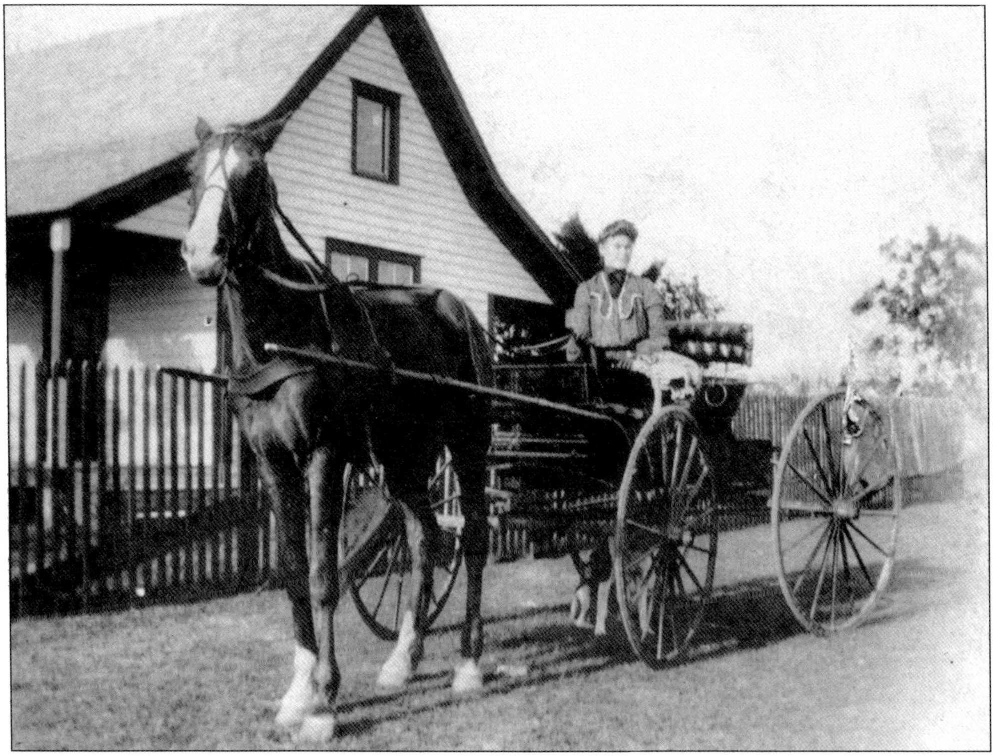

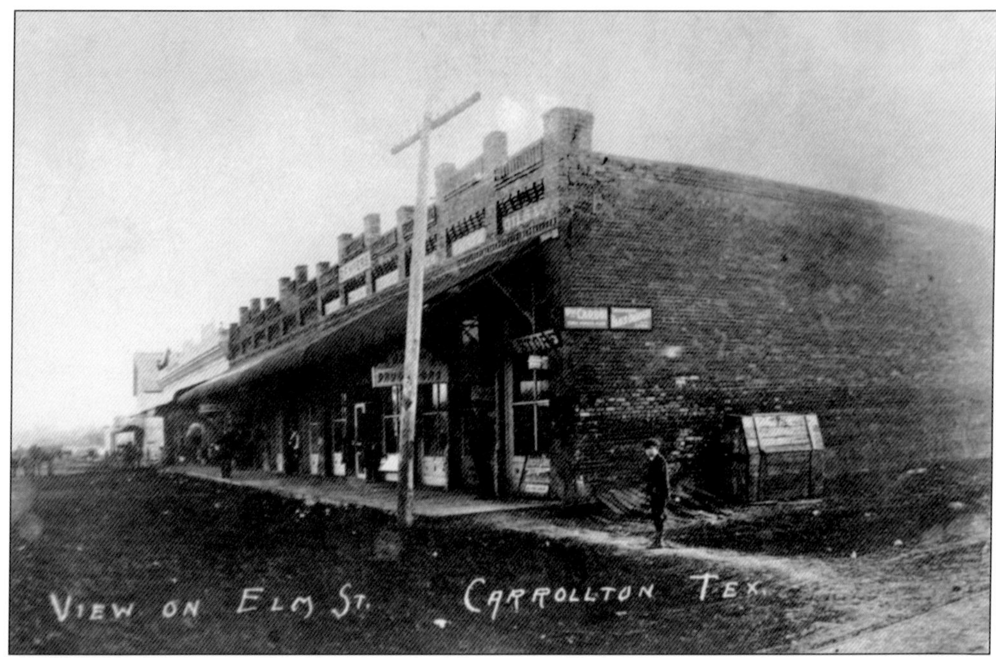

WEST SIDE OF SQUARE, 1908. This image of the west side of the square was taken in 1908 and was printed on a real-photo postcard that was sent by Laura Thompson to her daughter Myrtle Perry Padgett. This same year, a devastating flood destroyed homes located west of the square, closest to the Elm Fork of the Trinity River, and damaged many businesses on the square. (Courtesy of Fancy Oliver Tanner.)

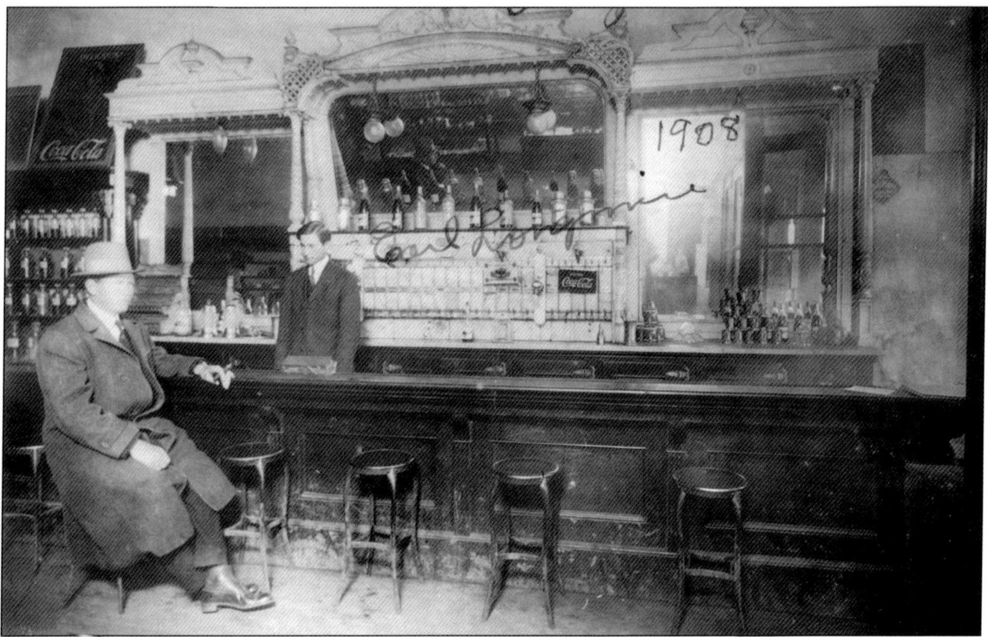

PERRY DRUGSTORE, 1908. This was the second business established by James Perry. It was located at Third and Elm Streets on the west side of the square. James Perry served as the druggist in Carrollton for 40 years. (Courtesy of A. W. Perry Homestead Museum.)

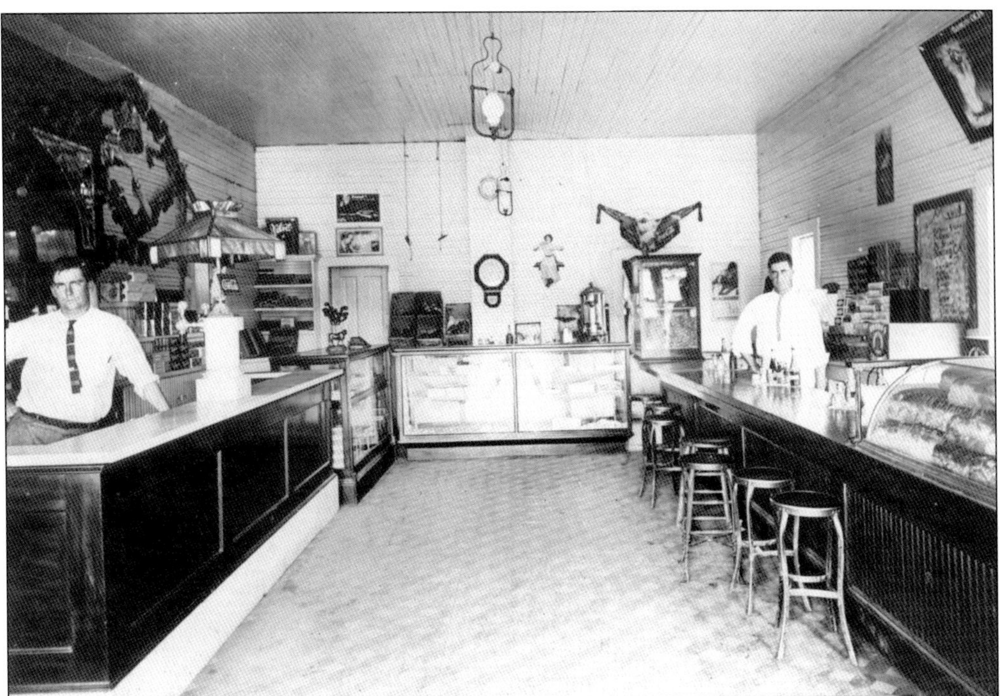

DAL CAR CAFÉ, C. 1913. The Dal Car (Dallas Carrollton) Café was located on the east side of the square where Frank Good's drugstore was in 1950, the Rainbow Pharmacy. Currently it is the space occupied by Sid's Rainbow Grill. The man on the left is G. W. Myers, and the man on the right of the photograph is identified as Otho Ogden. (Courtesy of A. W. Perry Homestead Museum.)

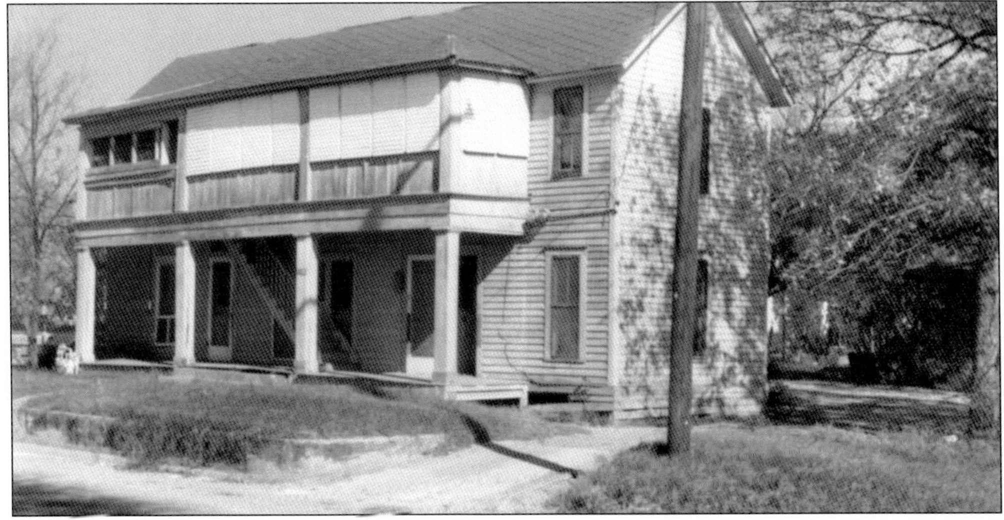

THE WORTH HOTEL. H. Moles established the first hotel in Carrollton so that his three daughters would have a means of support upon his death. The daughters operated it as a hotel for travelers and the occasional teacher who required boarding. It served as a restaurant to town residents as well. Eventually it became a private residence. The Worth Hotel was located on Denton Drive and Oak Street, south of the Cotton Belt Depot and railroad tracks. The structure was relocated to the Dallas Heritage Village in 1972 and was fully restored. (Courtesy of A. W. Perry Homestead Museum, Ogle Collection.)

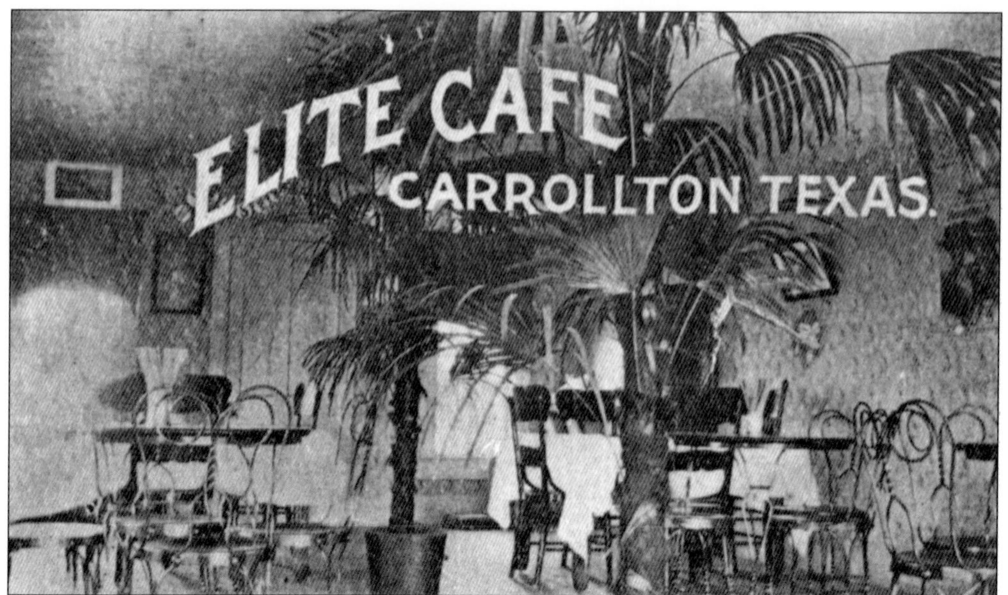

ELITE CAFÉ POSTCARD, 1912. The Elite Café was located on the east side of the square through the 1950s. This postcard was sent to a Jessie Meaders of Dallas, Texas, in 1912. (Courtesy of Ed Williams.)

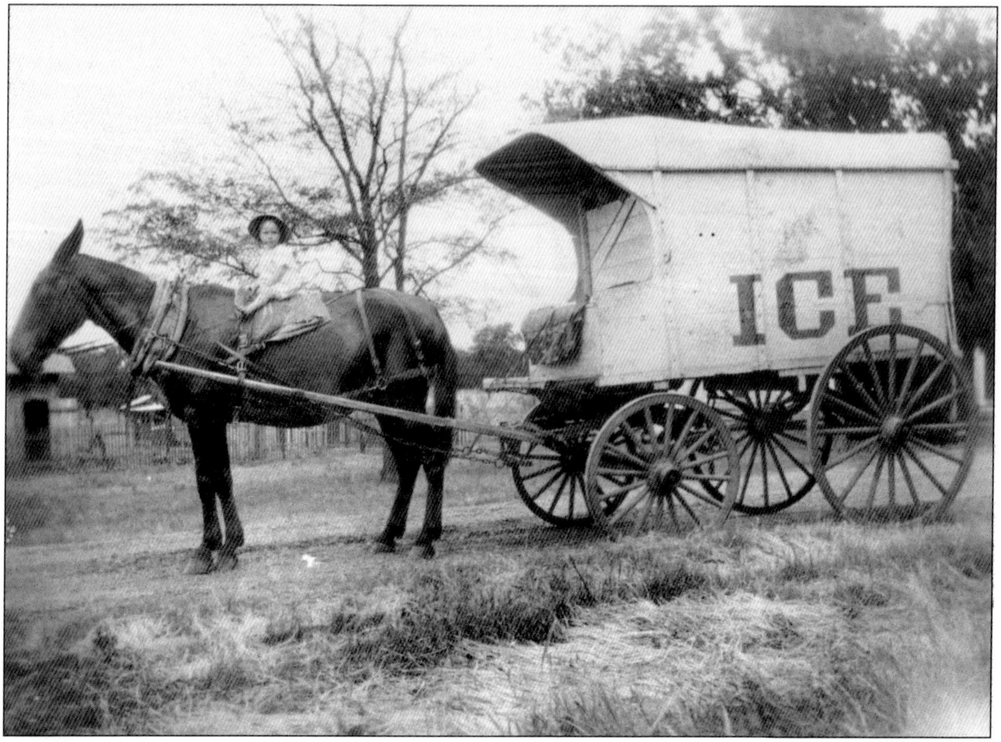

ICE WAGON, C. 1910. Ice wagon delivery service in Carrollton started around 1904 or 1905. This image from around 1910 shows Wade Clifton Myers posing with the horse that pulled the ice wagon operated by his father, G. W. Myers. The iceman would pick up ice from the icehouse and deliver it in large blocks to homes and businesses. (Courtesy of City of Carrollton.)

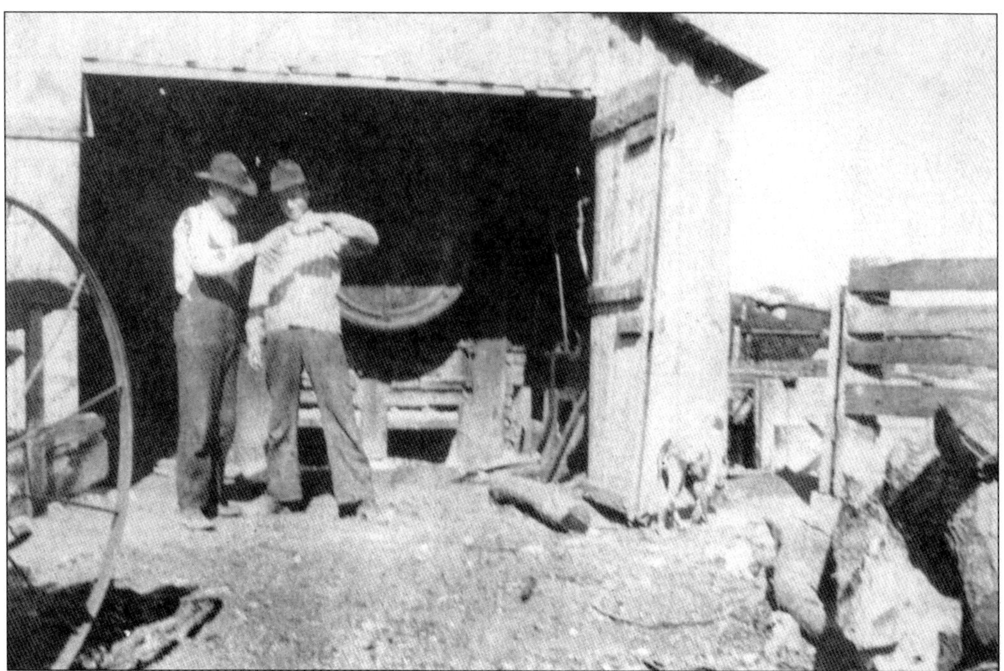

TENDING THE COTTON ENGINE. These images show men starting up and operating the cotton engine, or cotton gin, near the square. The cotton gin is a machine that would separate cotton fibers from its seedpods. Large amounts of cotton were farmed, processed, and shipped from the Carrollton area. Tending the gin was hard, hot work and required fuel to be almost constantly added to the wood-burning engine. Farmers would bring their cotton to the gin for it to be processed. An early advertisement for the Carrollton gin claimed that it could do 50 to 60 bales a day and would even operate at night, if needed, to accommodate everyone waiting. (Both courtesy of A. W. Perry Homestead Museum, Ogle Collection.)

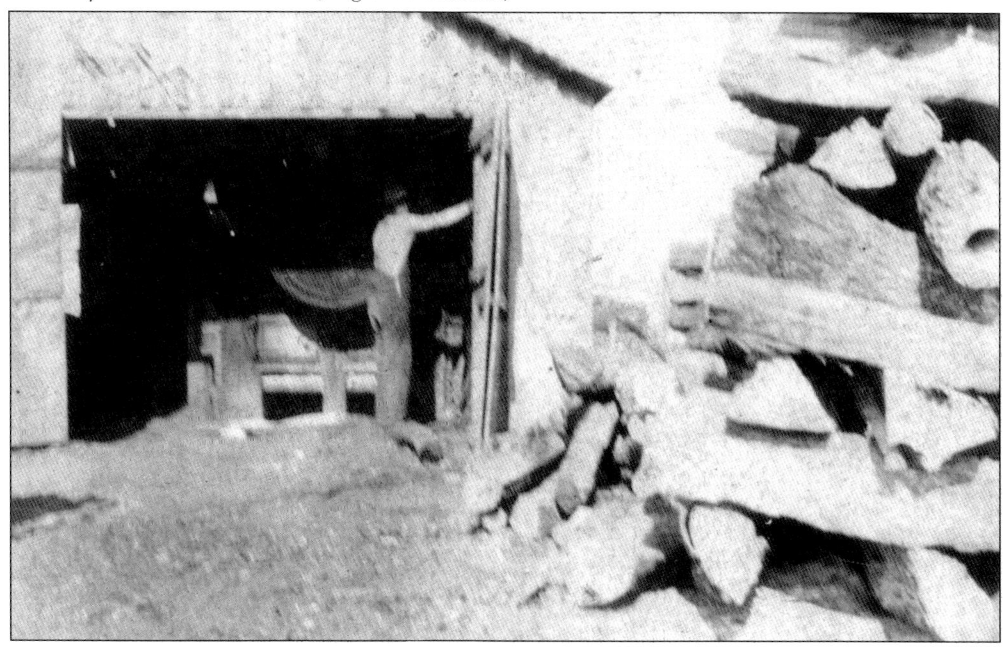

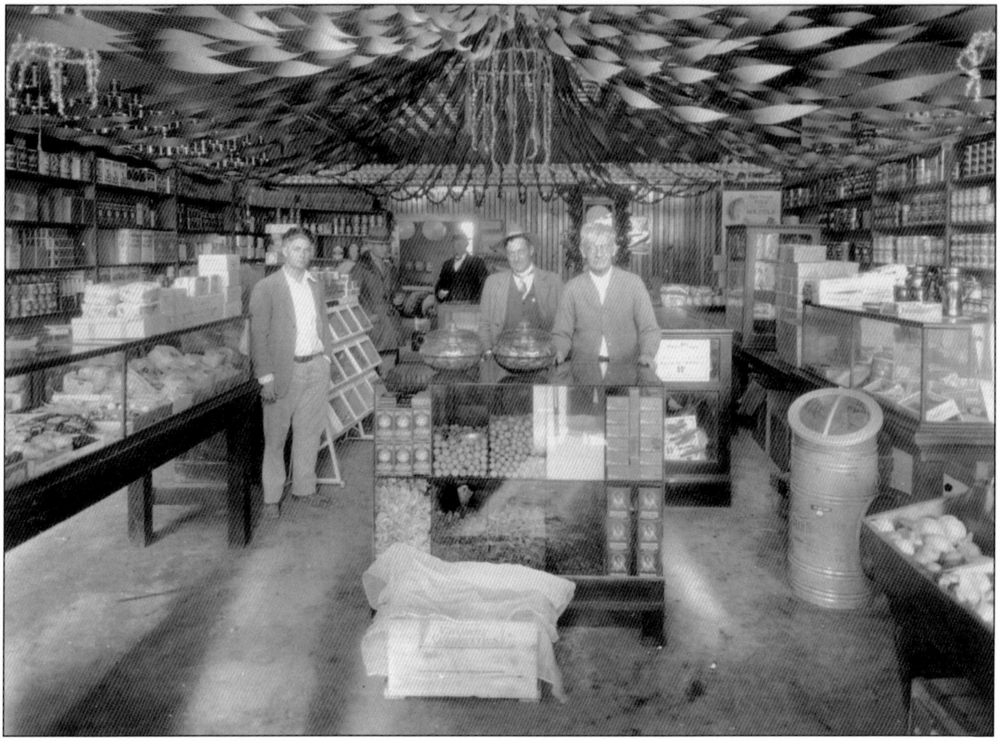

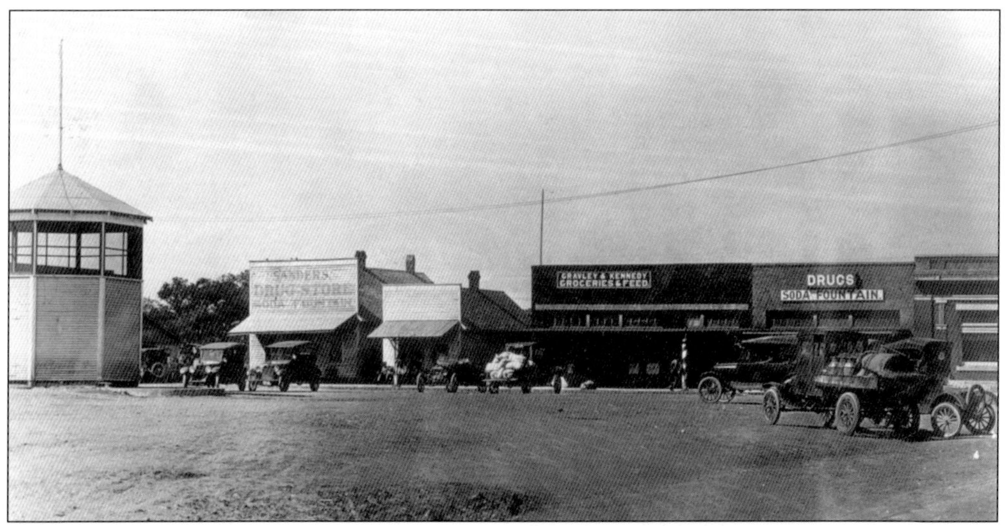

DAVIS AND PERRY GROCERY STORE AT CHRISTMAS, C. 1925. The store was located on the north side of the square. It is decorated for Christmas with crepe paper draped from the ceiling. The men are identified from left to right as Burnett Perry; Henry Noble; "Brother Jones," perhaps a local pastor and a Waples Platter salesman; and J. R. Davis. (Courtesy of Fancy Oliver Tanner.)

TOWN SQUARE, 1921. The edge of the bandstand in the center of the square can be seen on the left side of the image. The businesses from left to right are identified as Sanders Drug Store and Soda Fountain, Gravley and Kennedy Groceries and Feed, and another drug store and soda fountain. (Courtesy of City of Carrollton.)

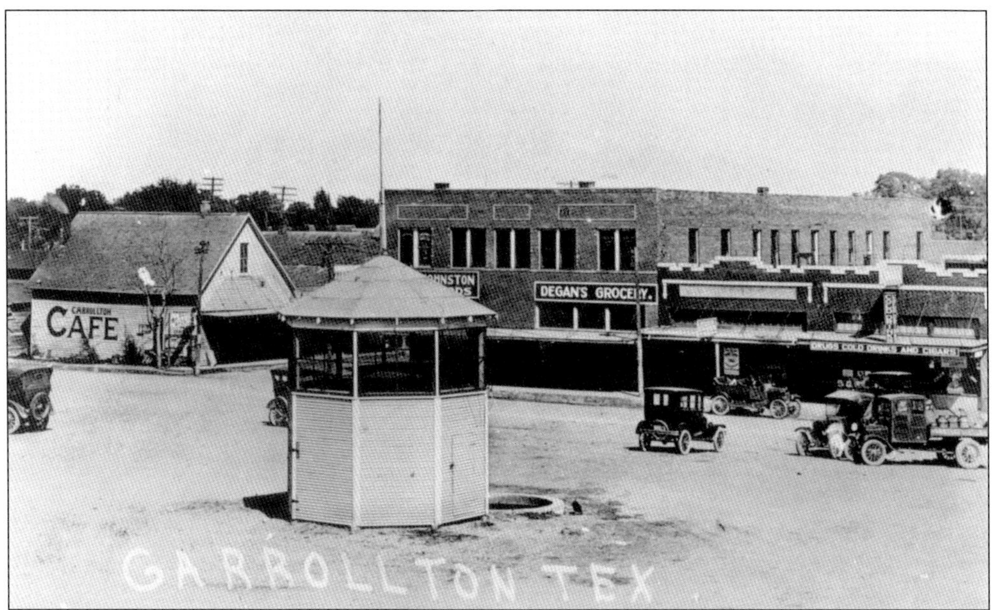

TOWN SQUARE AND BANDSTAND, 1923. This photograph shows the east side of the square. The Carrollton Café, owned by Oscar Wilkinson "Stogie" Fyke, is on the left. The bandstand is the white structure in the center and occupies the place where the gazebo would later be built. (Courtesy of A. W. Perry Homestead Museum, Ogle Collection.)

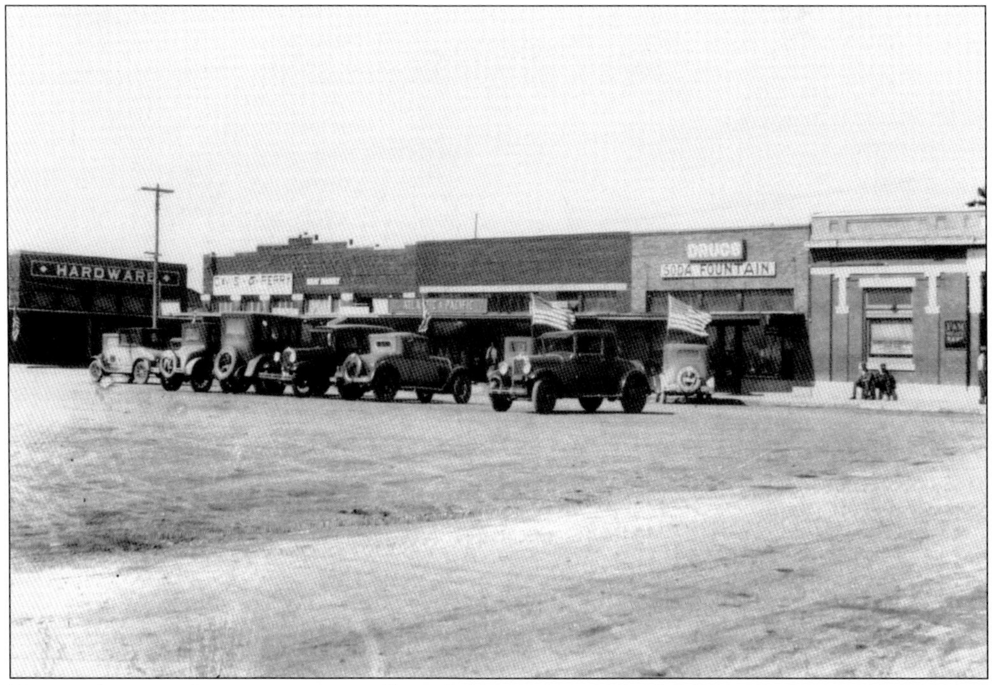

NORTH SIDE OF SQUARE, C. 1930. From left to right are the hardware store, Davis and Perry Grocery, and a drugstore and soda fountain. The far right of the image shows the front of the First State Bank of Carrollton building. (Courtesy of Fancy Oliver Tanner.)

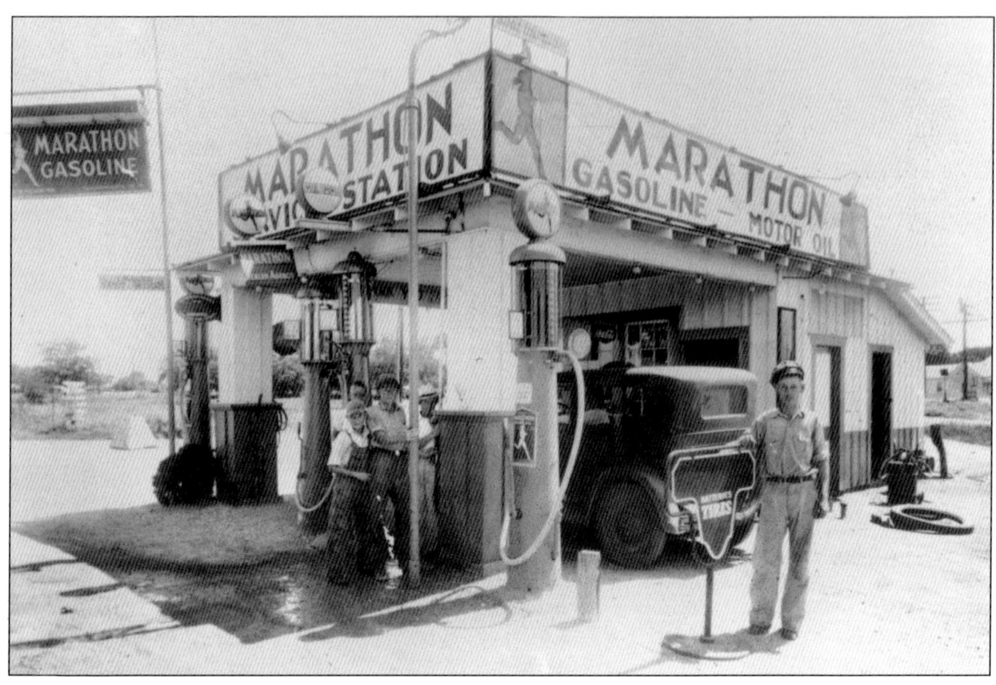

MARATHON SERVICE STATION, C. 1935. In the image above, Jack Ogle stands outside the Marathon Service Station, located on the southeast corner of Belt Line Road and Broadway. The three boys standing by the gas pumps are unidentified. In the image below, M. C. Kirkham sits on the fender of a car in front of the station in 1938. A reproduction of the Marathon Gas Station is on display at the Farmers Branch Historical Park in Farmers Branch. (Both courtesy of City of Carrollton.)

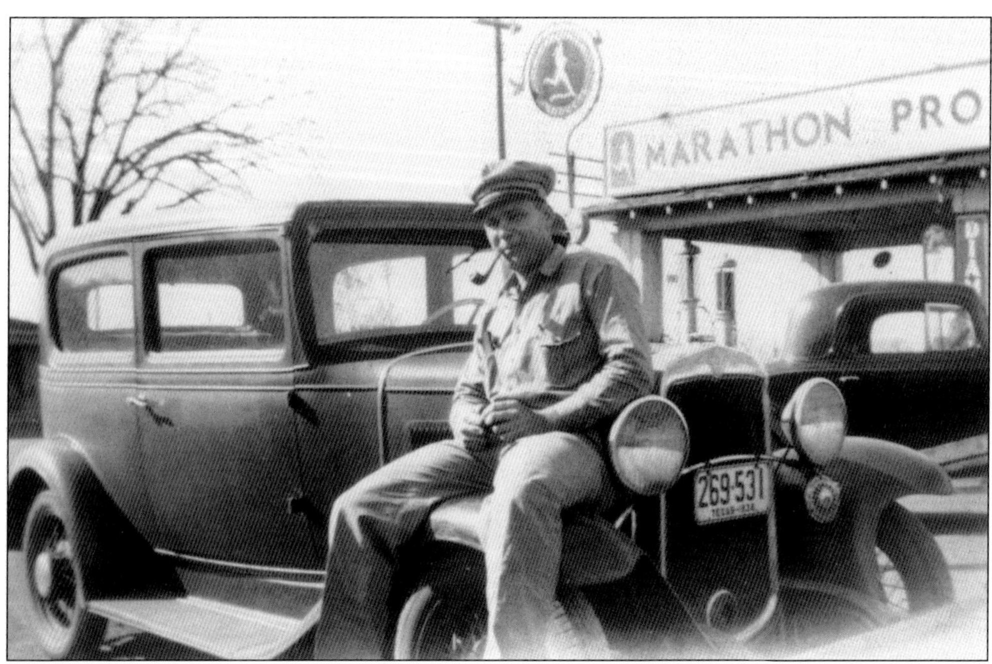

GEORGE FRANKLIN MYERS. George F. Myers was born in 1855 on his family's farm near the corner of present-day Josey Lane and Country Club Lane. A post office and a general merchandise store were located there until they were moved to the square once the railroads arrived. George Myers embraced new technologies. He was credited with having the first home telephone in Carrollton and the first Victrola for listening to music. He owned a general store, operated a cotton gin, was the postmaster, and built gas stations, cafés, and grocery stores. He opened a movie theater on the west side of the square and constructed an outdoor theater for the summertime. He organized fairs and exhibits for the town. At the 1922 Carrollton Country Fair, Myers displayed artifacts from his life in front of his store for an exhibit he called "From the Cradle to the Present." (Courtesy of A. W. Perry Homestead Museum, Ogle Collection.)

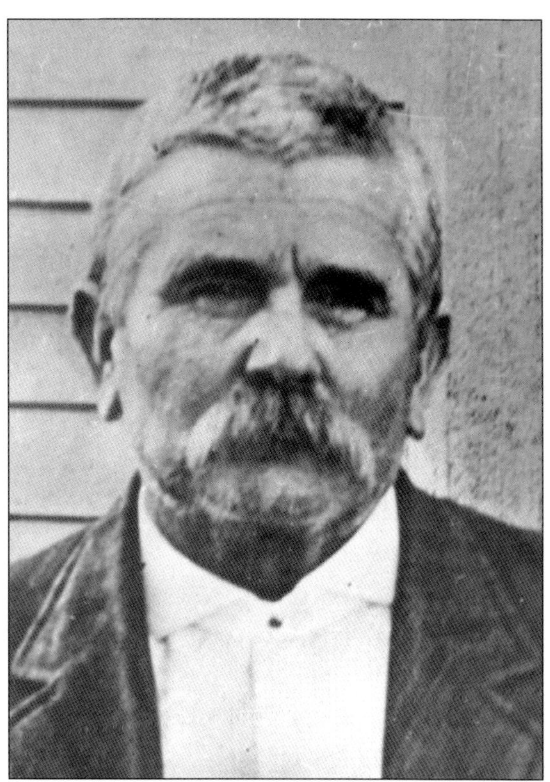

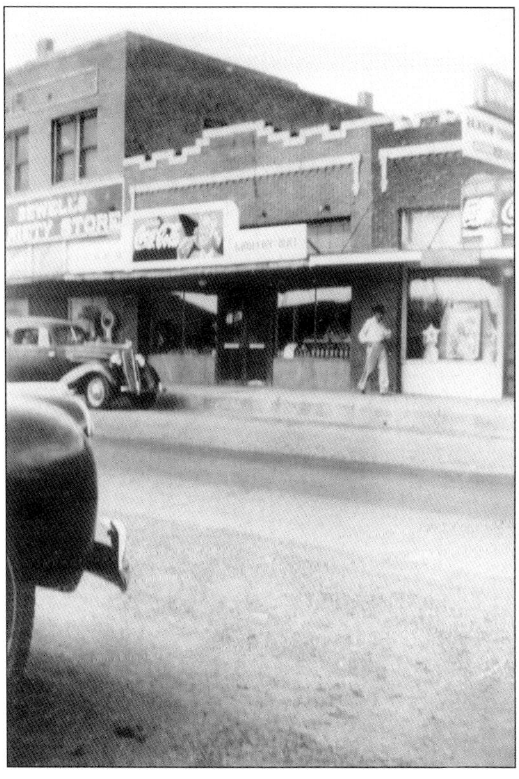

EAST SIDE OF SQUARE, 1940s. This is a view of Broadway on the east side of the square. Sewell's Variety Store, Perry Grocery, and Rainbow Pharmacy were the businesses located there at the time. These are the same buildings that occupy the east side of Broadway today. (Courtesy of Fancy Oliver Tanner.)

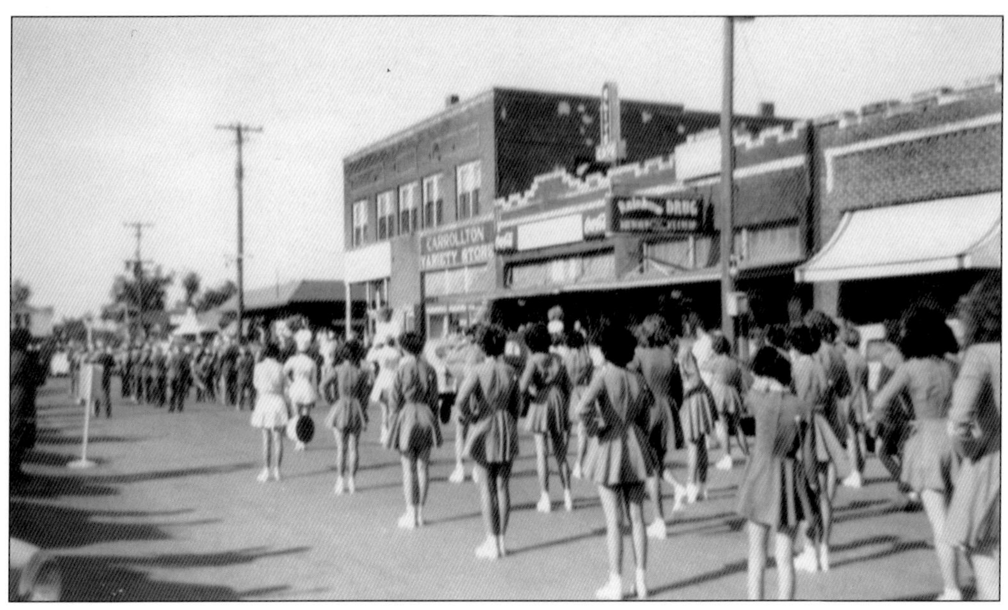

HOMECOMING PARADE ON BROADWAY, 1950S. A homecoming parade for Carrollton High School was held each year on the square. Businesses seen on the east side of the square behind the marchers, above, are the Carrollton Variety Store, Elite Café, Rainbow Pharmacy, and Perry's Foods. In the image below, the seniors of the class of 1950 proudly display their float, complete with a "Clean Up Mesquite" slogan to rally their team against the opponent. (Both courtesy of Fancy Oliver Tanner.)

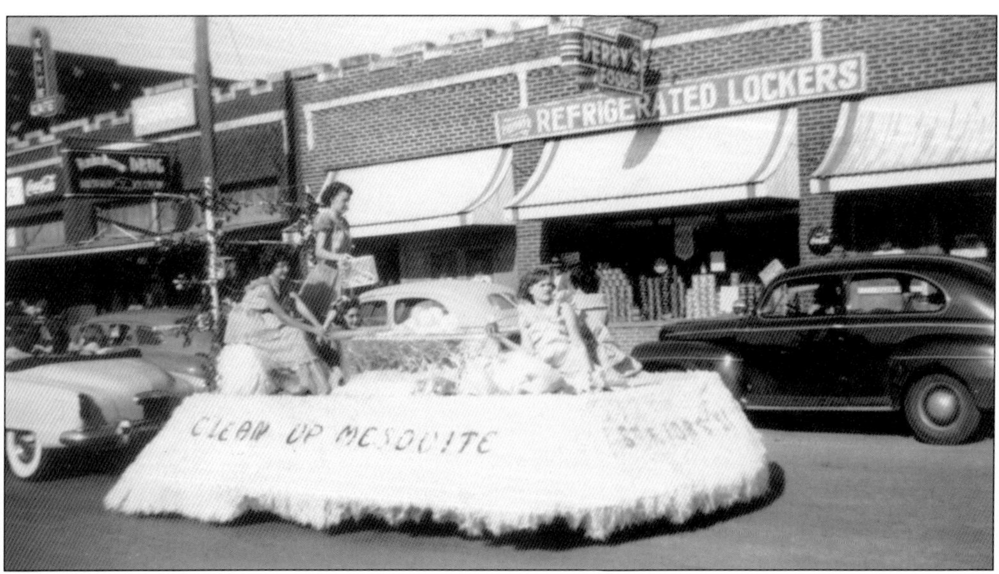

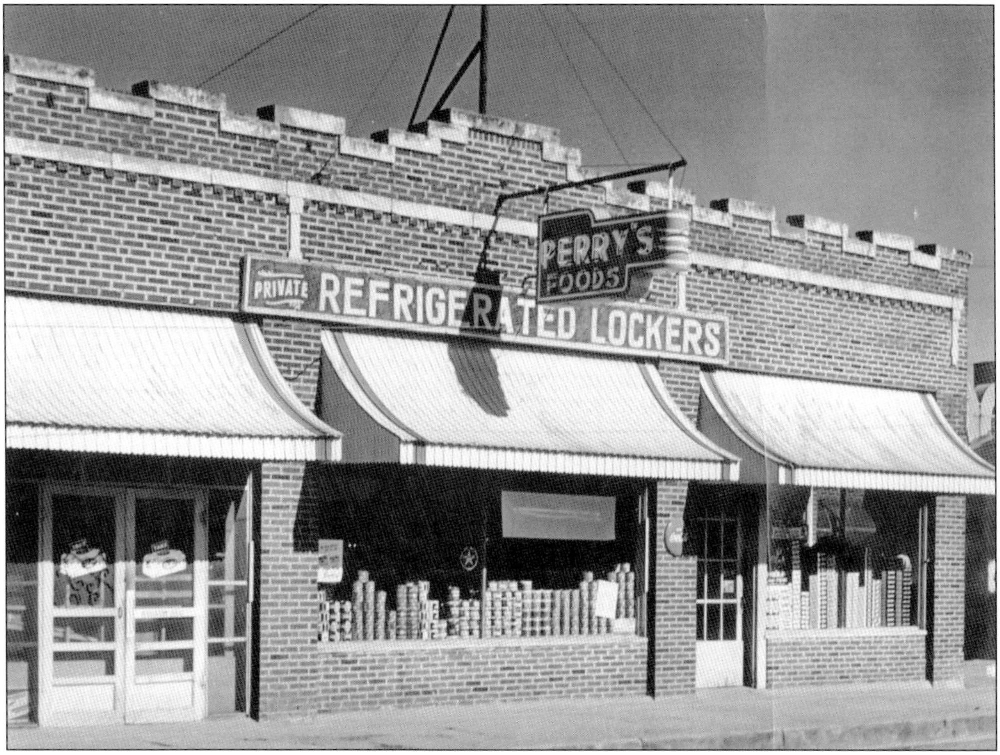

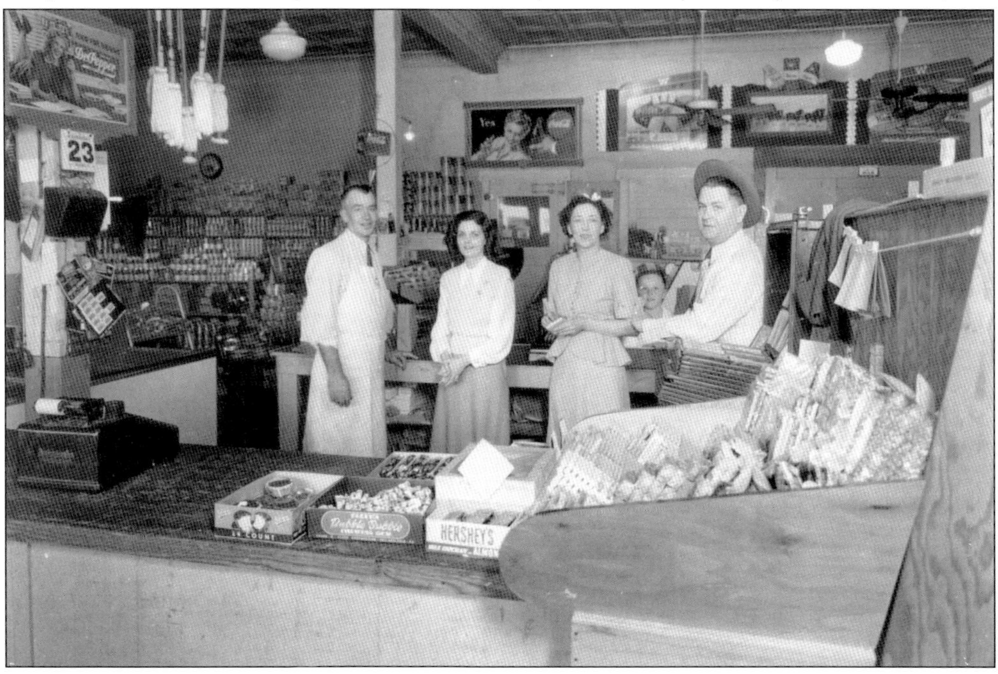

INTERIOR AND EXTERIOR OF PERRY'S FOODS, C. 1950. This store was located on the east side of the square at Broadway and Fourth Street. Pictured below are, from left to right, Lloyd (the store's butcher), Peggy Perry Oliver, Pearl Perry, and Burnett Perry. These photographs were taken of Perry's Foods before a subsequent remodel in 1953. (Both courtesy of Fancy Oliver Tanner.)

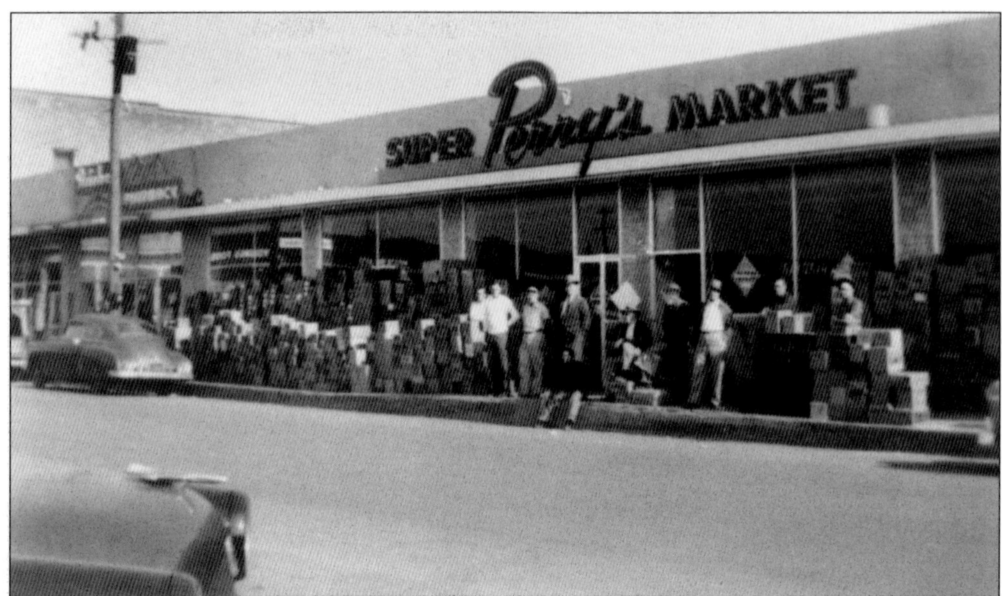

PERRY'S SUPER MARKET. Owner's Burnett and Eva Lee Perry remodeled Perry's Foods in 1954 and turned it into the more modern Perry's Super Market in the same location on the east side of the square. Burnett and Eva Lee returned from a vacation in June 1954 to the burned-out remains of their newly remodeled store. The above photograph was taken after the first remodel and subsequent fire when it was rebuilt and they were once again ready to move back in and reopen. (Both courtesy of Fancy Oliver Tanner.)

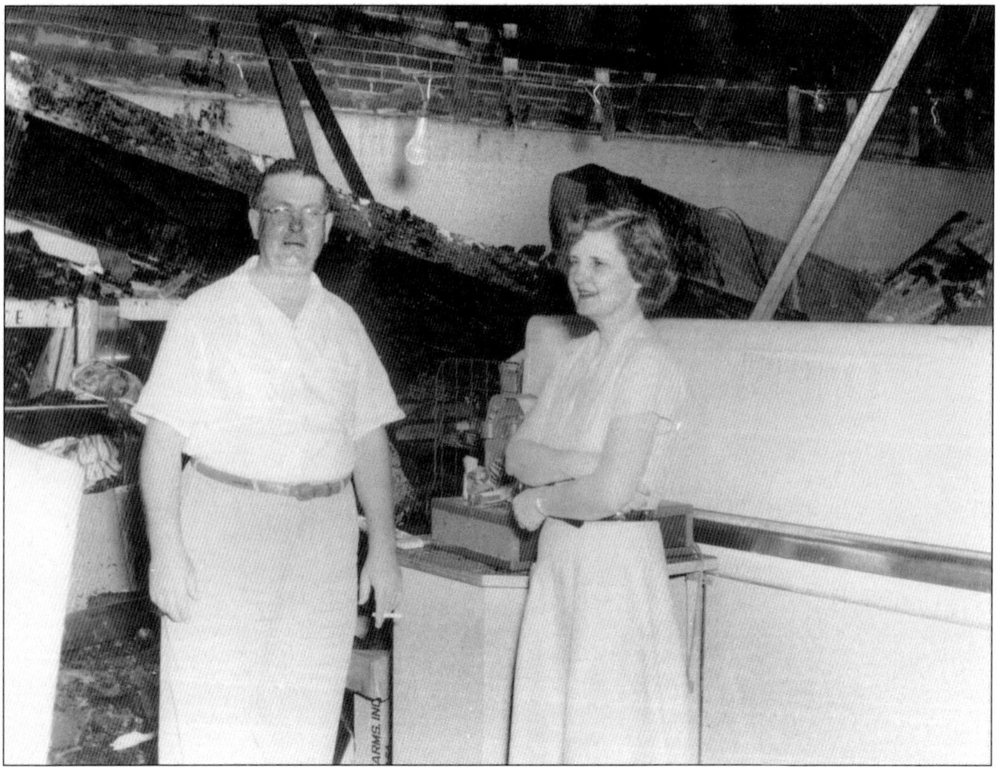

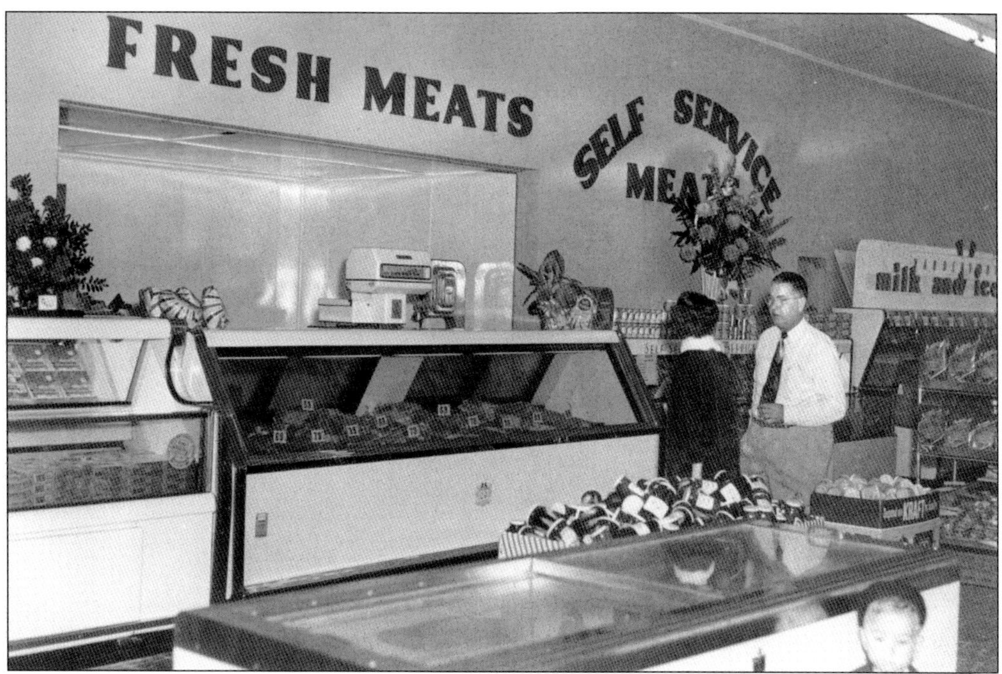

INTERIOR OF PERRY'S SUPER MARKET, 1954. These images are interior views of the supermarket after it was reopened. Above, owner Burnett Perry and his daughter Peggy Perry Oliver are touring the store during its grand reopening in November 1954. The image below shows the refrigerated portion of the store. The remodeled store had a green tile floor that is still present in the building, which is now used as an antiques mall. (Both courtesy of Fancy Oliver Tanner.)

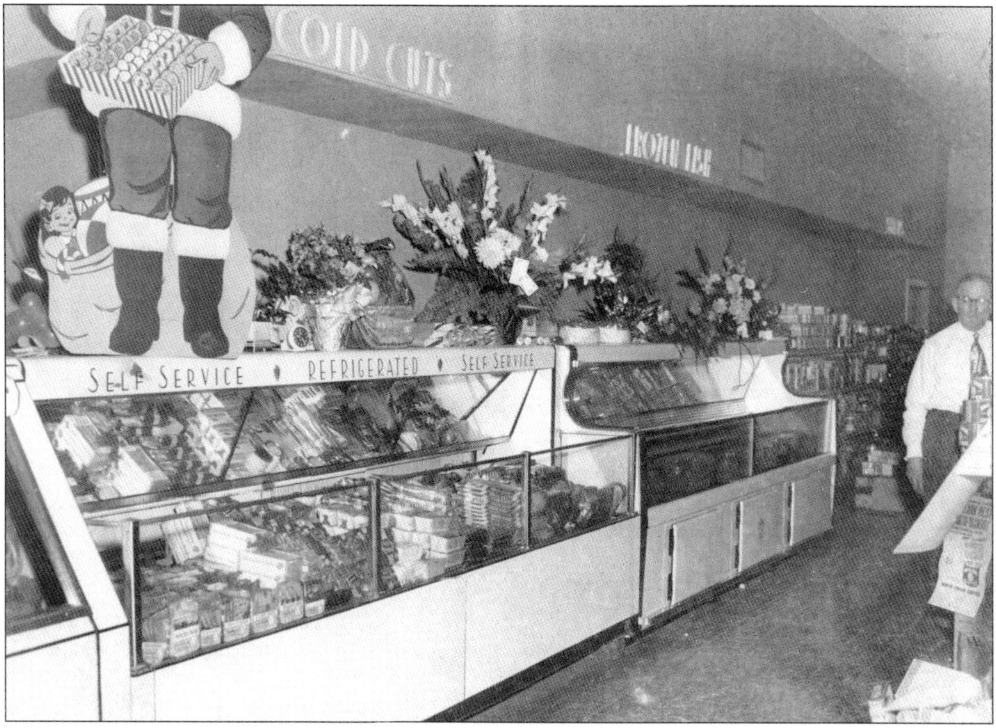

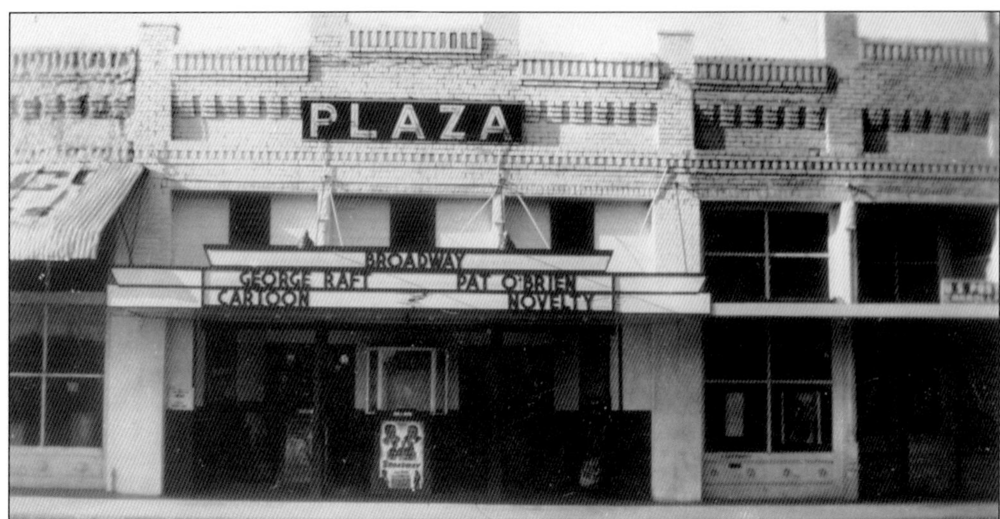

PLAZA THEATER, C. 1942. The first movie theater in Carrollton was actually a large white sheet nailed to the side of George Myers's store on the southeast corner of the square in the early 1900s. Myers later operated a theater on the west side of the square until the 1930s. A. R. "Cap" and Vera Perry Lowrey reopened the movie theater in 1940. This image shows that theater. The movie on the marquis is the 1942 *Broadway* starring George Raft and Pat O'Brien. (Courtesy of A. W. Perry Homestead Museum, Ogle Collection.)

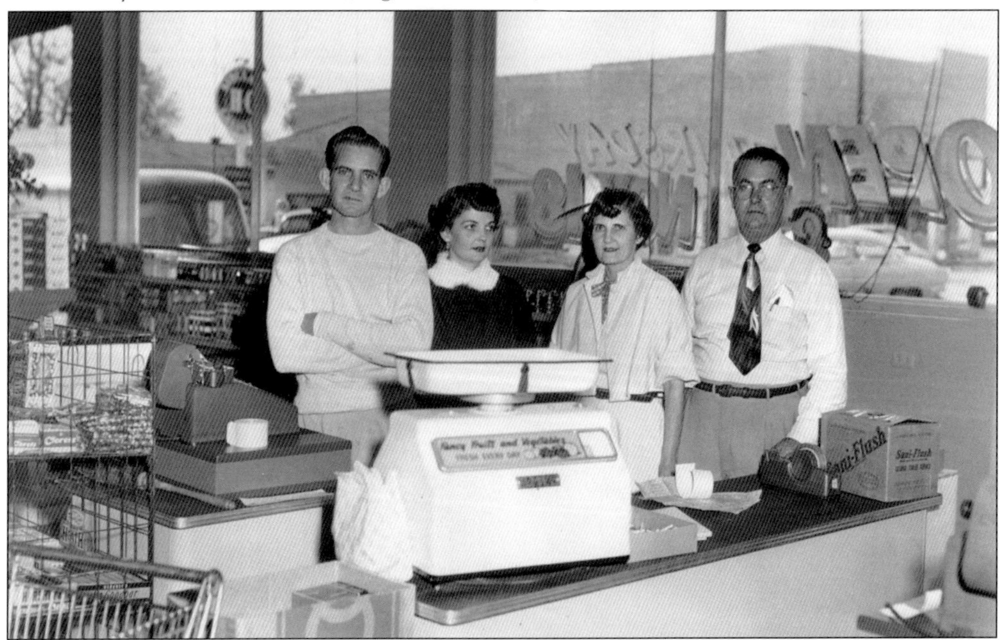

PLAZA THEATER SEEN THROUGH WINDOW OF PERRY'S SUPER MARKET. Vera Perry Lowrey's Plaza Theater can be seen out the store's window over the shoulders of those in the picture. Built in 1949, it replaced the Lowreys' first theater, shown in the previous photograph. According to city records, the new Plaza Theater was the first air-conditioned building in town. It is still located on the south side of the square and currently operates as an arts center. Individuals inside the store are identified from left to right as Edward Oliver, Peggy Perry Oliver, Eva Lee, and Burnett Perry. (Courtesy of Fancy Oliver Tanner.)

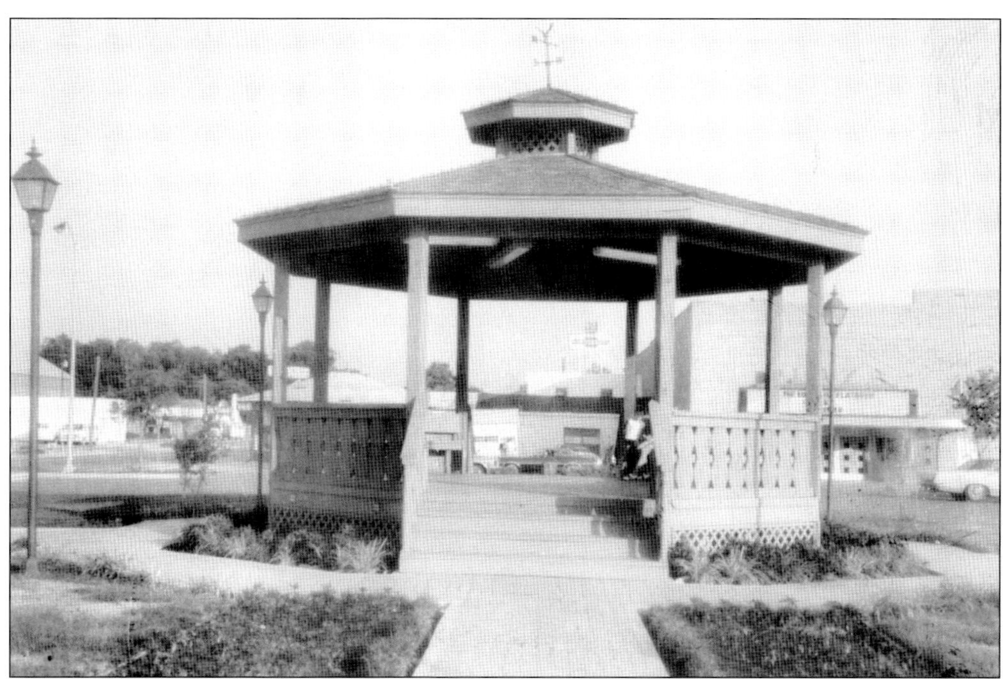

GAZEBO ON THE SQUARE, 1960S. The gazebo was first built as a bandstand in 1921. It marks the center of the square and was originally the location of an artesian well that served as the water supply for nearby homes and businesses. A pump and hand-pushed fire hose cart were stored below the bandstand in case of emergencies. It became a place for political speeches, concerts, dances, and the focal point for many other community celebrations. (Courtesy of A. W. Perry Homestead Museum, Ogle Collection.)

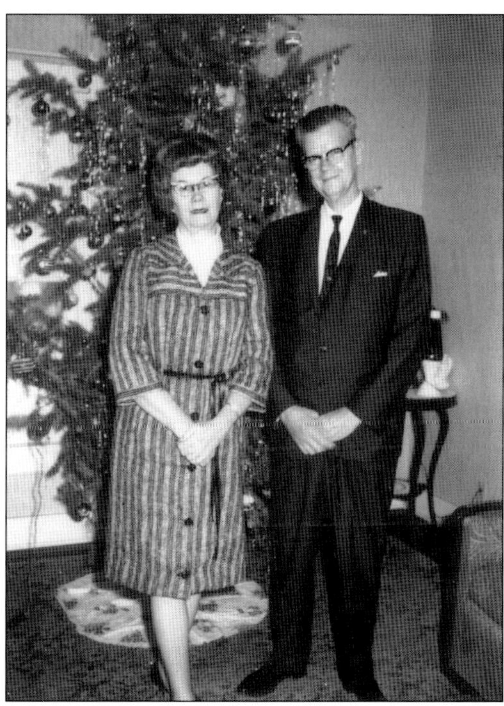

THE SQUARE AS THE COMMUNITY CENTER. Darrell and Eunice Myers were married on Christmas Eve in 1929 in the gazebo in the center of the square. A community Christmas tree was erected next to the gazebo in anticipation of the large holiday party. At the start of the festivities, Santa Claus called Darrell forward to accept the first gift, a blushing bride. After the ceremony, a 52-piece set of china was presented to the couple from the Carrollton Fire Department, and a silverware set was given to them by the businessmen's association. This image celebrates the couple's 37th wedding anniversary. (Courtesy of A. W. Perry Homestead Museum, Ogle Collection.)

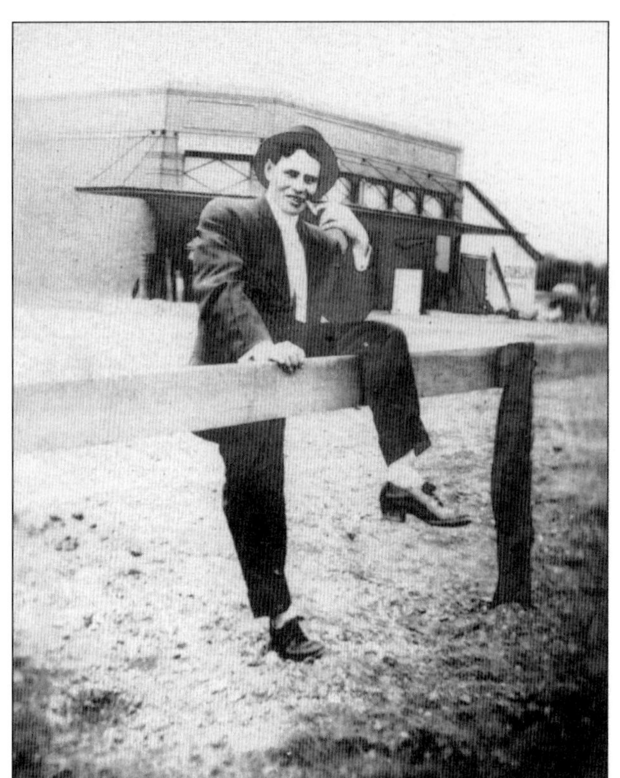

CARROLLTON HARDWARE STORE. The building behind the unidentified young man is the Carrollton Hardware store. A. W. Risien built the store sometime between 1900 and 1904 from brick manufactured by the Carrollton Pressed Brick Company. In 1915, Charley and Jerry Chastain purchased the business and continued to operate it as Carrollton Hardware. Roy Gravley became the sole owner of the business in 1933, after which it became known as Gravley Hardware. (Courtesy of Fancy Oliver Tanner.)

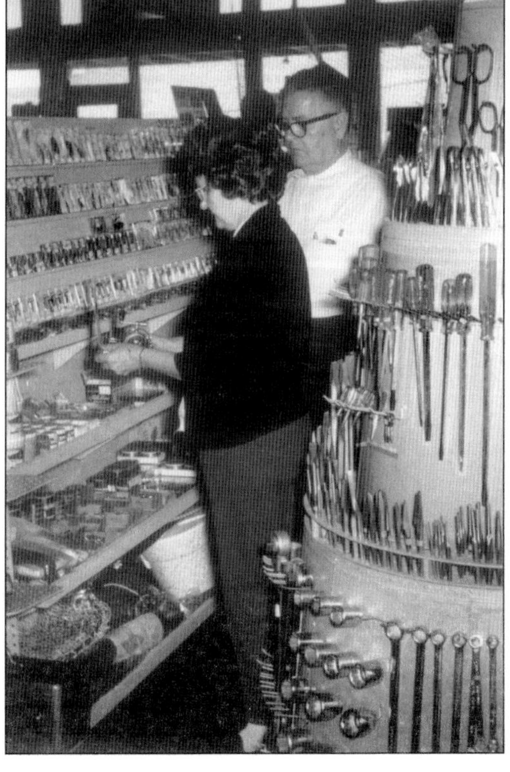

INTERIOR OF GRAVLEY HARDWARE, 1960S. Before big chain stores, Gravley Hardware provided citizens with everything they needed for home improvement and repairs. In 1966, owner Roy Gravley Jr. sold the business to his cousin Milburn Gravley, who ran the store until the early 1980s. Burnett and Eva Lee Perry are pictured browsing the aisles. (Courtesy of Fancy Oliver Tanner.)

Four

RINGING THE BELL
CHURCHES AND SCHOOLS

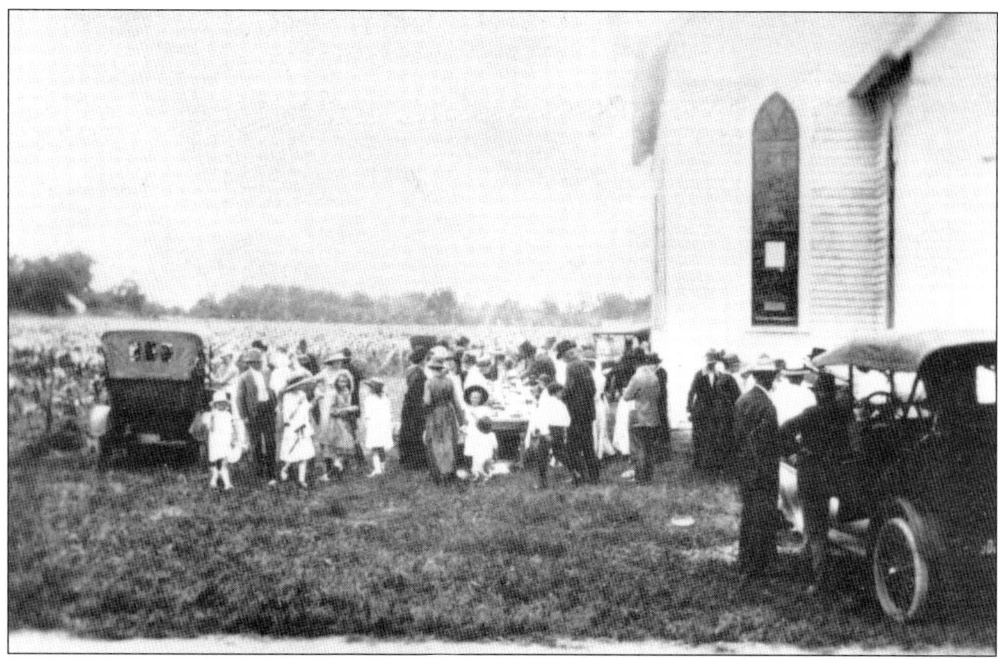

LUNCH ON THE GROUNDS OF THE UNION BAPTIST CHURCH, C. 1915. The Union Baptist Church was the earliest Baptist church established in Dallas County. Rev. David Myers led the first service in a pioneer cabin in 1846. The church moved from location to location throughout its early years. In 1896, a church building was constructed on land belonging to A. W. Perry where the Perry Cemetery exists today. This photograph was taken around 1915 after the church had been moved to Belt Line Road, then known as College Avenue. (Courtesy of A. W. Perry Homestead Museum, Ogle Collection.)

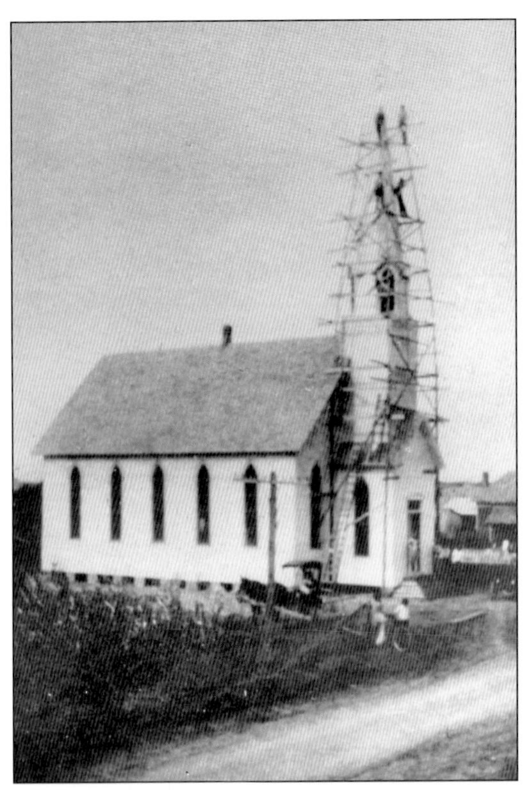

UNION BAPTIST CHURCH, C. 1911. The church was physically moved around 1911 to be closer to the homes and businesses surrounding the square and nearer to the railroad depot than its Perry Road location. Church members organized and funded the move. When the move was complete, a group of women were appointed to finish decorating. This "Ladies Aid" group, as it was referred to in the church's minutes, consisted of Ada Brake, Ollie Perry, Sally Myers, and Lura Fyke. They were responsible for selecting new wallpaper and fixtures for the building. (Both courtesy of A. W. Perry Homestead Museum, Ogle Collection.)

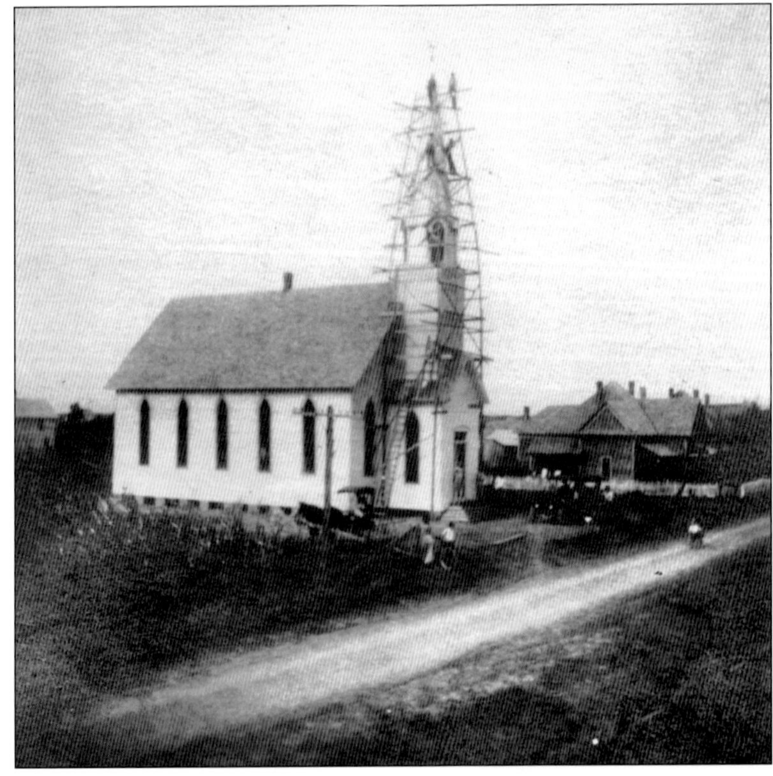

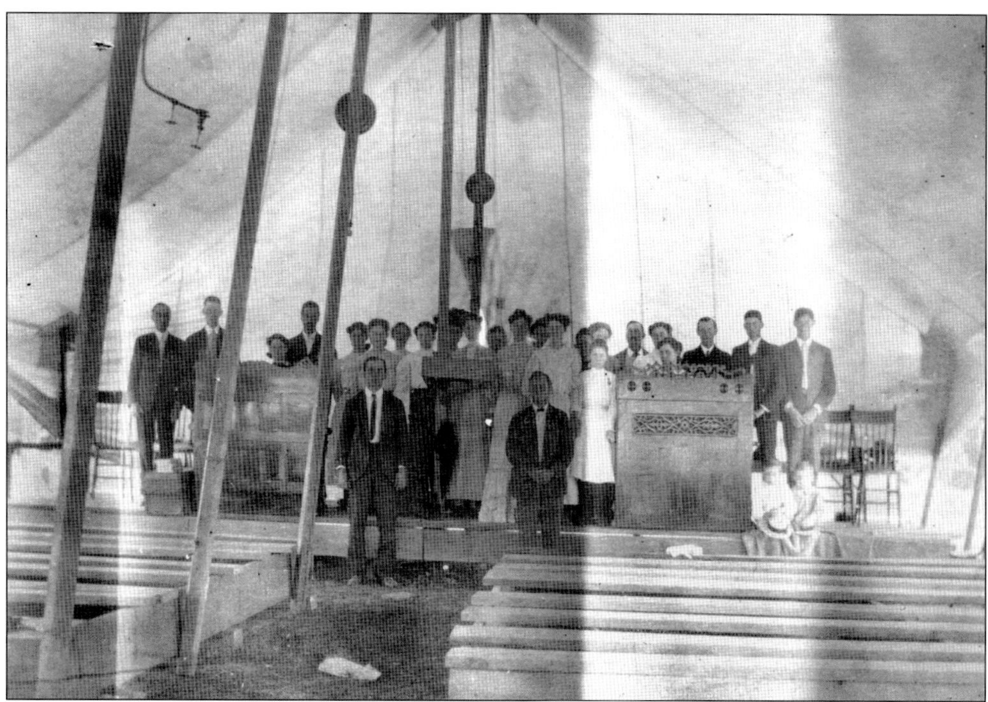

TENT MEETING, C. 1910. In the summer and before air-conditioning, tent meetings were often held on the lawn of a church. They were also held at the edge of town to draw in larger crowds in the hopes of attracting new members to the faith. In the center of the photograph, light from an open tent flap pours into the interior. The tent is complete with a piano for the service and a fire sprinkler system for safety. (Courtesy of A. W. Perry Homestead Museum, Ogle Collection.)

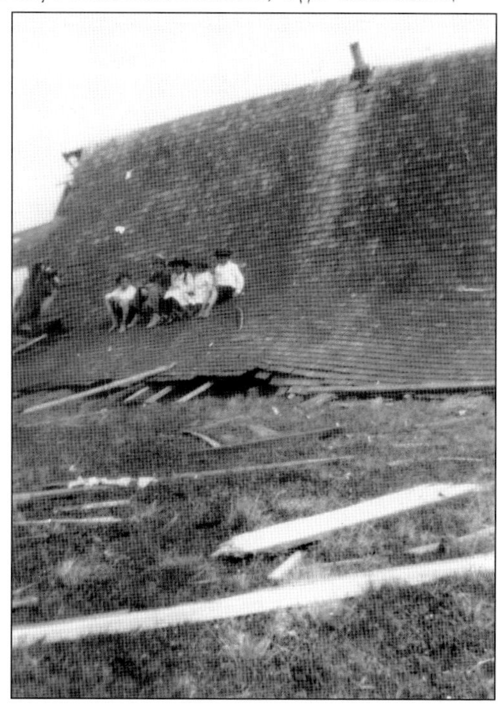

CEMETERY HILL UNION CHURCH, C. 1925. Cemetery Hill was the location of Union Church, but it was destroyed by a tornado in 1925 and was not reconstructed. However, historic Furneaux Cemetery remains and can be visited by those curious about this area of Carrollton and its early residents, many of which emigrated from England. William Furneaux had intended to establish the cemetery on his property but died suddenly before being able to finalize his plans. His family deeded property for the church and for Furneaux Cemetery after his passing. The children pictured sitting on the church's roof are Lee Watts, R. L. Brown, Bertie Bell Brown, Maxie Watts, and Johnie Watts. (Courtesy of A. W. Perry Homestead Museum, Ogle Collection.)

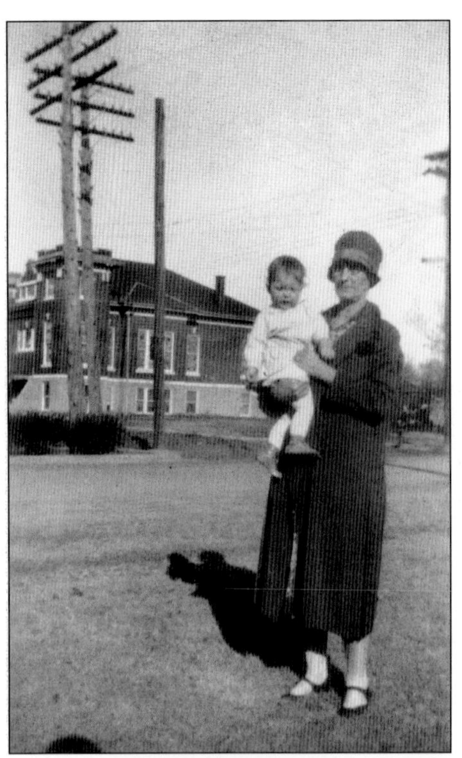

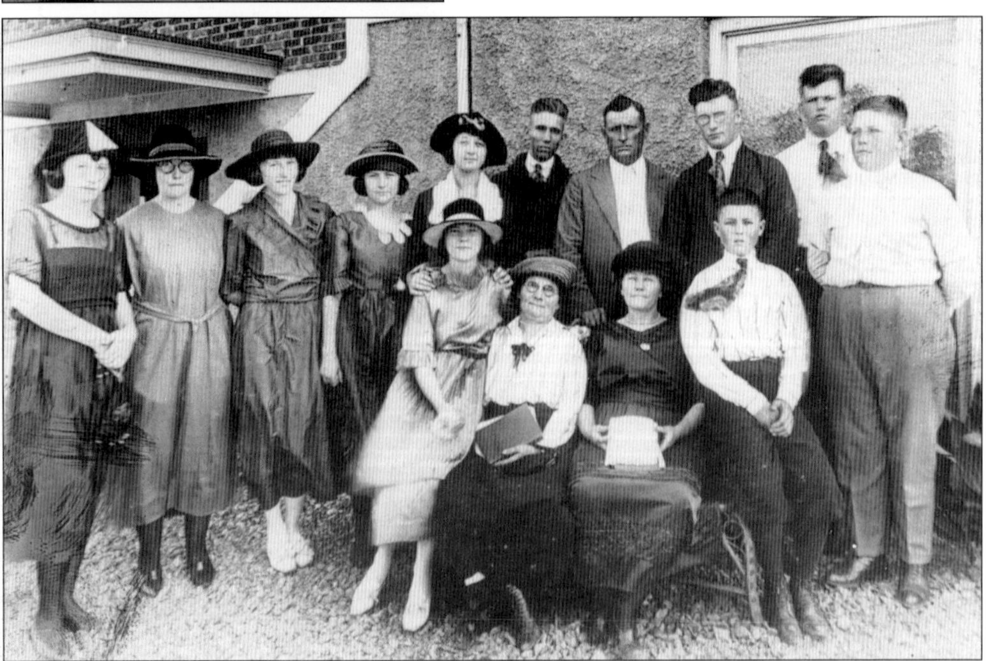

FIRST UNITED METHODIST CHURCH, 1930S. The First United Methodist Church's first meeting place was the attic of a store on the northeast side of the square. A wood-frame building was constructed in 1903, and the large redbrick building seen in this photograph was built around 1915 and was located on Belt Line Road at Jackson Street. (Courtesy of Fancy Oliver Tanner.)

FIRST UNITED METHODIST CHURCH SUNDAY SCHOOL CLASS, C. 1917. Pictured here from left to right are (first row) Louise Perry, Alice Padgett, Mrs. Andrew Jackson, and Boyd Huffines; (second row) Elsie Whitlock, unidentified, Faye Whitlock, Lula Gravley, Connie Hardcastle, Bennie Glidewell, W. T. Squibb, Chester Nowlen, Sidney Noel, and Arthur E. "Fat" Gravley. (Courtesy of City of Carrollton.)

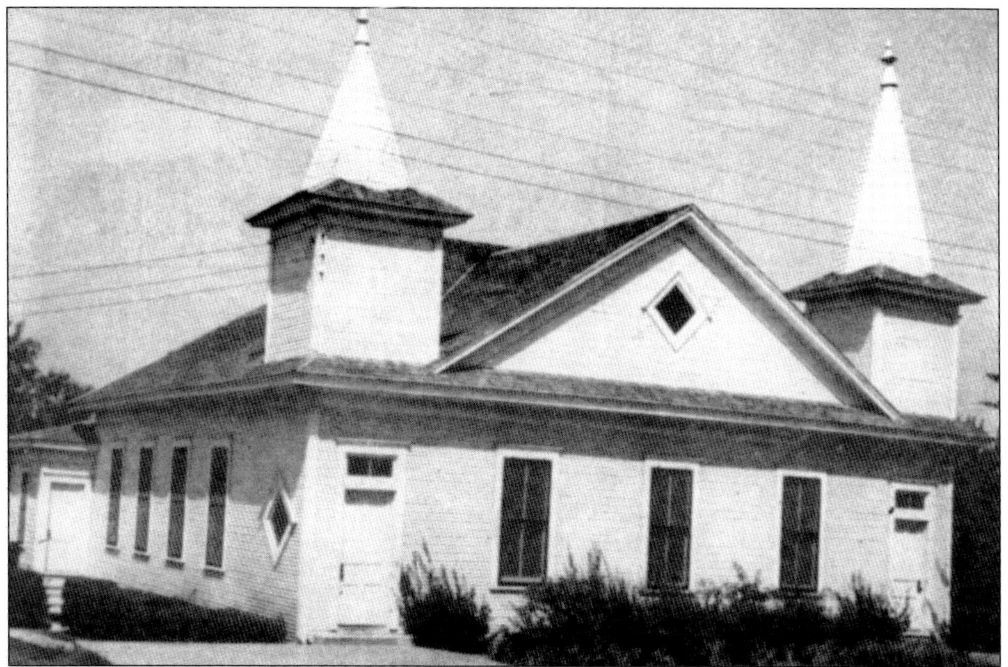

FIRST BAPTIST CHURCH POSTCARD, 1913. Located at the corner of Erie and Walnut Streets, the church was first organized in 1909. Its members wanted a church closer to their homes and the main part of town than Union Baptist Church, so they created a second Baptist church for the growing community. (Courtesy of A. W. Perry Homestead Museum, Ogle Collection.)

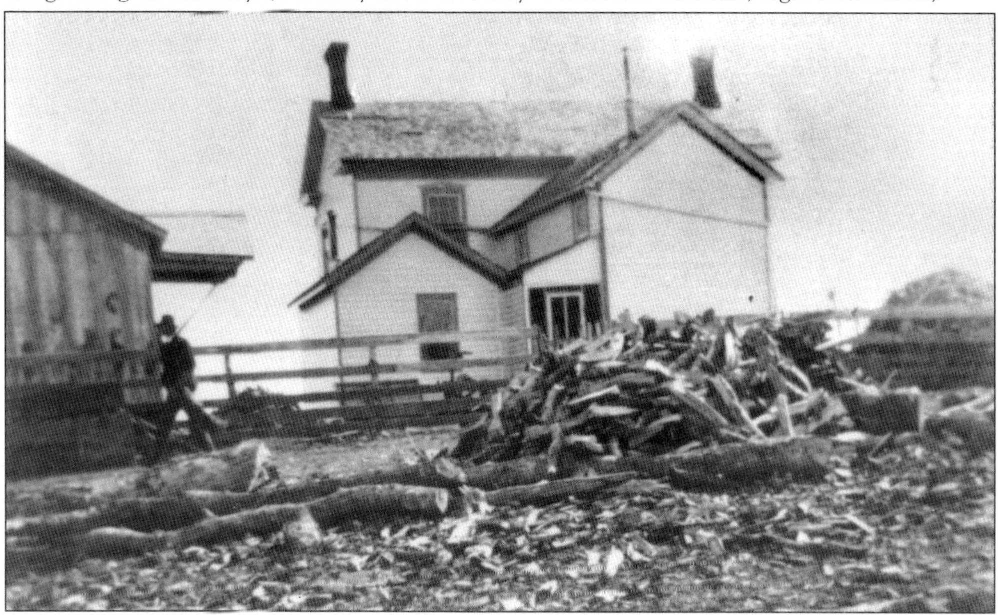

WOOD LOT AT THE MORGAN SCHOOL, TOR HILL, C. 1890. Schools were often organized by and held in churches. Schools in private homes of area residents were also common. Margaret Oliver Morgan opened a private school on her family's farm, "Tor Hill." Subjects at Morgan's school included arithmetic, grammar, geography, history, and dictation. Girls also learned needlepoint. (Courtesy of A. W. Perry Homestead Museum, Ogle Collection.)

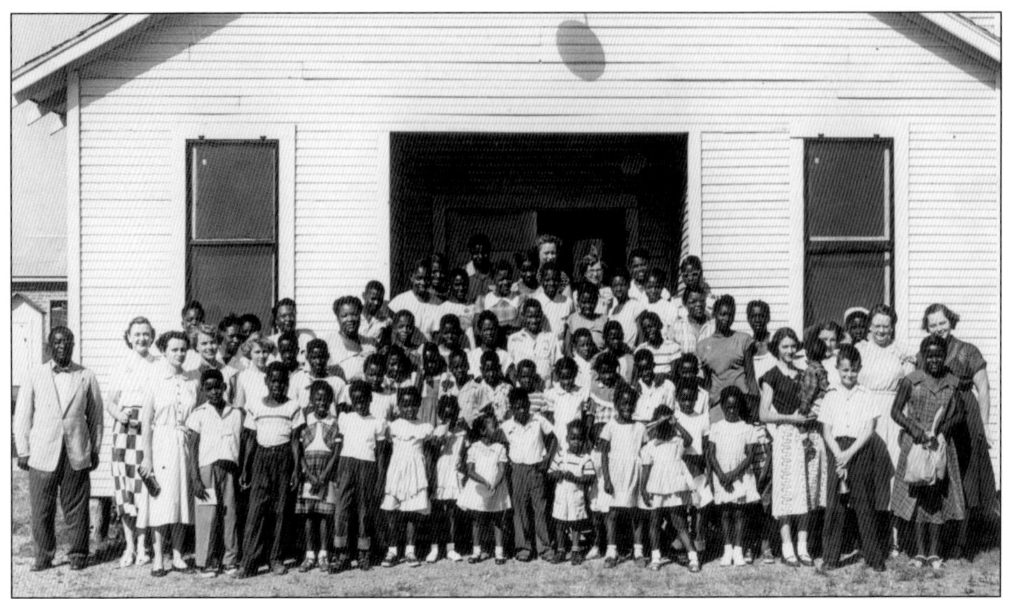

Simms Chapel African Methodist Exchange. Simms Chapel AME was established in 1890 and was led by the Reverend Wash Simms, who delivered such intense, fiery sermons he was nicknamed the "Black Angel." The congregation was moved to West College Avenue in 1939 when Highway 77, now Interstate 35, was constructed. (Courtesy of Willie Rainwater.)

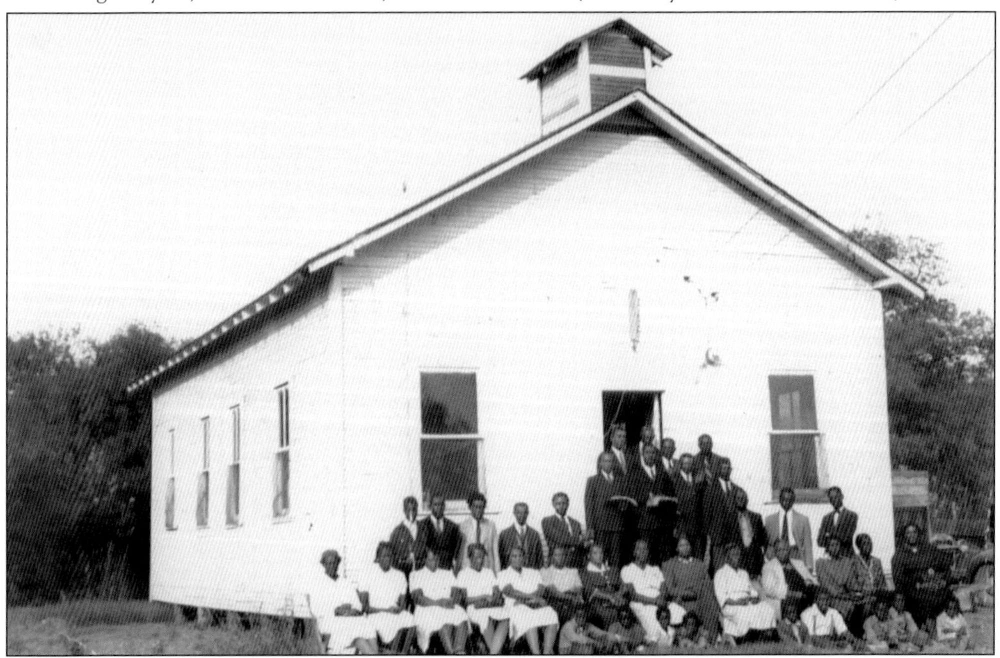

St. John's Baptist Church, c. 1955. Established after the Civil War on land donated by the Union Baptist Church and its minister, David Myers, St. John's is the oldest African American church in Carrollton. This image from the 1950s shows a Bible school class sponsored by the Ethyl Hardy Business Women's Circle of the First Baptist Church. St. John's Baptist Church is located north of Crosby Road on South Broadway. (Courtesy of A. W. Perry Homestead Museum, Ogle Collection.)

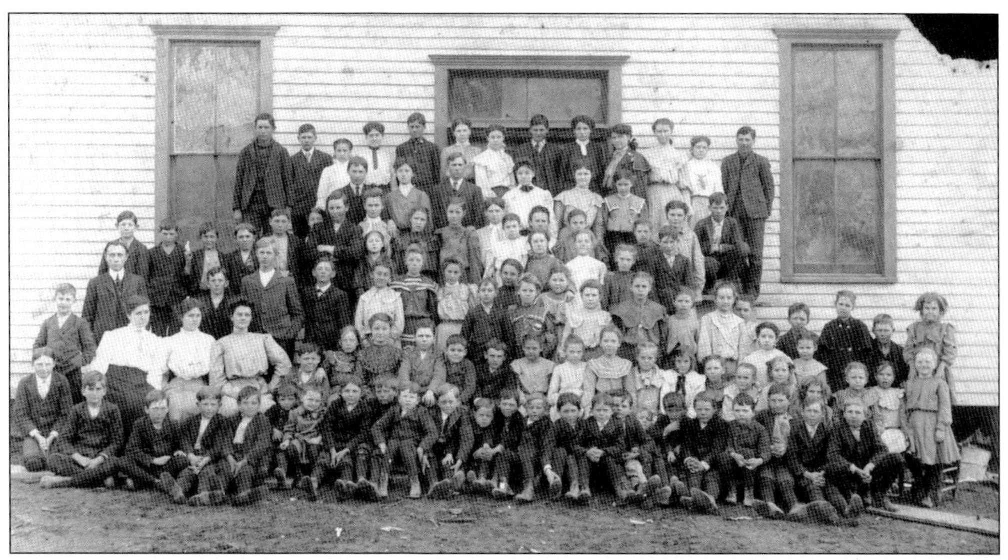

CARROLLTON SCHOOL, C. 1903. A new, two-story, five-room school building located at the corner of what is now Belt Line Road and Erie Street opened for the 1902 school year. It was built on a 9-acre site donated by A. W. Perry. Advertisements were sent out to surrounding communities to attract additional students who could find board with private families for $10 per month. Grade levels included primary first through fourth, grammar or intermediate grades fifth through seventh, and high school, which consisted of grades 8 through 10. (Courtesy of Hal Simon, Nix family collection.)

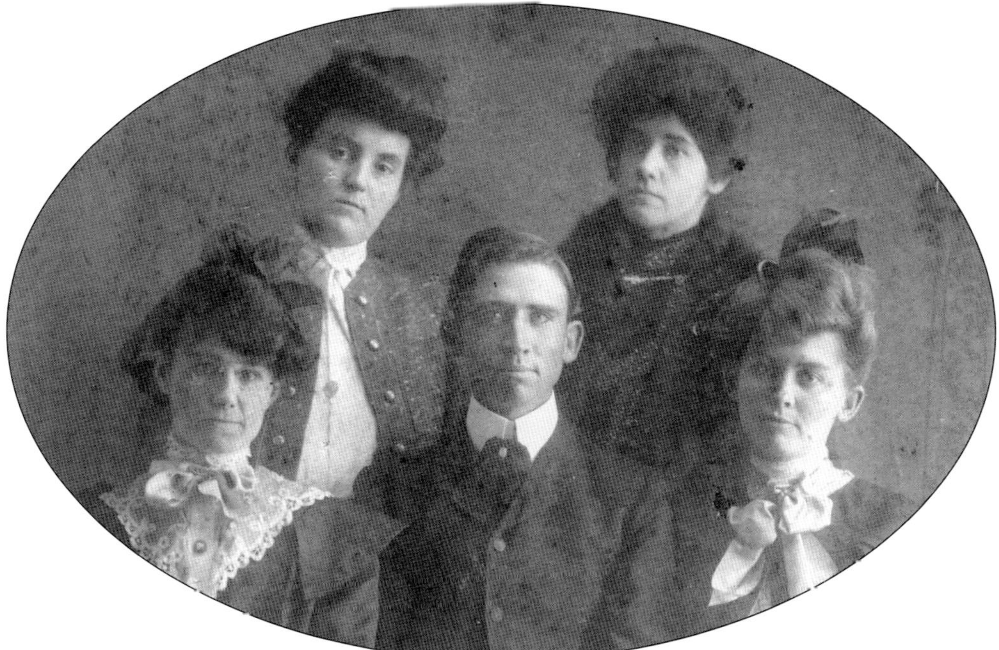

CARROLLTON SCHOOL FACULTY, C. 1902. The teachers of Carrollton's first public school included Nora Blalach, W. T. Squibb, and Amy Squibb. Even after public schools were opened, parents still paid tuition to help cover the cost of books and the teachers' salaries. (Courtesy of A. W. Perry Homestead Museum, Ogle Collection.)

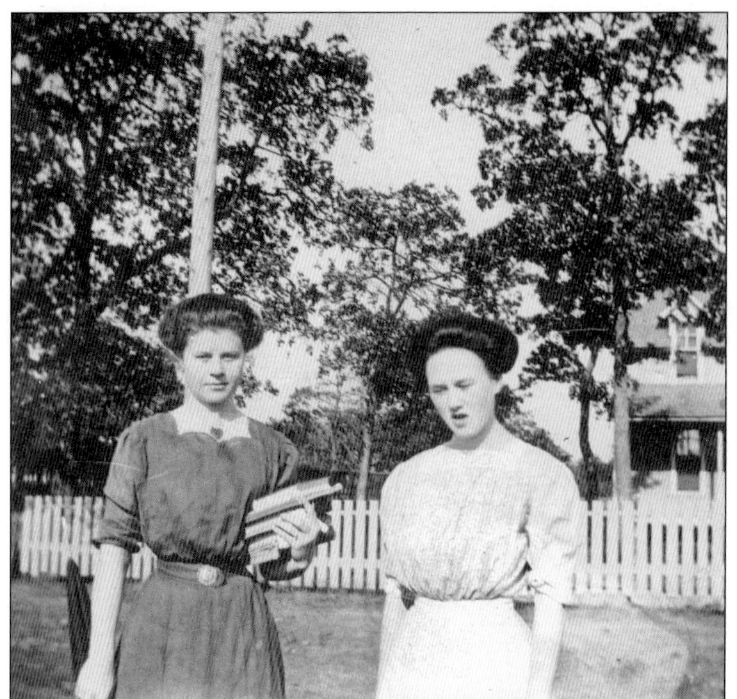

GOING TO CLASS, c. 1900. Many of the teachers were young, unmarried women. Sometimes they were from the local community, and sometimes they were from surrounding or more distant towns and boarded with local families while they taught during the school year. The women in this photograph are unidentified. (Courtesy of A. W. Perry Homestead Museum, Ogle Collection.)

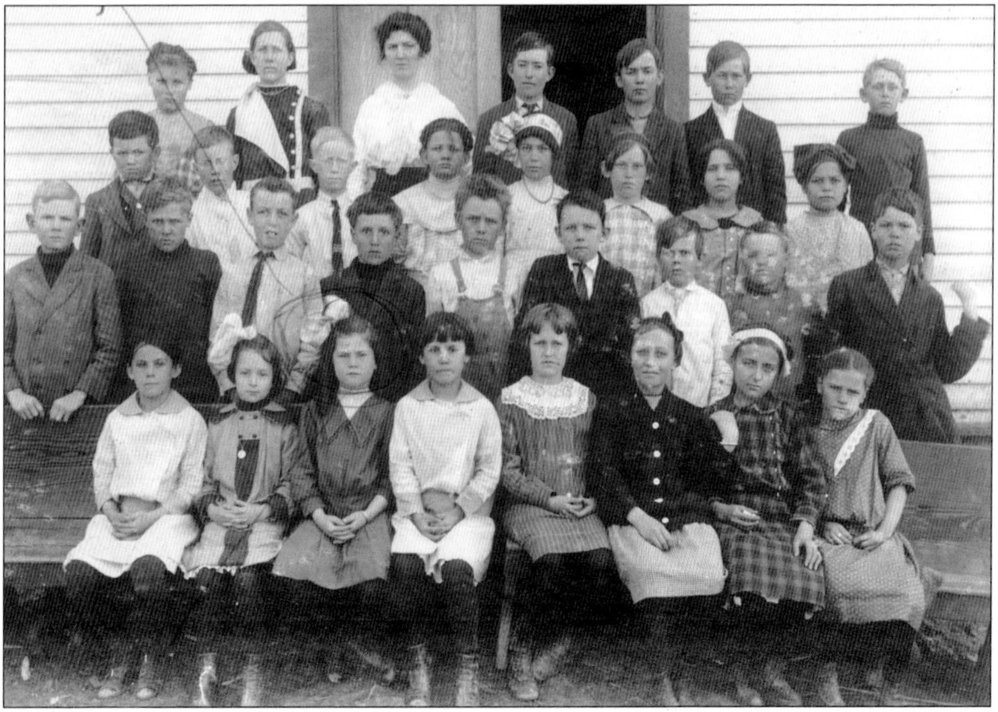

CARROLLTON SCHOOL, c. 1915. The school accommodated students of all ages through the tenth grade. The building had two stories with four classrooms on the first floor along a central hallway. A large auditorium with a stage was located on the second floor. (Courtesy of A. W. Perry Homestead Museum.)

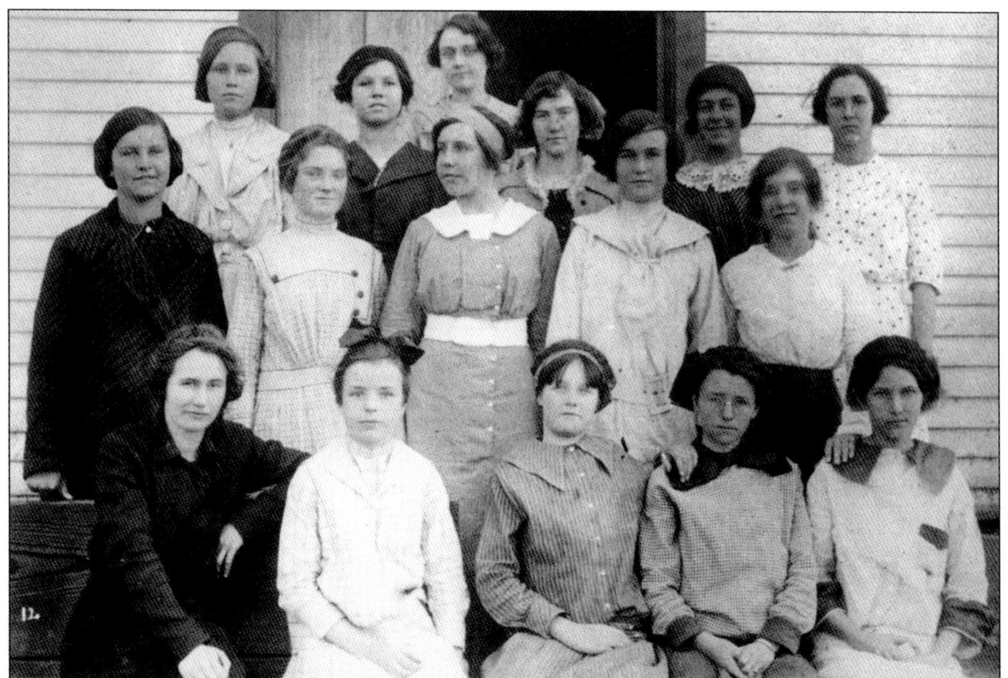

OLGA STEINMAN'S CHORAL CLUB, 1910s. Carrollton School's choral club members included Pauline McClendon, Jewel Rieley, Connie Hardcastle, Susie Wills Sanders, Alma Moore, Nannie Lane, Ella Belle Myers, Esther Gravley, Averil Brake, Willie Jackson, Emabel Brake, Vera Perry, Aline Chambers, and Carrie N. (Courtesy of A. W. Perry Homestead Museum, Ogle Collection.)

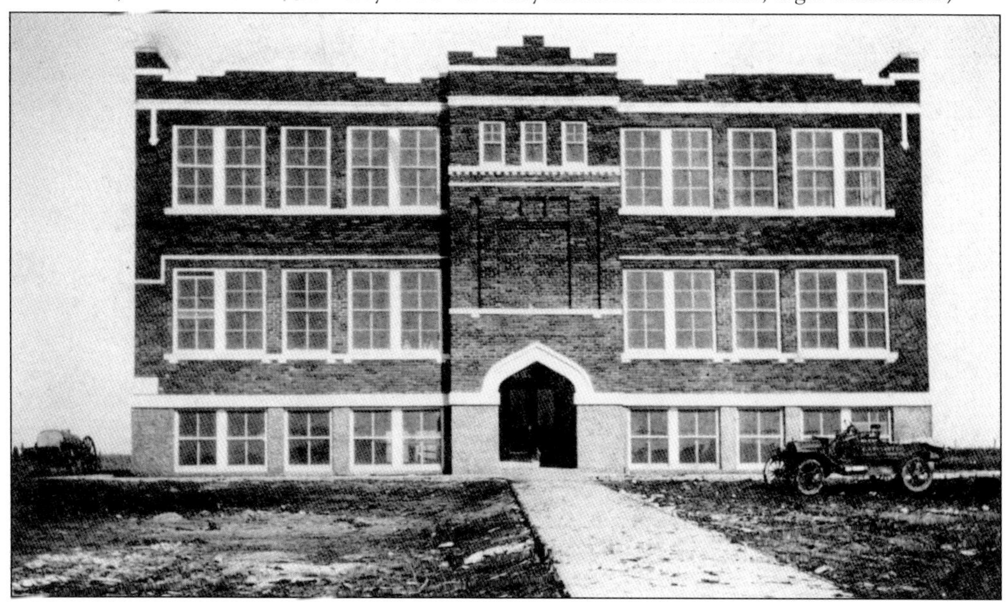

CARROLLTON'S OLD REDBRICK SCHOOL, C. 1916. In 1914, a bond election was passed by citizens to build a new brick school for Carrollton's students at a cost of $12,500. In 1916, the new school was completed. It was located on Belt Line Road where the gymnasium of DeWitt Perry Middle School is now and was known locally as "Old Red." (Courtesy of A. W. Perry Homestead Museum, Ogle Collection.)

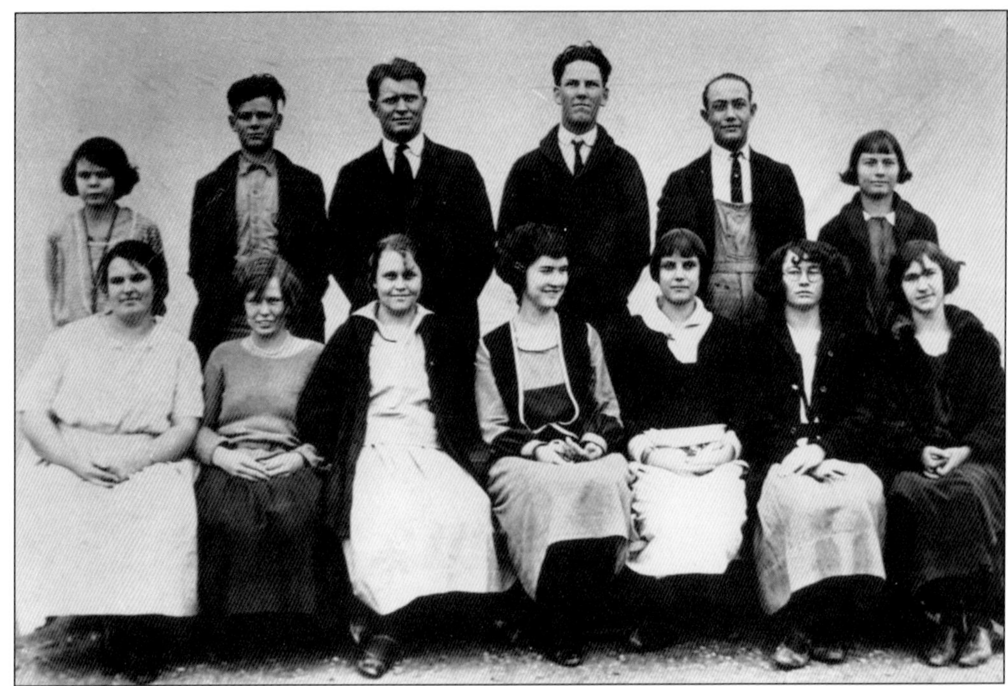

CARROLLTON'S JUNIOR CLASS, C. 1924. Members of the junior class of the school included those pictured here, from left to right, (seated) Janie Stark, Frances Kirksey, Juanita Brake, Ona Mae Carloy, Edna McAnally, Berie Louq, and Tessie Seamans; (standing) Jewel Jordan, Darrell Myers, Ed Lowe, principal Clarence Verbick, Jay Needham, and Eura Fyke. Not pictured are Eunice Fyke and Margie Mayes. (Courtesy of A. W. Perry Homestead Museum, Ogle Collection.)

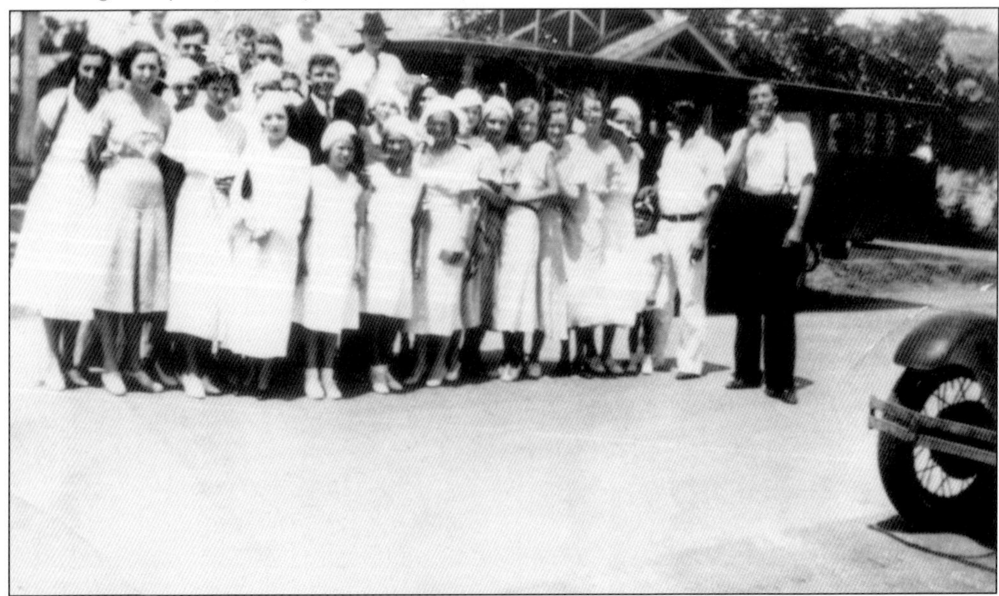

CARROLLTON'S FIRST SCHOOL BUS. The Studebaker bus can be seen in the background of the photograph. The bus driver, Roy Gravley, poses in front of the new vehicle, which served as Carrollton's first school bus. Unlike then, a no-smoking rule is strictly enforced on today's school buses. (Courtesy of A. W. Perry Homestead Museum, Ogle Collection.)

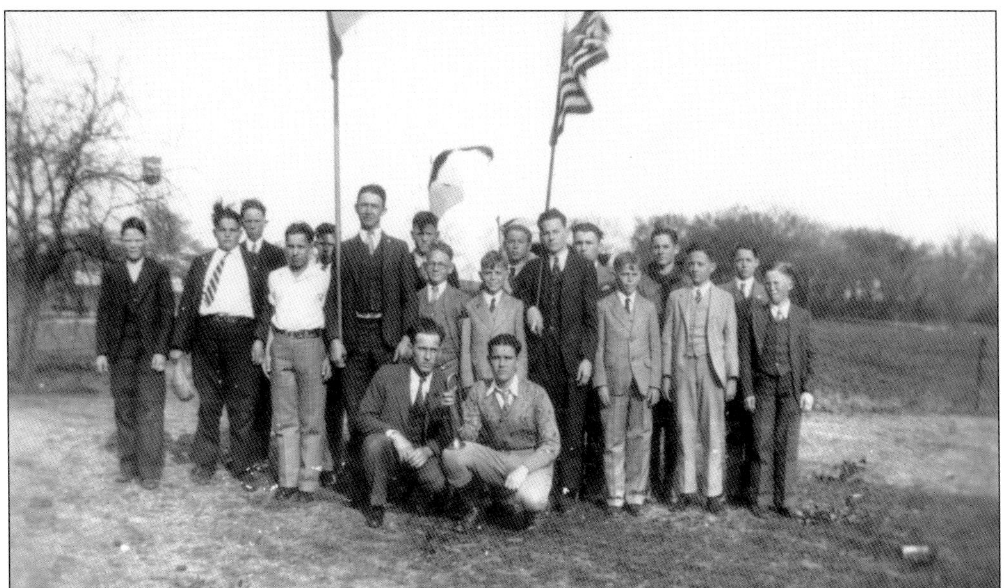

BOY SCOUT TROOP NO. 320, C. 1930. The first Boy Scout troop in Carrollton was organized around 1926. Troop No. 320 was led by Gola Bailey and A. W. "Bubba" Clem, who are pictured kneeling in the center of the photograph. Many local men assisted the boys with completing their badges by sharing their expertise in subjects like swimming, hiking, plumbing, masonry, leatherworking, dairying, and many others. (Courtesy of A. W. Perry Homestead Museum, Ogle Collection.)

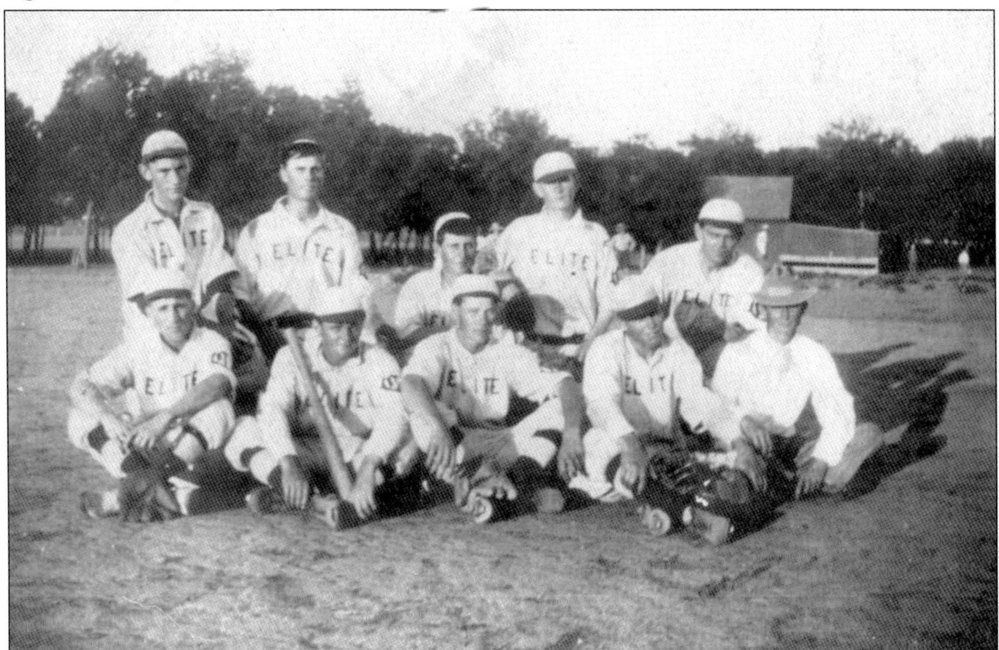

CARROLLTON ELITE BASEBALL TEAM, C. 1917. The town baseball team was sponsored by the Elite Café, located on the square. The pronunciation of "Elite" was recorded on the back of the photograph as "EE-light." This picture was taken sometime before World War I. (Courtesy of City of Carrollton.)

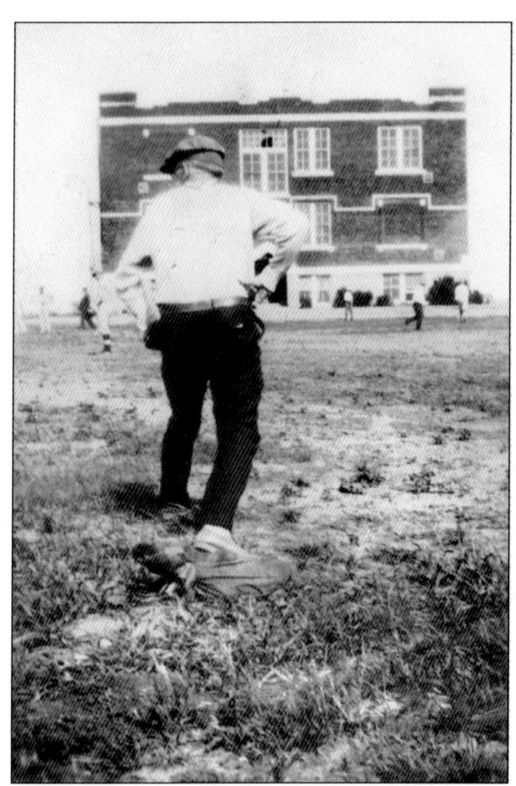

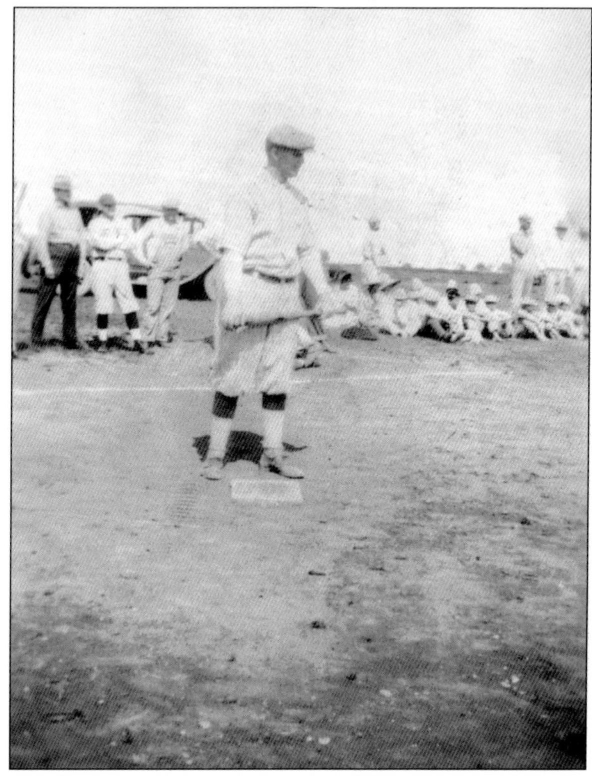

BASEBALL GAME, 1928. Burnett Perry, below, is the man at-bat during a baseball game in front of the Old Red school in 1928. The school yard was a gathering place for sporting events even before organized interscholastic athletics existed on a regular basis. This game took place between adults in the late 1920s. The man in the image to the left is identified only as Roy. (Both courtesy of Fancy Oliver Tanner.)

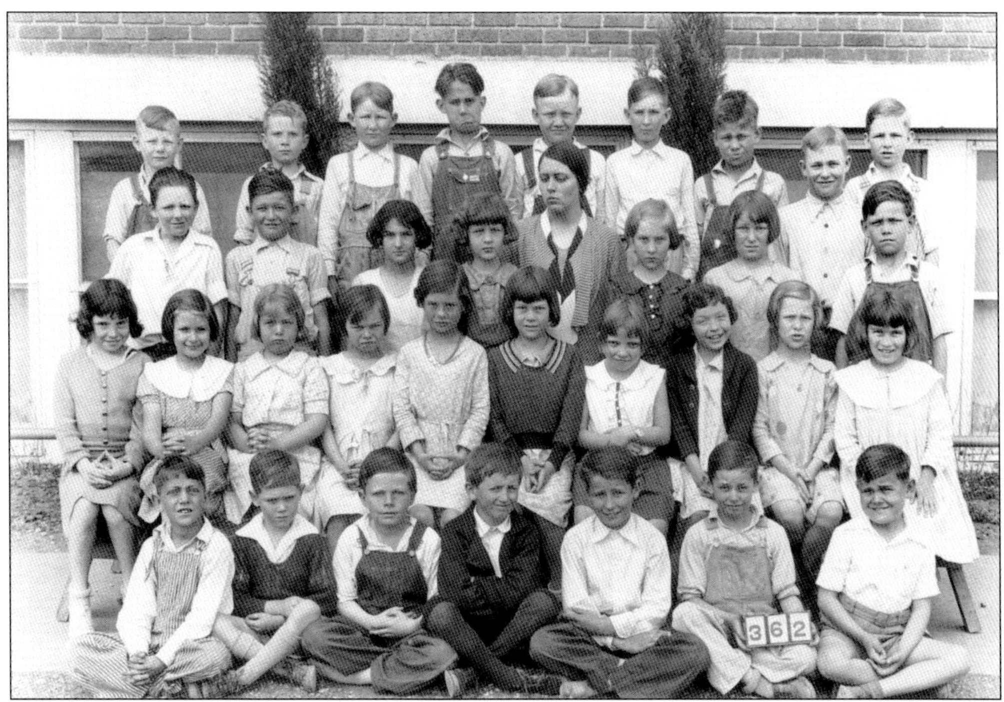

CARROLLTON ELEMENTARY SCHOOL. Old Red became Carrollton's elementary school when the Carrollton High School opened in 1936. The building was razed in 1966 to make room for an expansion of the newer building. (Both courtesy of A. W. Perry Homestead Museum, Ogle Collection.)

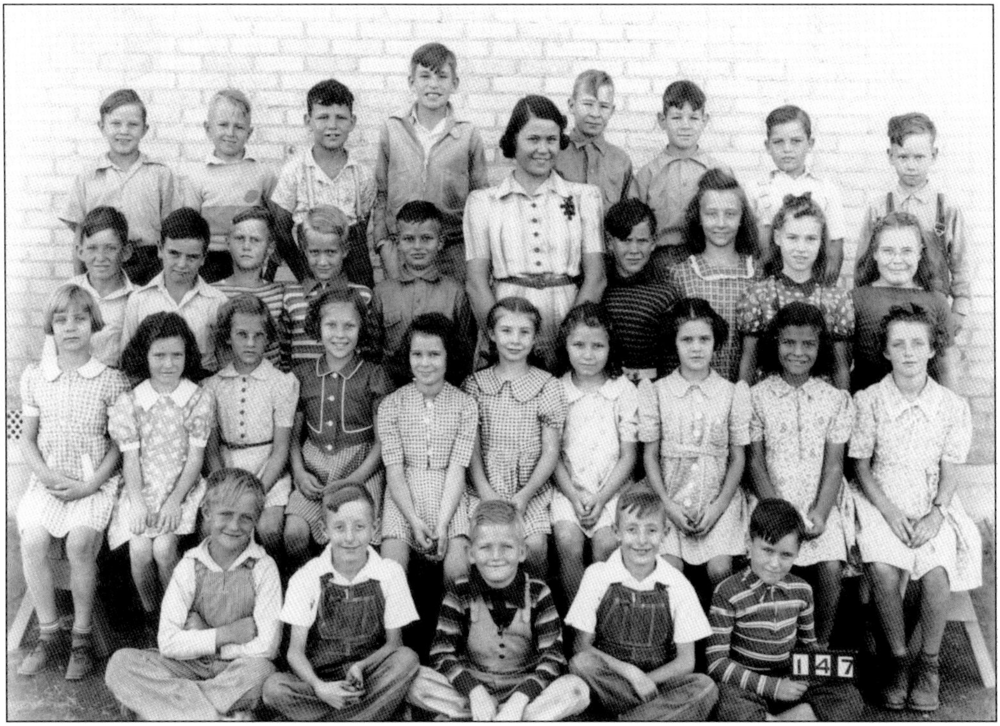

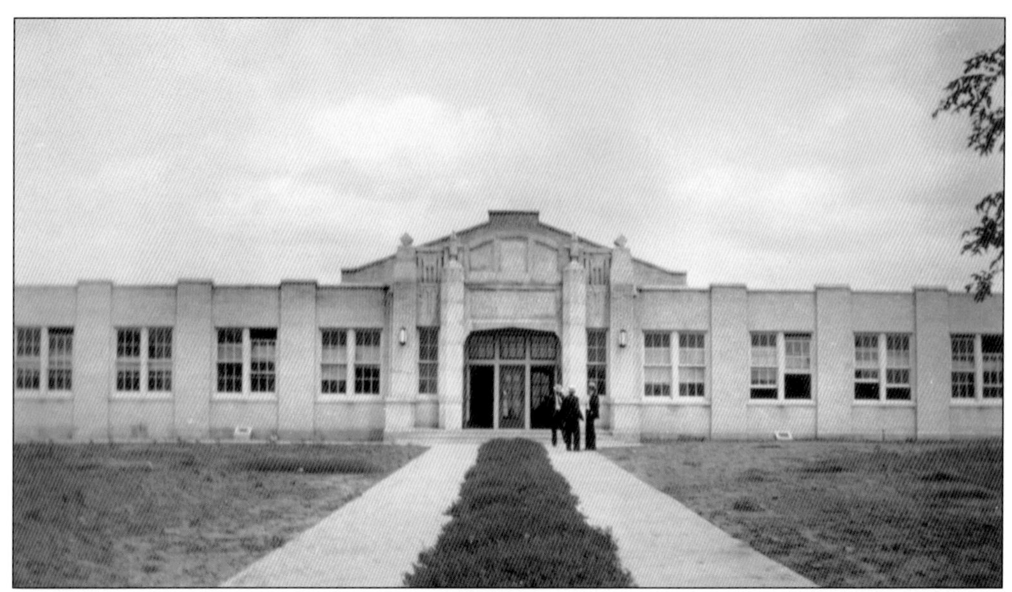

DeWitt Perry High School. Opened in 1936, the building remains as the oldest school in the Carrollton Farmers Branch School District. Constructed on land donated by DeWitt Perry and his sister Harriet Perry Warner, the school was referred to as Carrollton High School, and the school mascot was the hornet. In 1962, it became DeWitt Perry Middle School after R. L. Turner High School opened on Josey Lane and Crosby Road. (Both courtesy of Howard J. Cox.)

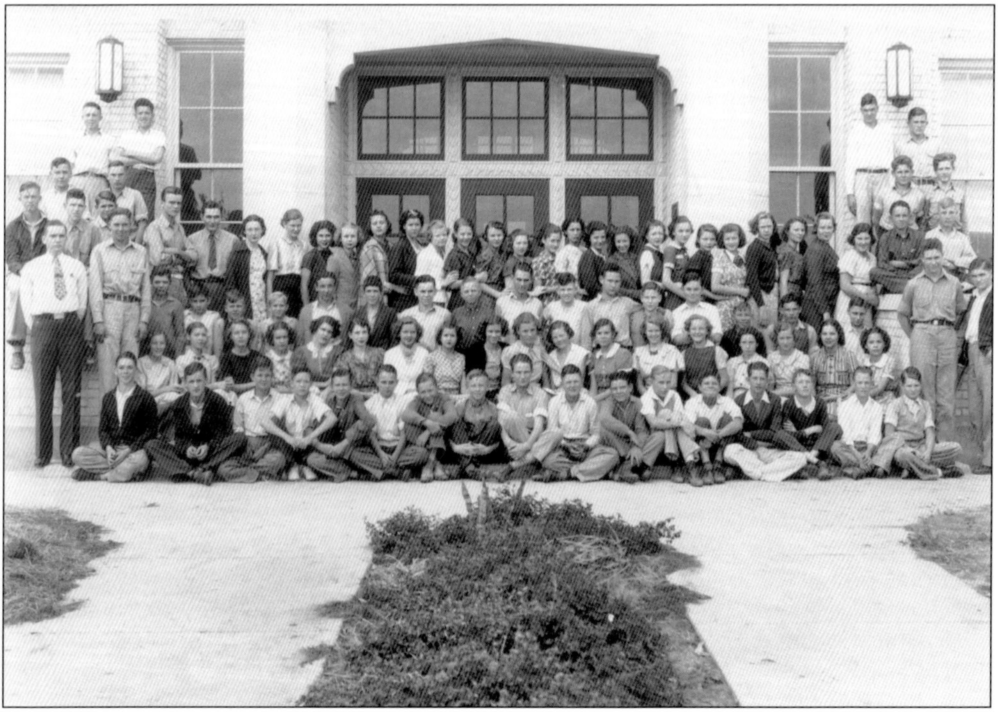

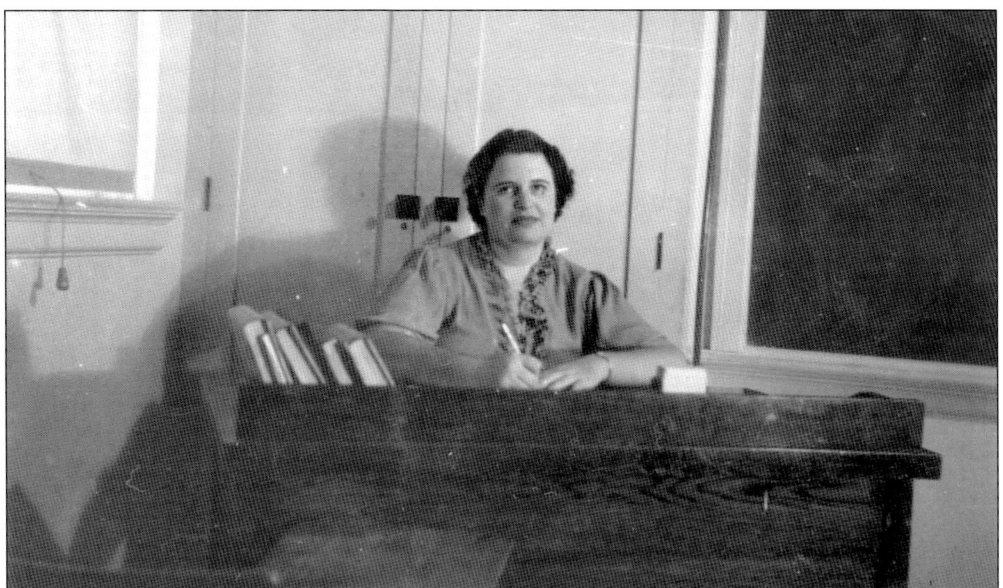

TEACHER JANIE STARK. Stark was a beloved teacher in the Carrollton schools from 1928 to 1952. She graduated from Carrollton High School and went on to earn degrees from what is now the Texas Women's University in Denton and worked toward a master's degree from the University of Texas at Austin. She taught Spanish and math courses. From 1952 to 1962, she left the classroom to be the full-time secretary for the school, which included assisting the superintendent and the board of trustees. (Courtesy of Howard J. Cox.)

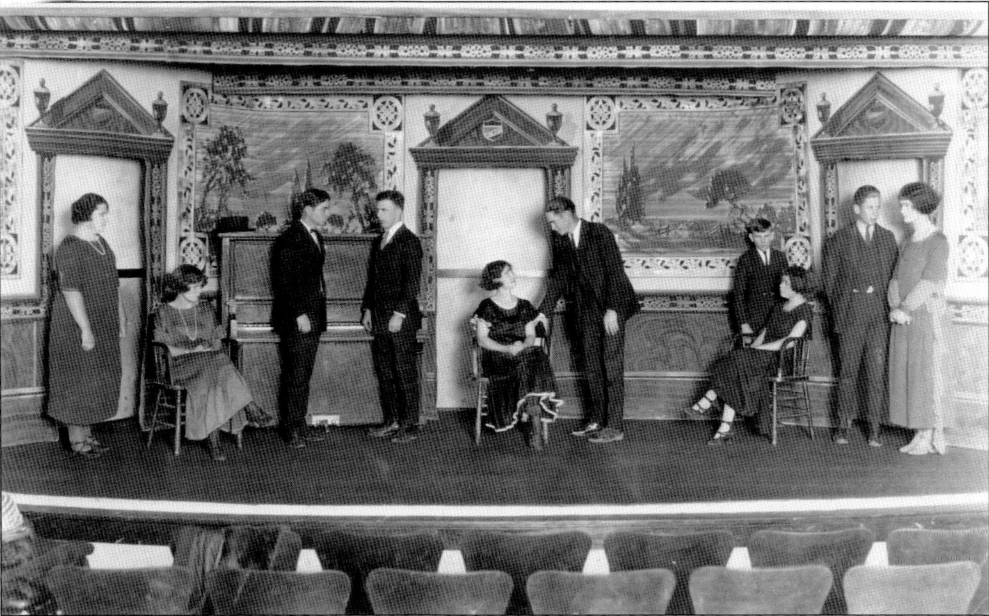

SCHOOL PLAY, 1930s. Janie Stark was not only a teacher and staff member, she also devoted herself completely to the students. She served as the senior class sponsor and supported many other extracurricular activities, including the annual senior class play. Each year, she coached the drama class in interscholastic competitions and organized class celebrations and trips. (Courtesy of A. W. Perry Homestead Museum, Ogle Collection.)

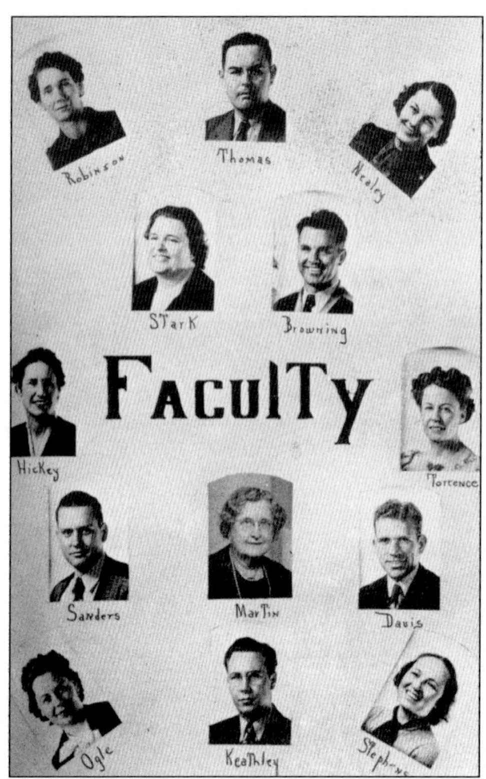

FACULTY AND FACILITIES, 1939. The *Silver Lion* was the title of the school's annual, first published in 1939. Teacher Janie Stark led the effort to make its publication possible. These pages from the yearbook show the school's faculty for that year as well as Carrollton's school facilities. Photographs of the tennis court and football field, the bus drivers, and various clubs were featured. (Both courtesy of Howard J. Cox.)

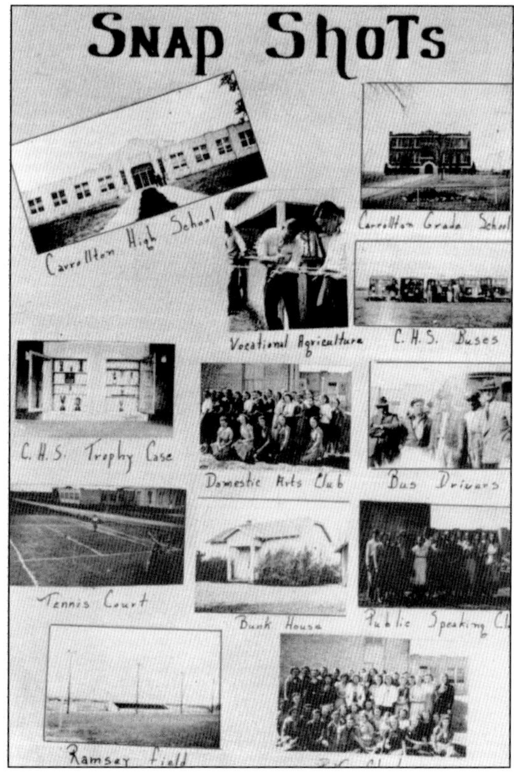

CARROLLTON HIGH SCHOOL PEP
SQUAD, 1939. The pep squad supported
the school's sports teams and provided
general spirit for the school during pep
rallies and parades. The young Irene
Carver was the group's mascot, and
Marion Good was the sweetheart of the
squad. Others in the group are listed
as they appeared in the 1939 yearbook.
(Courtesy of Howard J. Cox.)

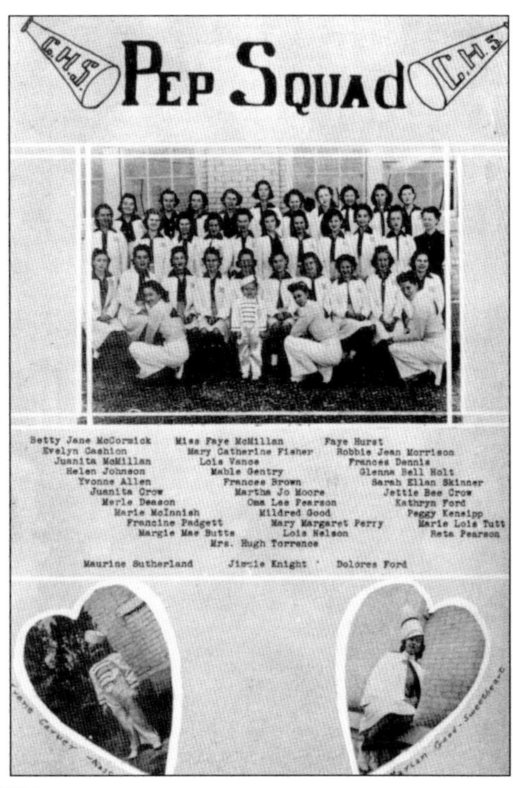

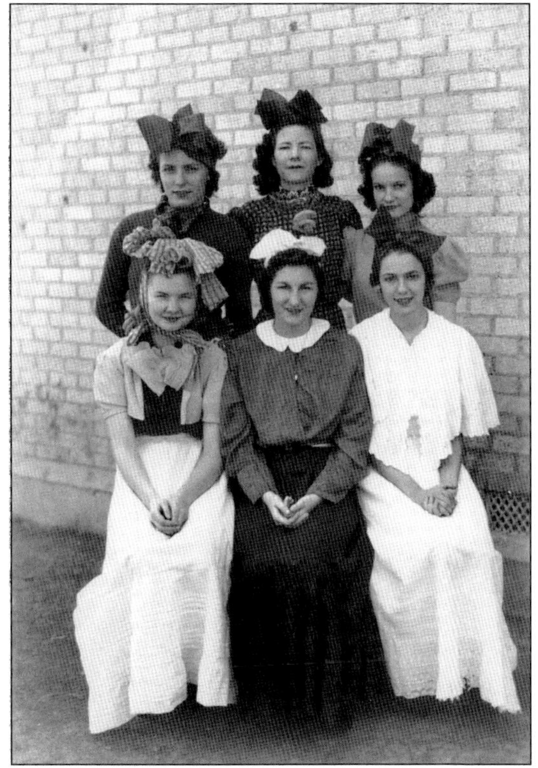

SENIOR CLASS SPEECH RECITAL,
1939. Pictured are the members of
the dramatic club for Carrollton High
School. Pictured from left to right
are (first row) Charlotte Perry, Julia
Ledbetter, and Joy Cox; (second row)
Kathryn Collins, Marie McInnish, and
Margaret Towery. The group presented
a performance in the school auditorium
that featured dramatic speeches and a
short play titled *Cinderella's Marriage*.
(Courtesy of Howard J. Cox.)

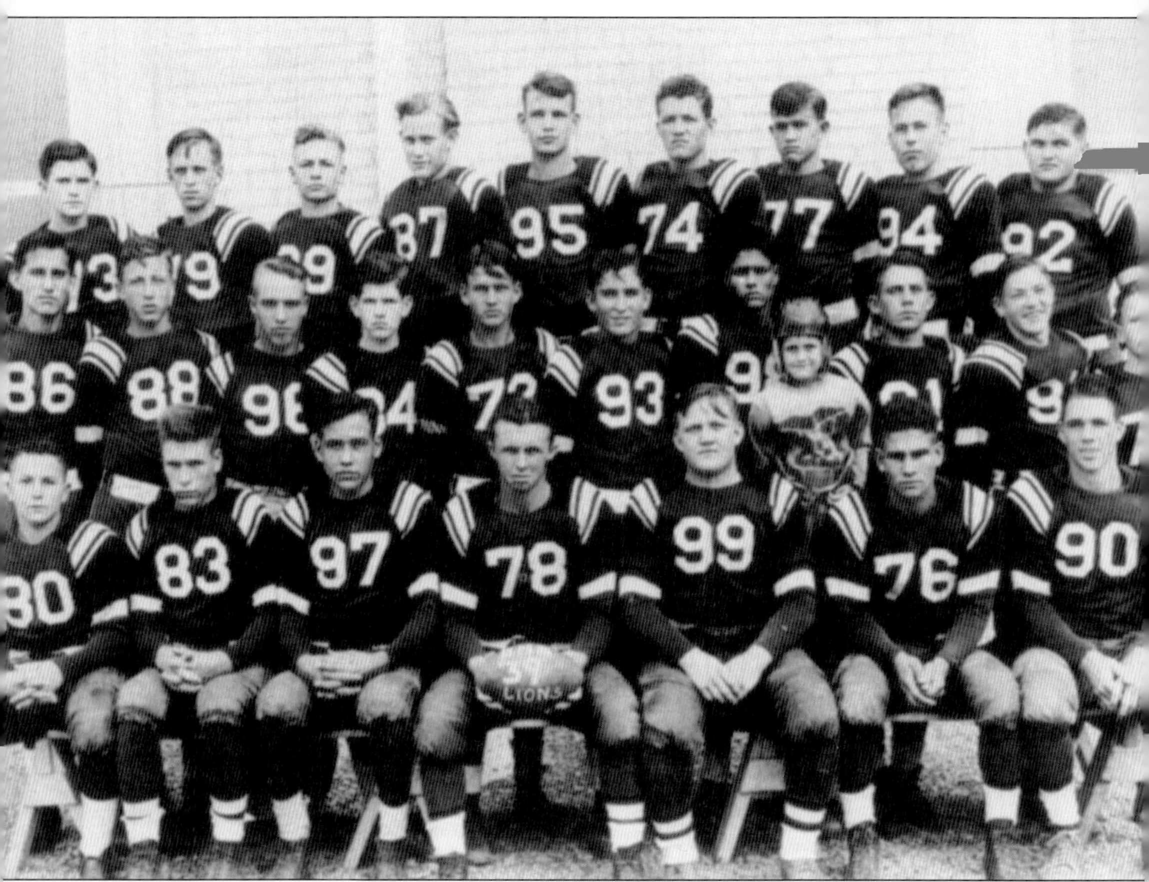

CARROLLTON HIGH SCHOOL FOOTBALL TEAM, 1940. Interscholastic athletics did not begin until the mid-1910s. Before the establishment of school sports, organized community teams in sports like baseball played each other. In 1916, the Dallas Athletic Association met and made plans for schools to compete against each other in the upcoming year in the areas of girls basketball, boys baseball, declamation contests, and spelling contests. Football was well established by 1920. The young boy in this photograph was the team's mascot. (Courtesy of Howard J. Cox.)

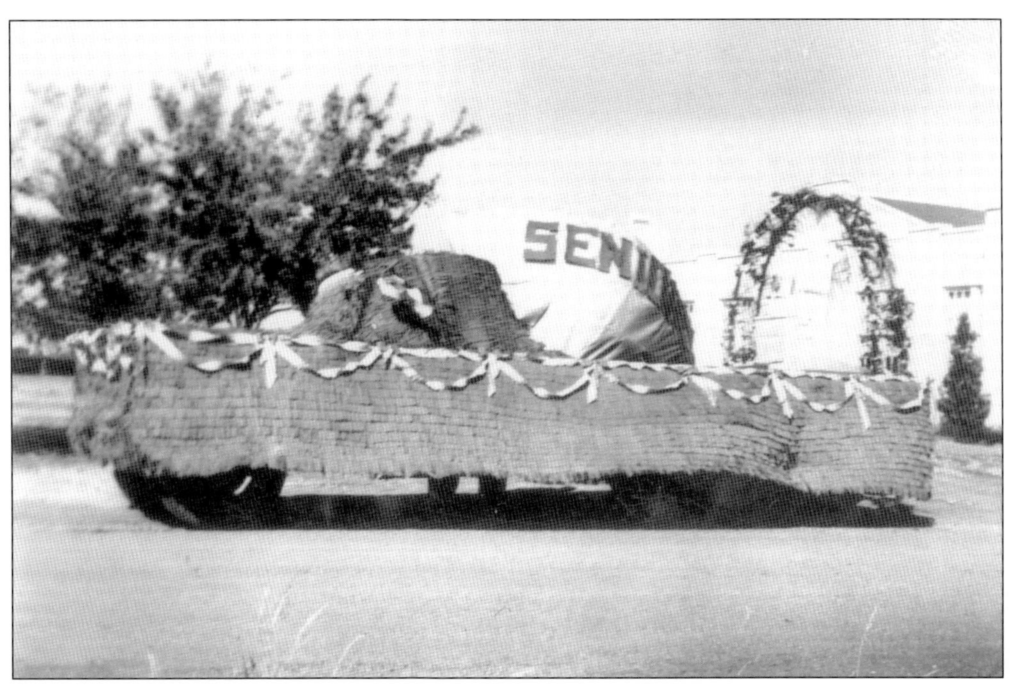

JUNIOR AND SENIOR HOMECOMING PARADE FLOATS, C. 1940. The annual homecoming parade for Carrollton High School was held each year on the square. The junior and senior classes each made elaborate floats to show their spirit and support for their team. The senior float (above) is constructed of elaborate crêpe paper decorations. The junior float (below) appears to be a tribute to the town's rural heritage as students ride on a rustic wagon pulled by horses. (Both courtesy of Howard J. Cox.)

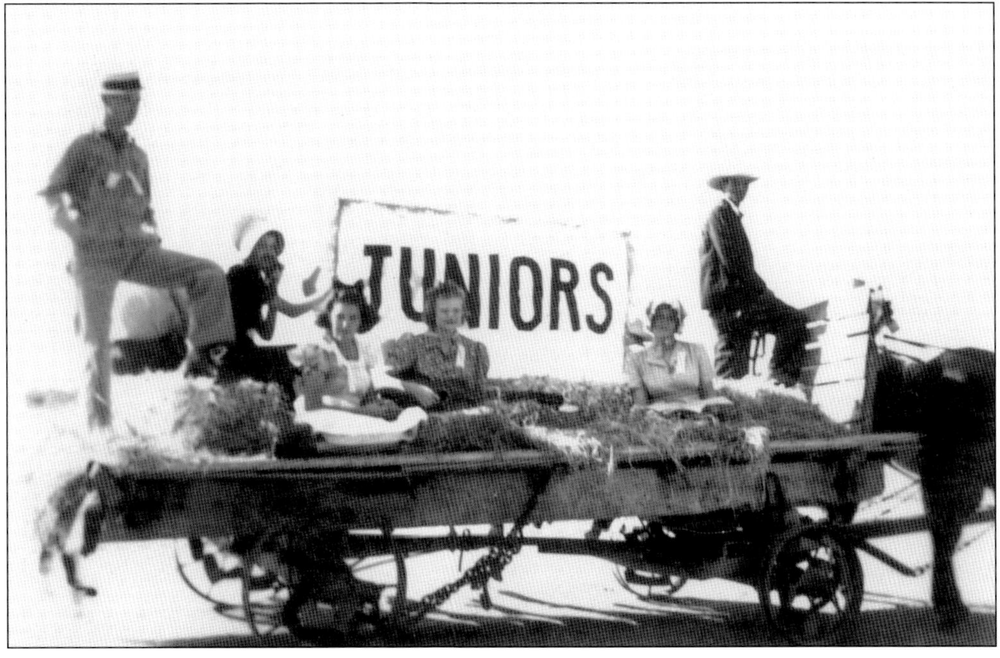

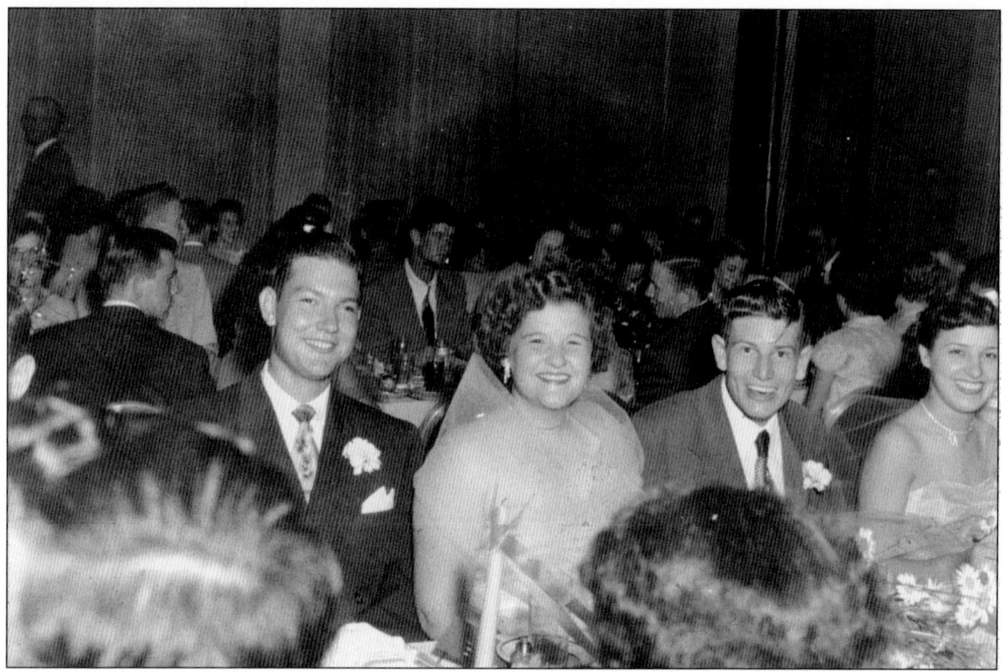

BANQUET AT COLUMBIAN CLUB, 1950S. This class banquet was held at the newly opened Columbian Club, a country club located east of Josey Lane and north of Belt Line Road. The site was complete with a golf course, tennis courts, and a clubhouse for its members, and it was also rented out for private parties. (Both courtesy of A. W. Perry Homestead Museum, Ogle Collection.)

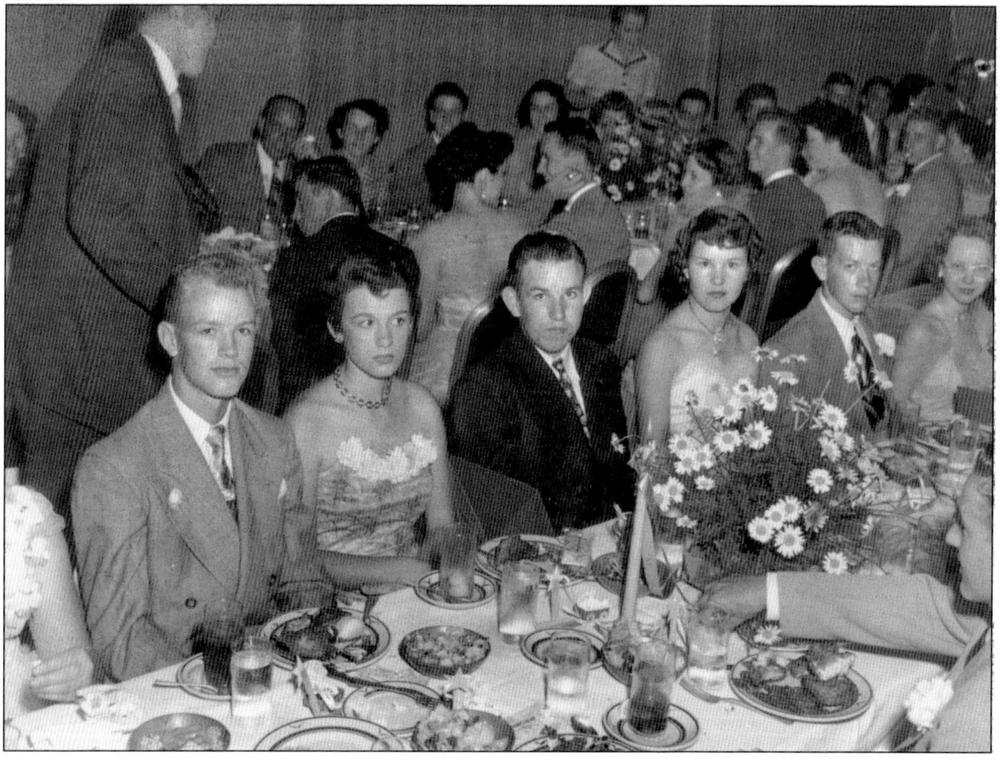

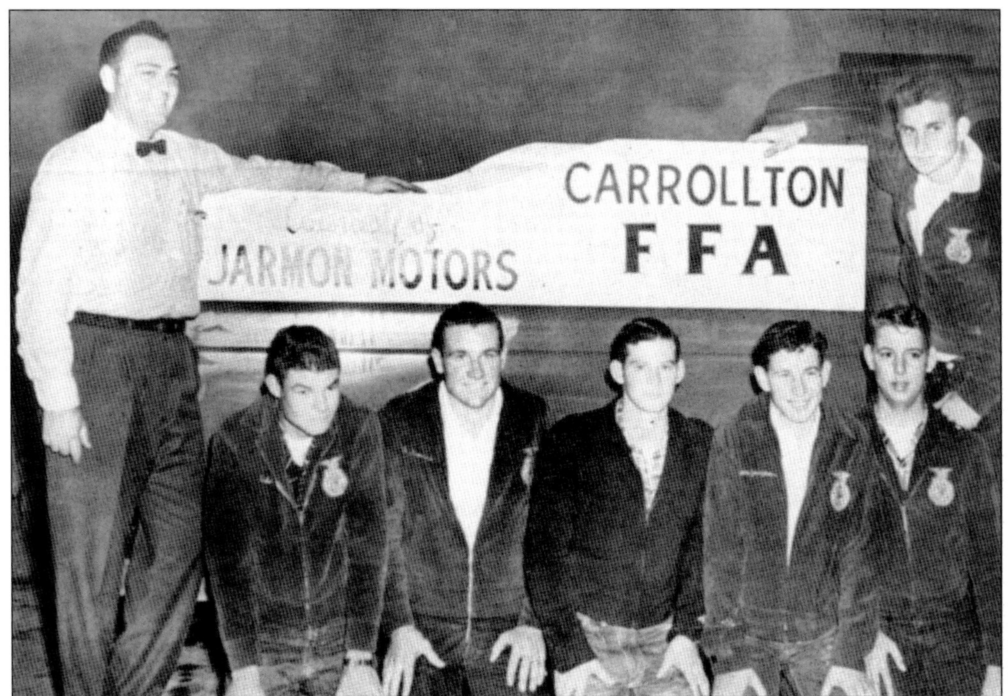

CARROLLTON FUTURE FARMERS OF AMERICA, SPONSORED BY JARMON MOTORS, 1950S. Carrollton's Future Farmers of America (FFA) was established in 1936 by Ralph Sanders, the agricultural teacher at Carrollton High School. In 1949, Sam Bagley took over leading the FFA and greatly expanded the program. He is pictured here with FFA members. (Courtesy of A. W. Perry Homestead Museum, Ogle Collection.)

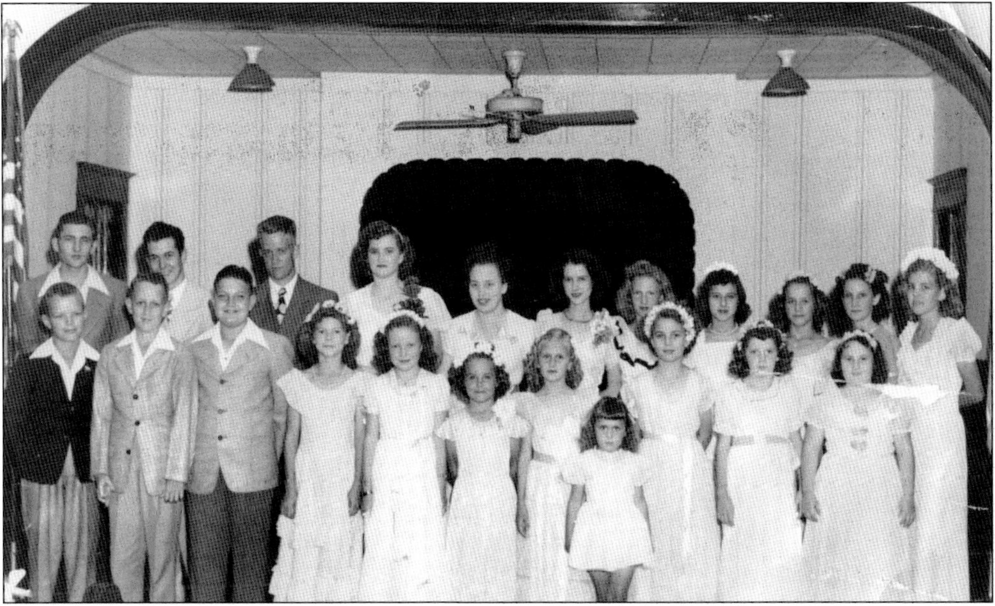

LOVING'S PIANO CLASS, 1950S. This nostalgic photograph shows the piano class of Jewel Loving, who was an active member of the First Baptist Church in the 1950s. (Courtesy of A. W. Perry Homestead Museum, Ogle Collection.)

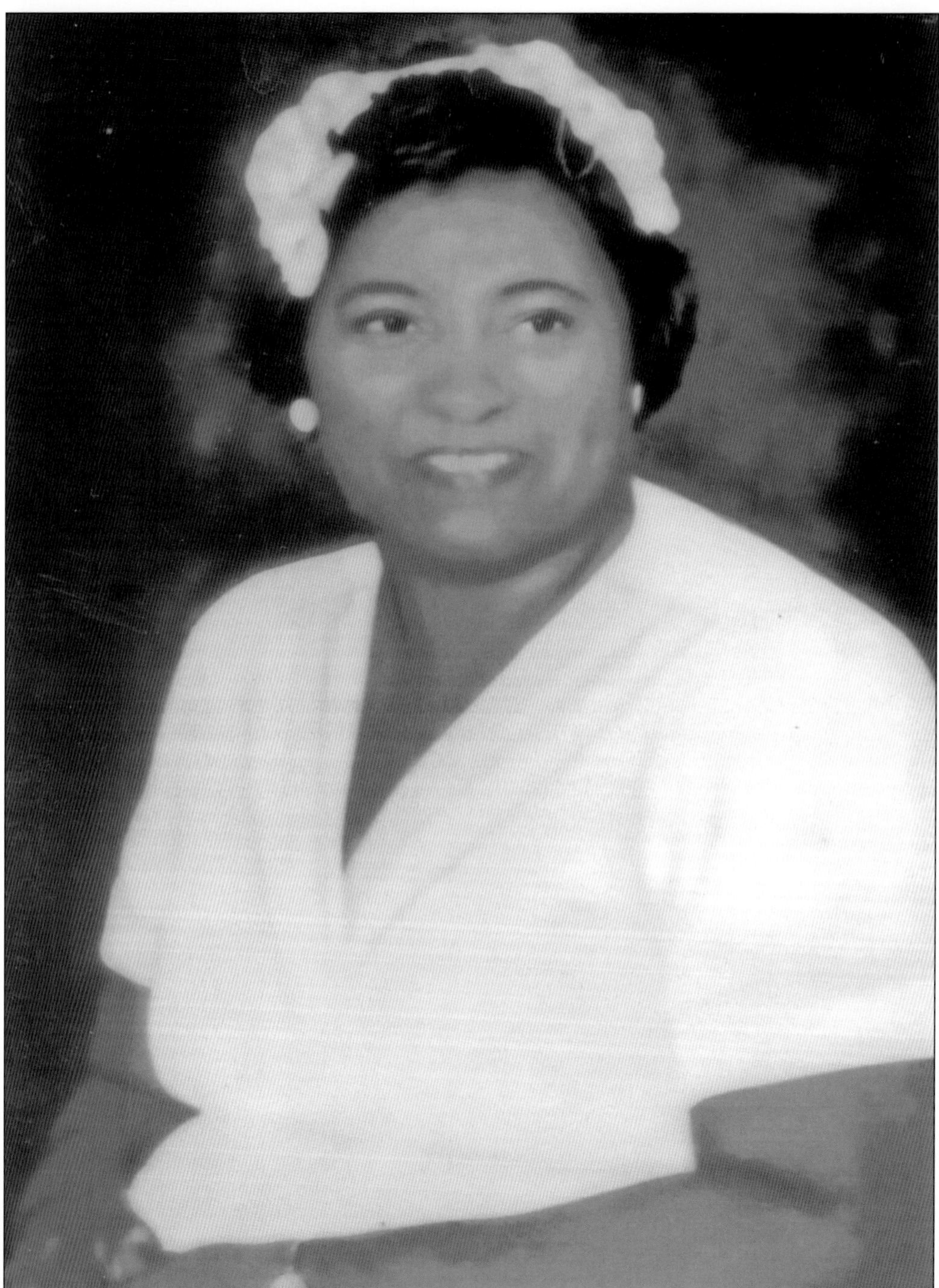

ANNIE HEADS RAINWATER. In 1963, Carrollton's schools were the first in Dallas County to be integrated. On behalf of her two youngest daughters, Annie Rainwater sued the Carrollton Farmers Branch School District to allow black students to attend school in Carrollton. Before integration, black students attended Jessie Bush Elementary and were later bused to a segregated high school located in Denton. In 1993, the memory of Annie Rainwater was honored when the Carrollton School District named its newest elementary school after her. (Courtesy of Willie Rainwater.)

Five

WATER'S EDGE
ELM FORK OF THE TRINITY RIVER

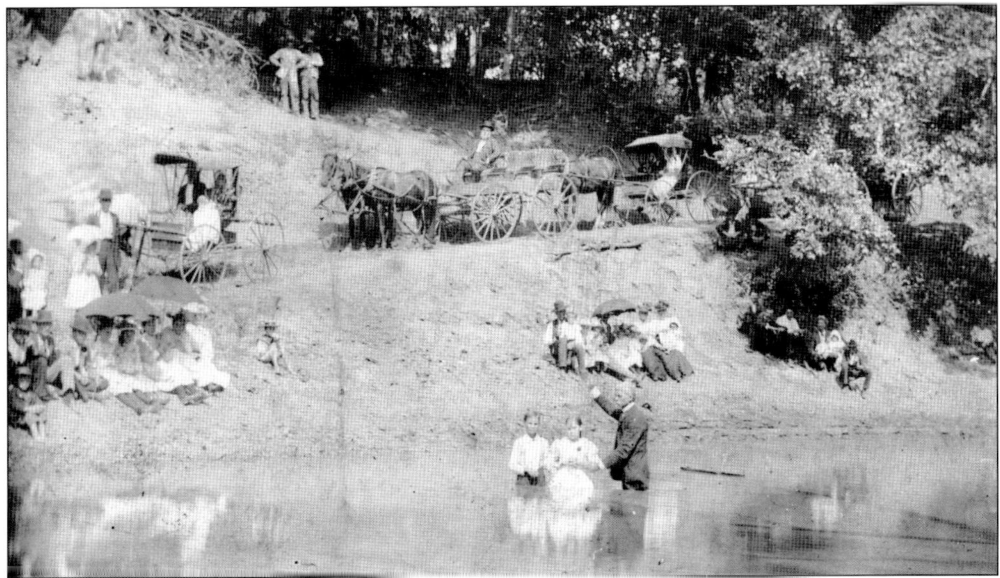

BAPTISMS IN THE ELM FORK OF THE TRINITY RIVER, 1898. The Caddo Indians called the river Arkikosa in Central Texas and Daycoa closer to the Gulf Coast. Spanish explorer Alfonso De León named the river La Santísima Trinidad, meaning "the most holy trinity," in 1690. Eventually, the river simply became known as the Trinity. Because of its proximity to the town, churches in Carrollton frequently used the river for baptism services. This image is from 1898 and shows twin brother and sister Wade and Willie Fyke in the river with the preacher, Elihu Newton, of Union Baptist Church. Families and church members line the banks of the Elm Fork to watch the services. (Courtesy of A. W. Perry Homestead Museum, Ogle Collection.)

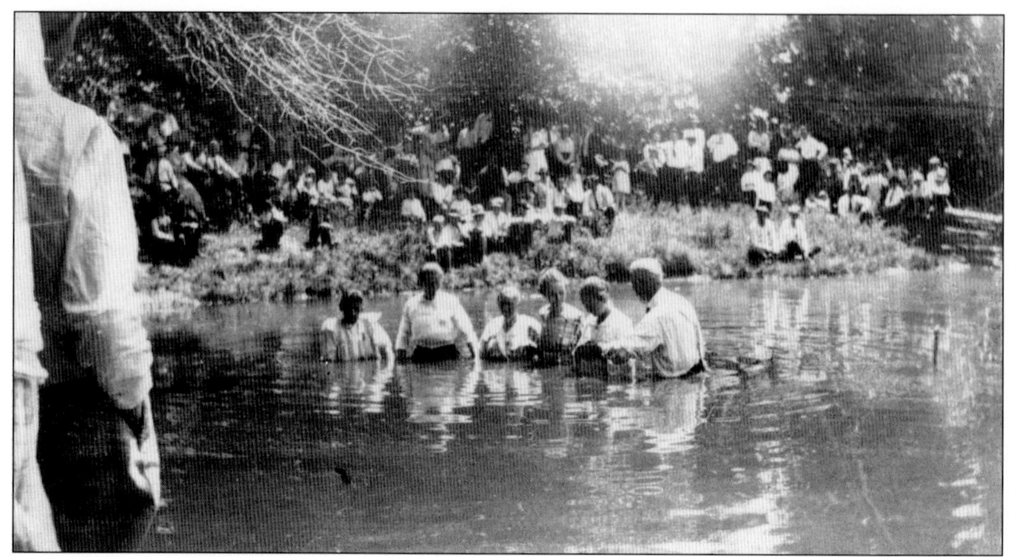

BAPTISMS IN THE ELM FORK OF THE TRINITY RIVER, C. 1900. These images were taken slightly later than the previous image but show a much larger group of people on the banks of the river. It appears that much of the town is in attendance to witness the baptisms and join in the day's celebrations. The Trinity River is made up of three main forks, the West and East Forks and the Elm Fork. The Elm Fork of the Trinity flows south from the east side of Gainesville and Denton toward Dallas. The three main forks of the river join near Dallas, and from there it continues to flow southeastward and eventually reaches Galveston Bay and the Gulf of Mexico.

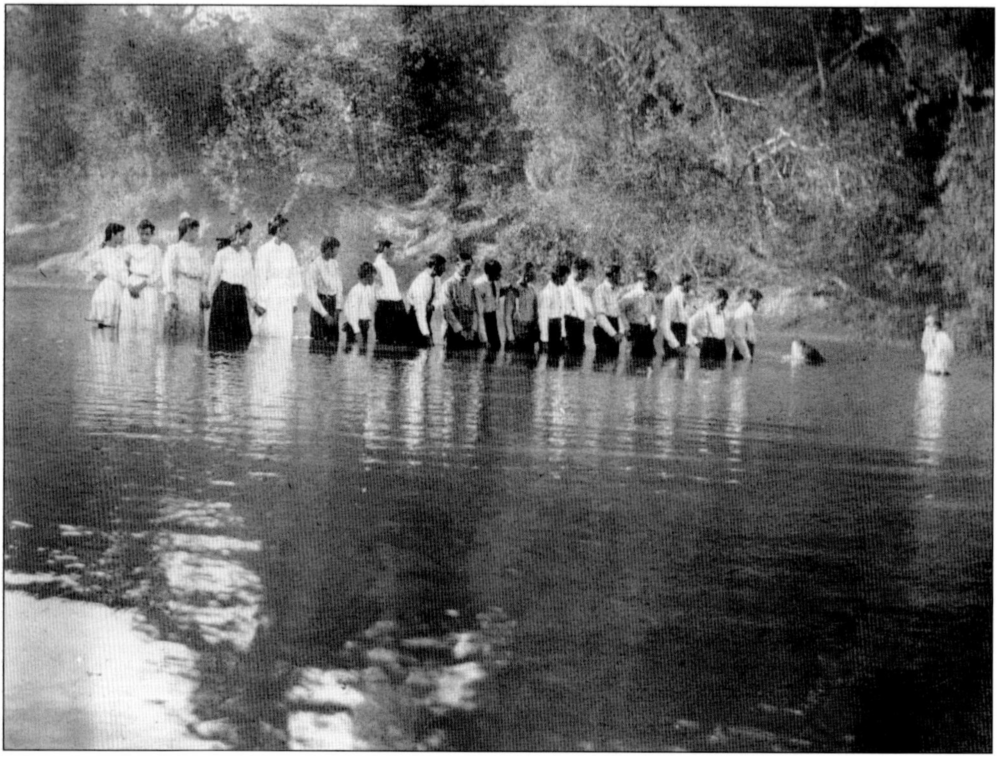

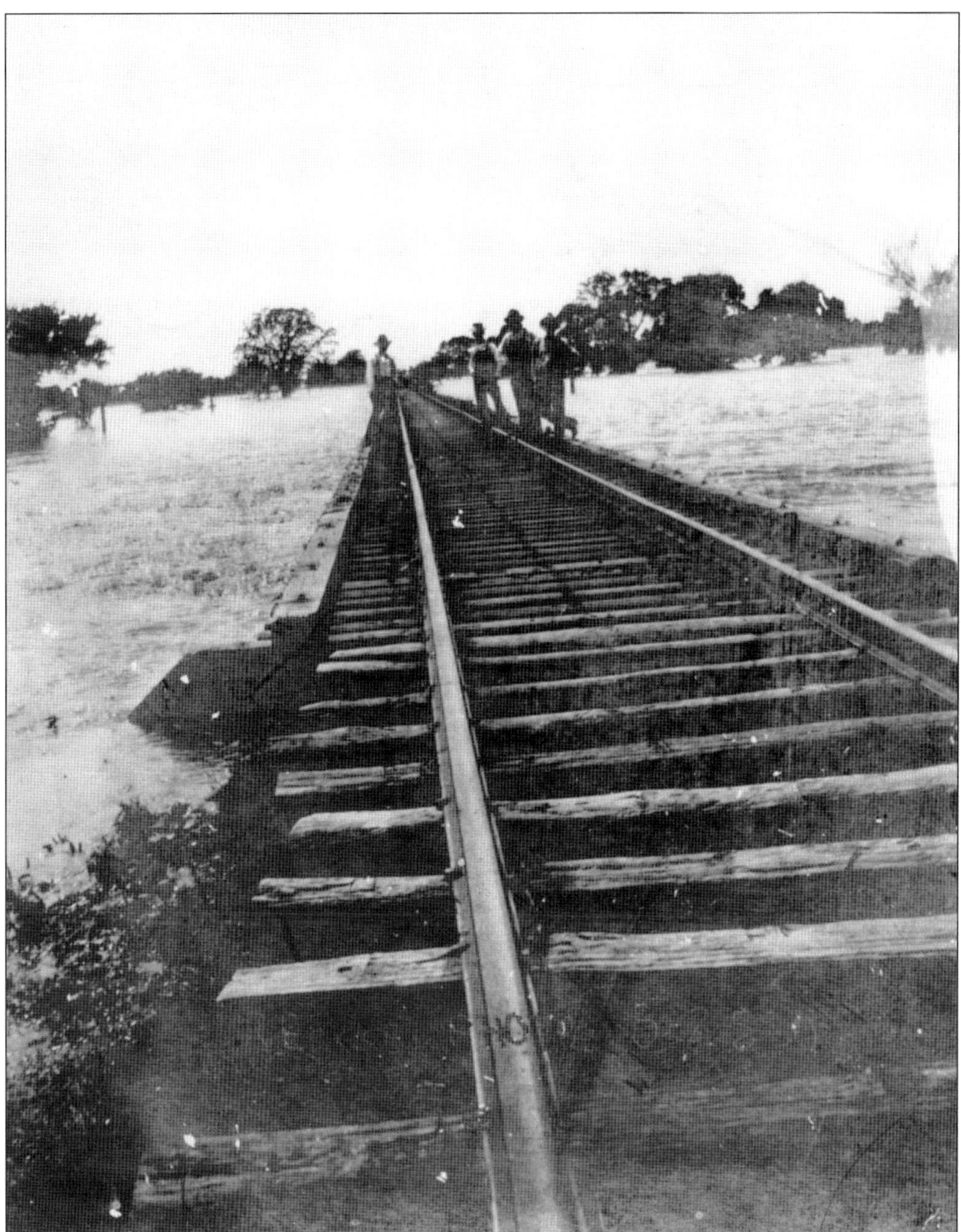

THE FLOOD OF 1908. Widespread flooding had been recorded in 1844, 1866, 1871, and 1890, but none of those before or since reached the magnitude of the flood of 1908. Torrential rain started in the local area on May 23, 1908, and continued throughout the night and into the next day. There were also intense rains in the entire watershed area of the Trinity River, and the swollen river quickly overflowed its banks. On May 26, the depth of the Trinity River in Dallas was at a record 52.6 feet and measured 1.5 miles wide. Ray Fyke took several photographs of the flood damage in the Carrollton area. This photograph shows a group of men standing on the railroad bridge that crossed the river; the floodwaters were just inches from covering the tracks. (Courtesy of Hal Simon, Nix family collection.)

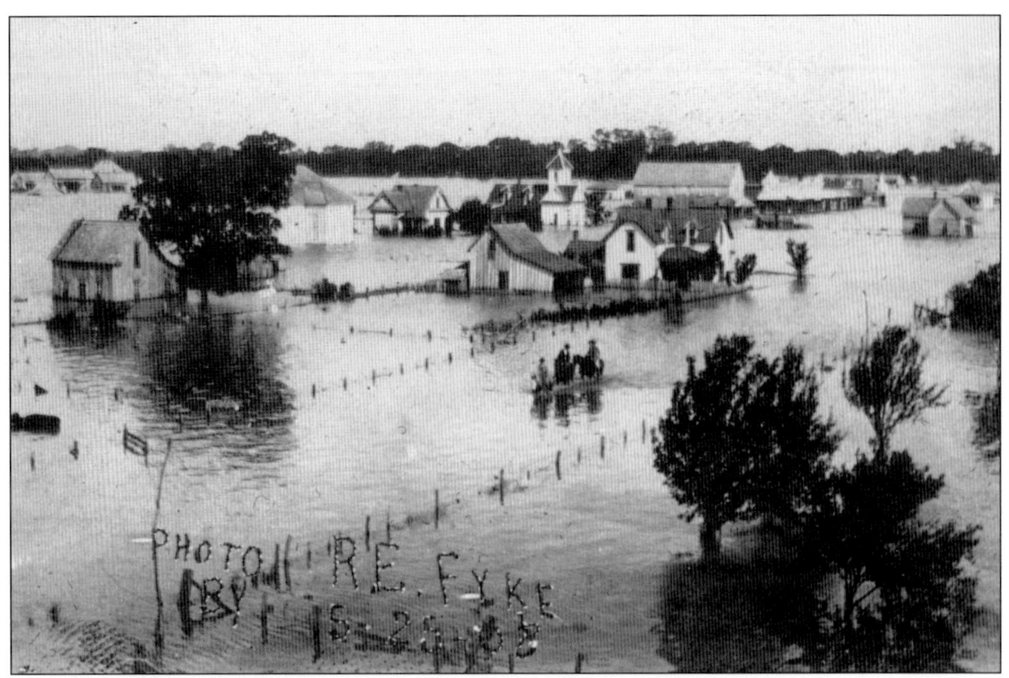

HOMES AND BUSINESSES DURING THE FLOOD OF 1908. A group of men on horseback wade through the floodwaters in Carrollton. The countryside was described at the time as looking like a large lake. Families living west of town and, therefore, closer to the river were devastated. Particularly hard hit were the many African American families. People lost their homes, crops, and livestock to the flood. (Courtesy of A. W. Perry Homestead Museum, Ogle Collection.)

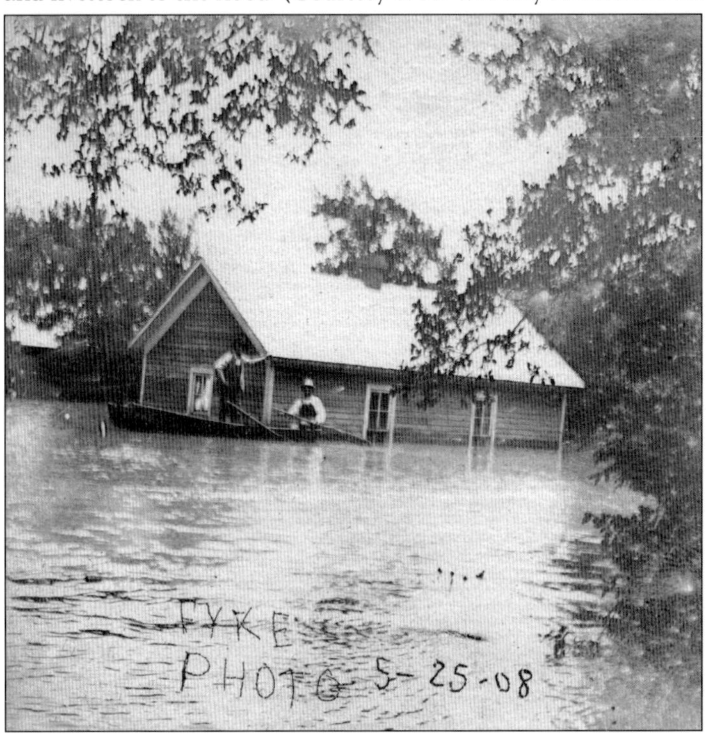

RISING WATERS, 1908. Men in boats were used to rescue families from their homes as the floodwaters rose. Cords of wood that had once been neatly stacked up outside homes and businesses had now become part of large debris islands where wildlife and livestock sought refuge. (Courtesy of A. W. Perry Homestead Museum, Ogle Collection.)

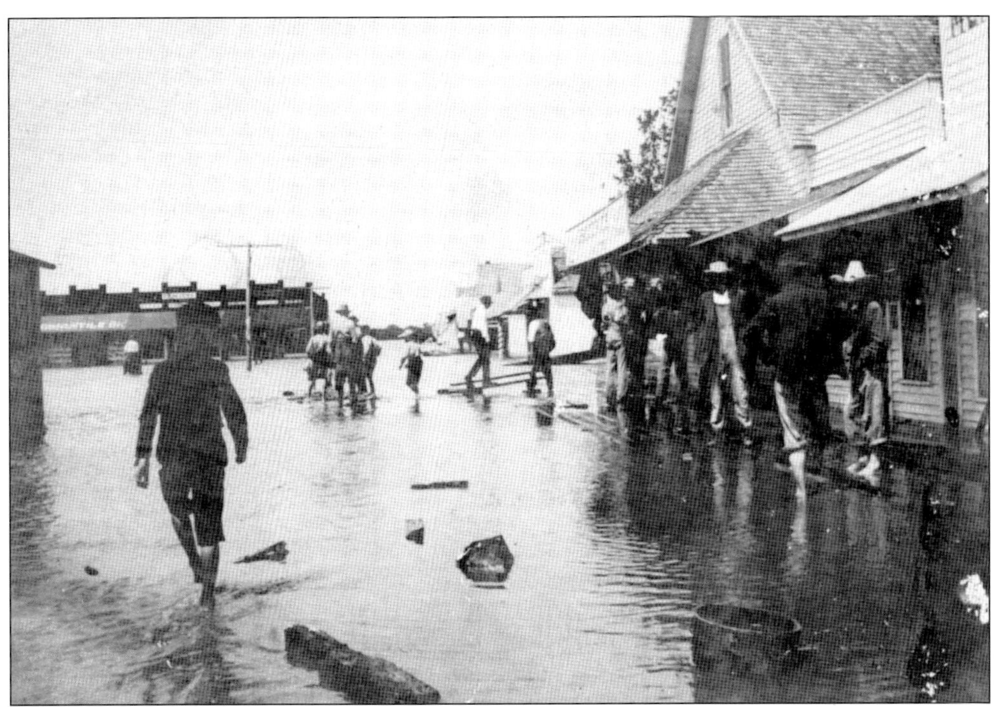

TOWN SQUARE DURING THE 1908 FLOOD. During the widespread flooding in north central Texas, rail service was suspended, and mail was not delivered for a week. Telephone lines were out for two days. Loads of dirt and gravel were piled outside of the bank on the southwest side of the square in an attempt to keep the water out. When the floodwaters subsided, Carrollton was faced with the task of cleaning up. Carrollton east of the Katy railroad tracks was spared because it was on higher ground. Businesses on the west side of the square saw 2 to 3 feet of water. The floodwater left behind debris, mud, and an abundance of snakes in homes and businesses. One local business owner, George Myers, described finding snakes on the shelves and in the bins of his general merchandise store after the flood. (Both courtesy of Hal Simon, Nix family collection.)

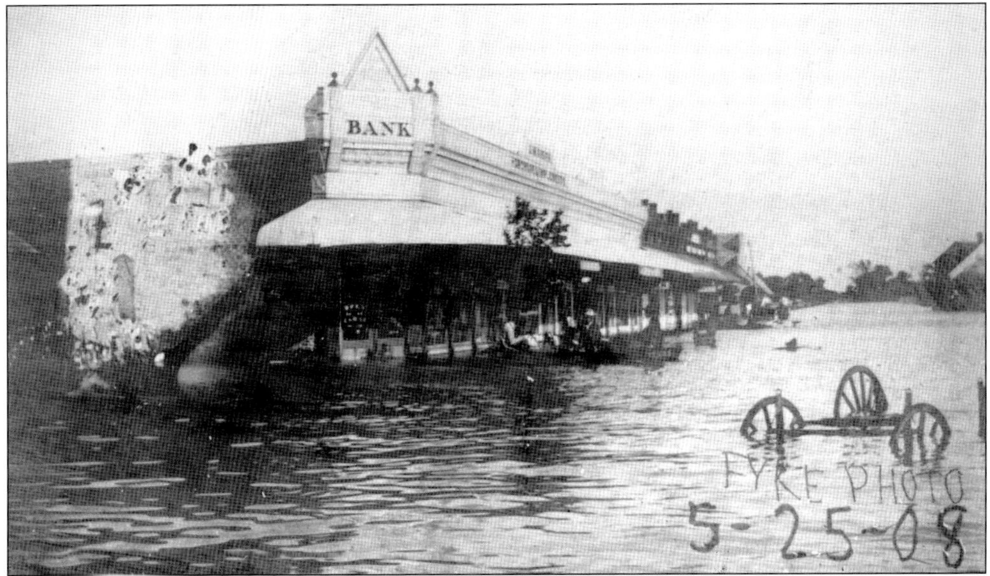

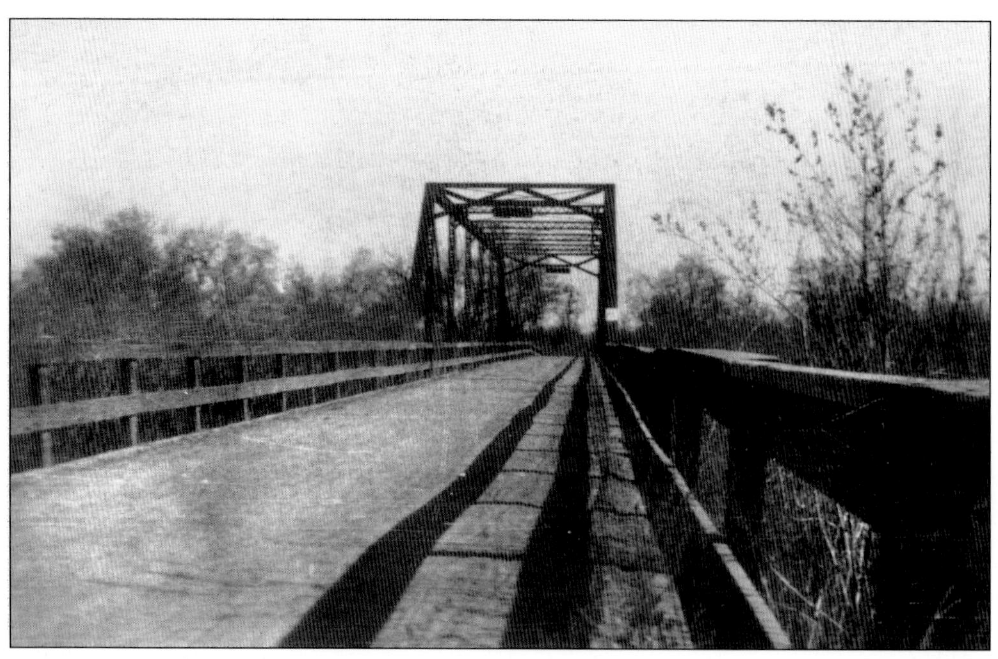

CARROLLTON DAM AND BRIDGE OVER ELM FORK, 1924. In 1912, Carrollton's municipal board voted to get bids for the construction of a concrete dam. The main purpose was not the prevention of flooding though. It was built to hold water from the river for consumption by the community. According to an article in the *Dallas Daily Times Herald*, the Carrollton Dam was completed in 1914. It had a storage capacity of 180,000,000 gallons and was similar in size to Dallas's Bachman Lake. Its construction cost the city $34,000. The reservoir created by the dam became a popular recreation spot. (Both courtesy of Fancy Oliver Tanner.)

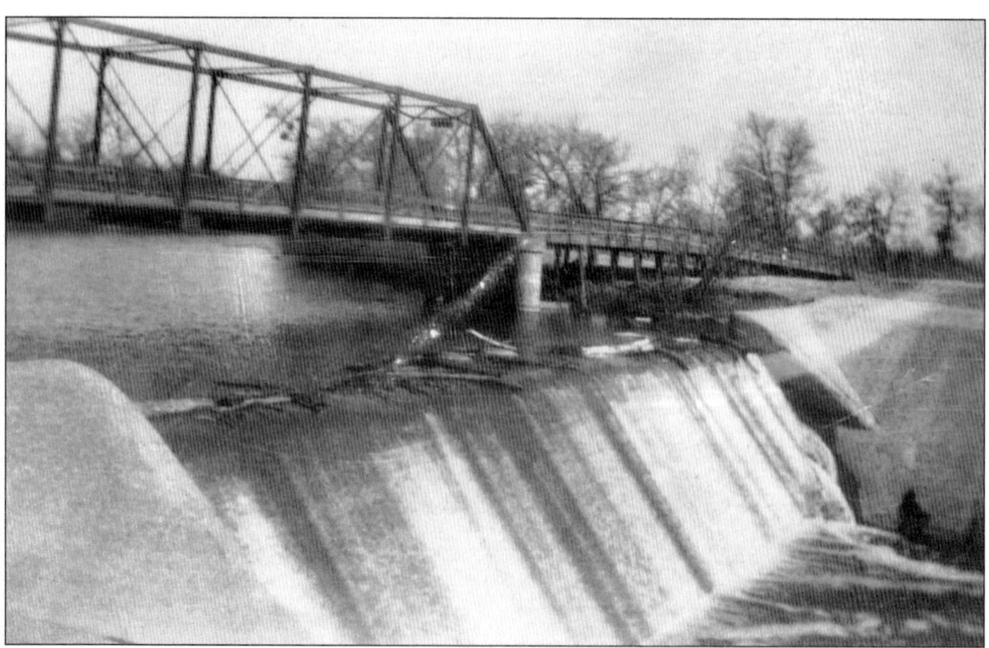

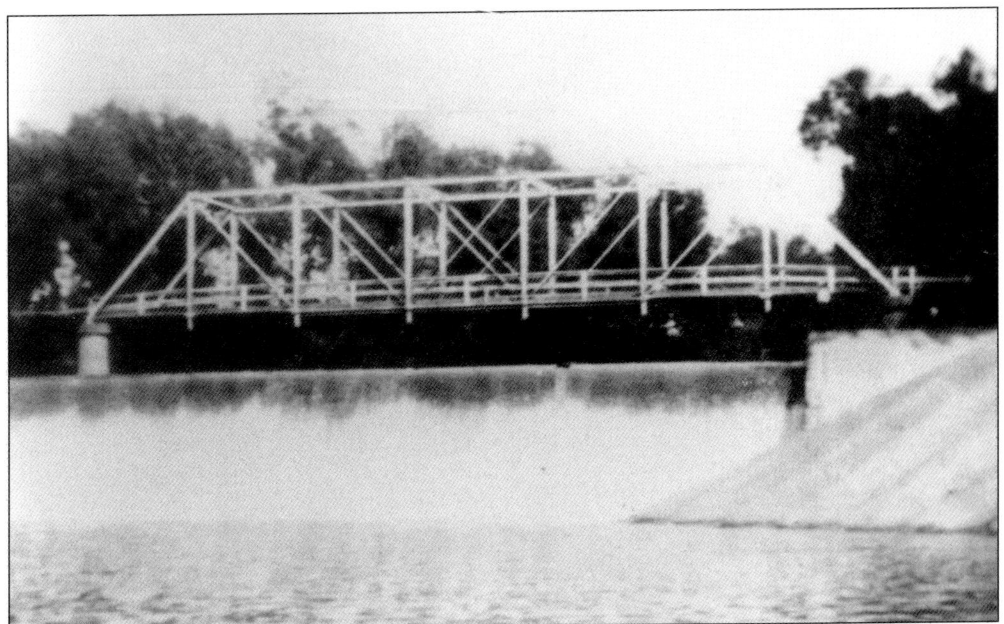

CARROLLTON DAM AND BRIDGE OVER THE ELM FORK. This image shows a full-length view of the bridge and dam. At the time of its construction, the concrete dam was touted as an example of some of the finest engineering in Texas. (Courtesy of A. W. Perry Homestead Museum, Ogle Collection.)

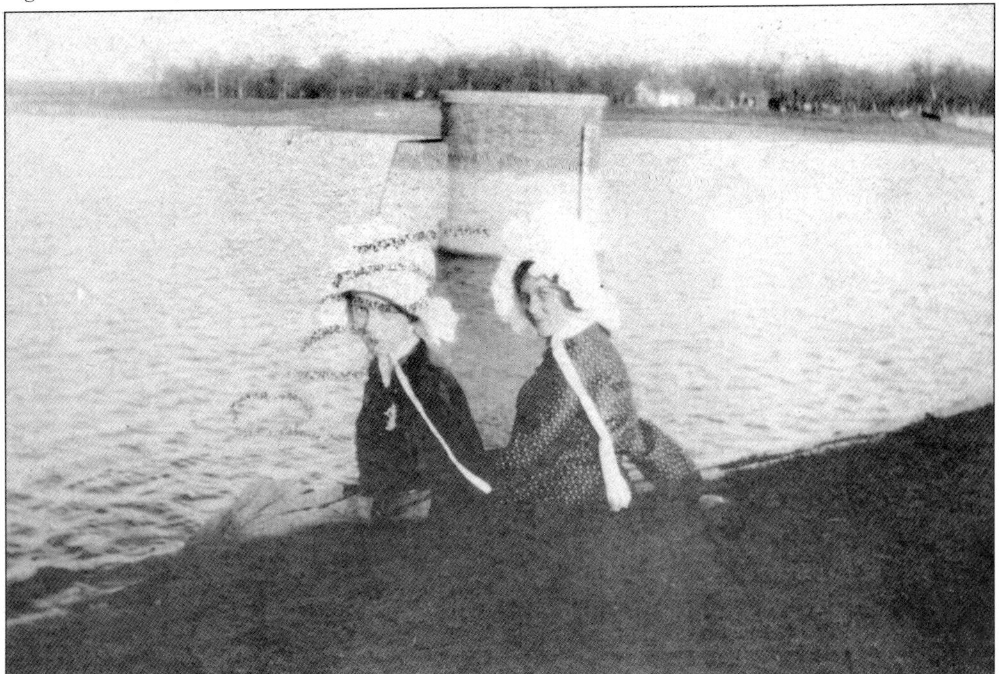

A DAY AT THE DAM, C. 1915. As a means of recreation, many local people would retreat to the area around the Carrollton Dam to fish and picnic. Locals Sarah Myers and Alma Gillians seem to be enjoying a relaxing sunny day at the Carrollton Dam. (Courtesy of A. W. Perry Homestead Museum, Ogle Collection.)

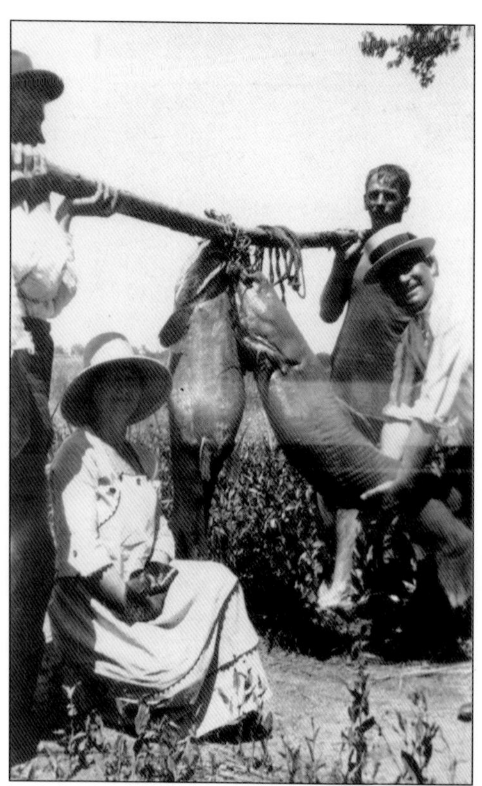

COMMUNITY FISH FRY, C. 1915. Mr. and Mrs. Jerry Chastain and Ashley Webb pose with two large catfish that were caught in the Elm Fork of the Trinity River. Church picnics and fish fries along the banks of the river were held often. Jerry Chastain, shown kneeling, served as one of Carrollton's first mayors after it was incorporated in 1913. He was mayor from 1917 to 1919. (Courtesy of A. W. Perry Homestead Museum, Ogle Collection.)

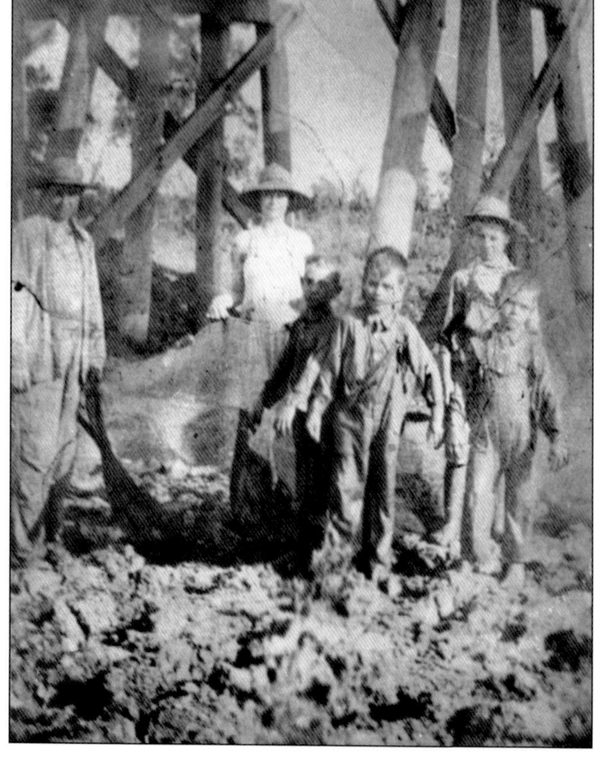

CROW FAMILY FISHING. Fishing in the Elm Fork of the Trinity River was a popular summer pastime. The large Crow family lived just west of town, close to the river. This image shows part of the Crow family standing below a railroad trestle with a large fish they had just caught in the river. (Courtesy of A. W. Perry Homestead Museum, Ogle Collection.)

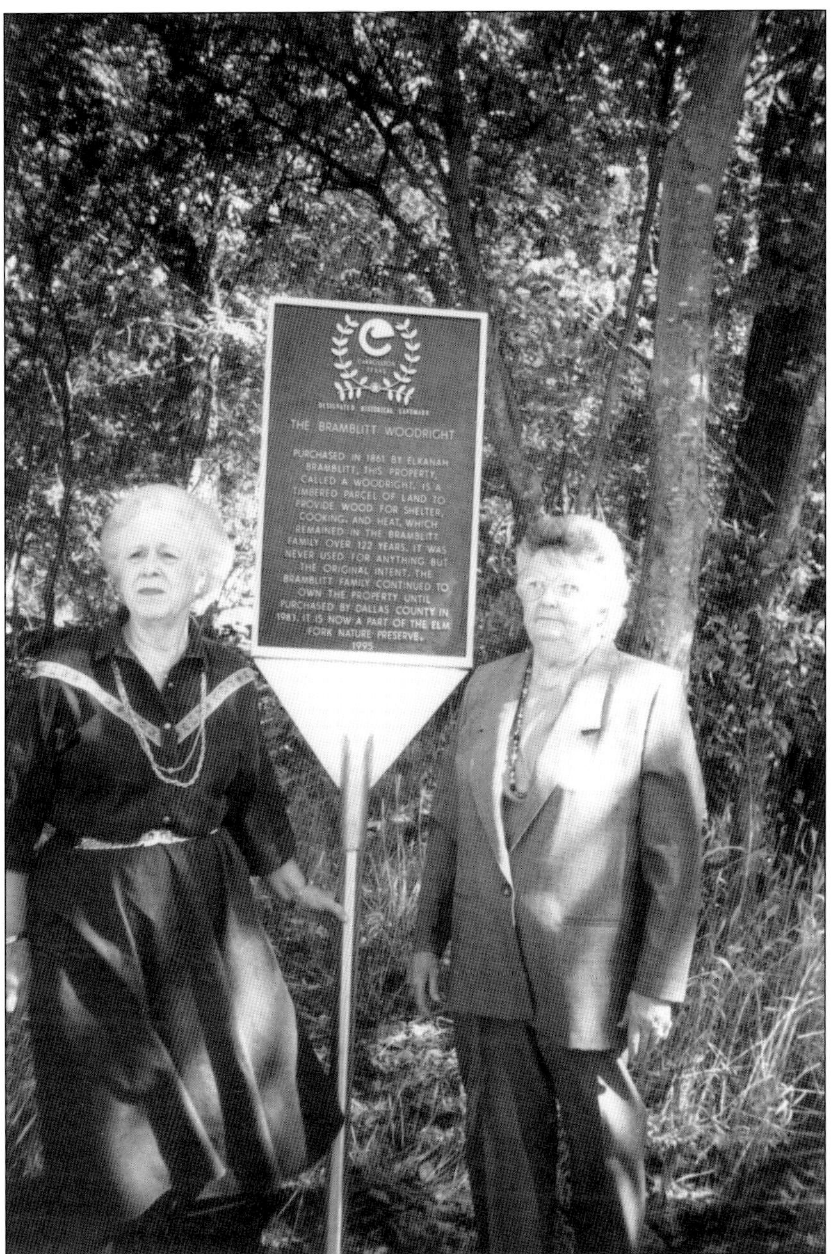

BRAMBLIT WOODRIGHT. Elkanah Columbus Bramblitt emigrated from Virginia in 1859. His property was in Addison. In 1861, he purchased 40 additional acres of land close to the river near present-day Sandy Lake Road as a wood right. Families camped at their wood rights for several days to cut timber to take back to their homes to be used as fuel for heating and cooking. He was a pastor of several Baptist churches in the area at various times. Other professions he held included carpenter and cattle driver. The Bramblitt family continued to own a 10-acre portion of the land for more than 122 years until it was sold to Dallas County to establish a park. Peggy Perry Oliver, who researched and wrote the historical narrative for the property, and another member of the city of Carrollton's Historic Preservation Advisory Board stand in front of the historical marker for the site at its dedication ceremony. (Courtesy of Fancy Oliver Tanner.)

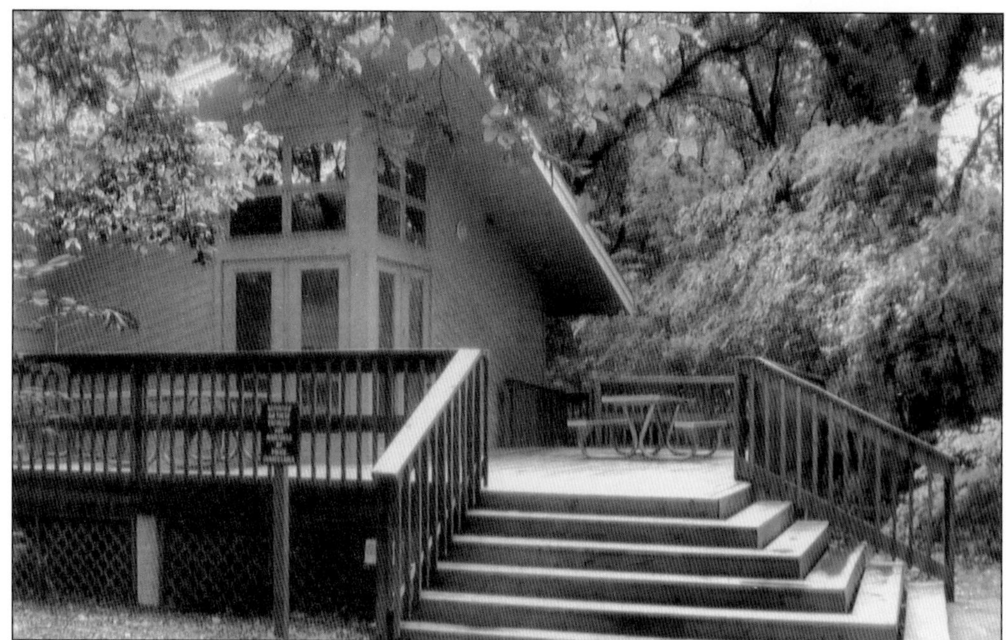

ELM FORK NATURE PRESERVE, 1990S. The land was never clear-cut, and in 1986 the City of Carrollton and Dallas County used the land to create the Elm Fork Nature Preserve. It consists of 40 acres of virtually undisturbed land in the center of the McInnish Sports Complex south of Sandy Lake Road. Volunteers and the city constructed and opened an interpretive building and cut a mile-long looped trail for visitors to enjoy. (Courtesy of City of Carrollton, Elm Fork Nature Preserve.)

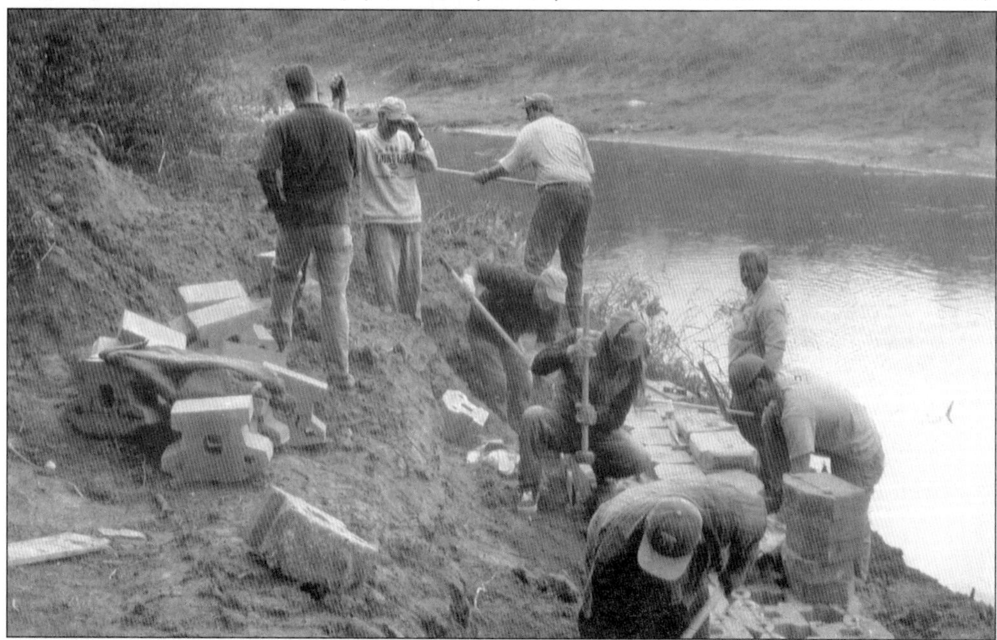

ELM FORK OF THE TRINITY RIVER CANOE LAUNCH, C. 2005. Volunteers from the community and local businesses constructed a series of steps that lead down to the river to provide access for canoeing. This river access point is located south of Belt Line Road on Elm Park Drive. (Courtesy of City of Carrollton, Elm Fork Nature Preserve.)

Six

GRIT AND GLITZ
JOSEY RANCHO

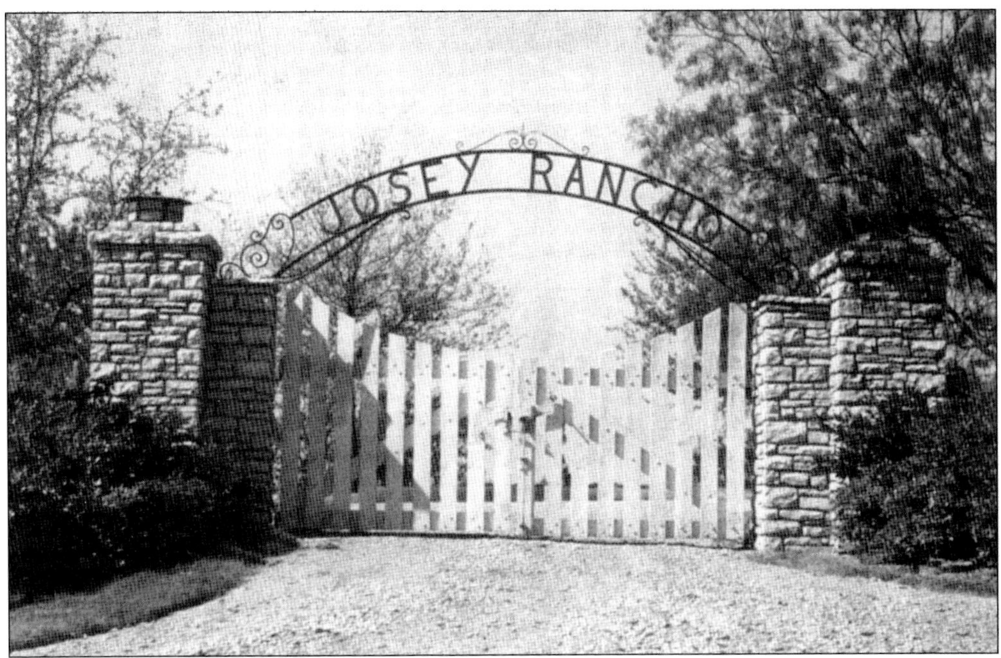

JOSEY RANCHO ENTRANCE, 1950S. In the 1930s, oilman "Colonel" C. W. Josey and his wife were living at the Adolphus Hotel in Dallas when they purchased 70 acres in Carrollton. Construction of a large home and barn on the site was completed in 1939. The Joseys continued amassing land in the area, and the Rancho Oil Estate eventually became a sprawling 1,000 acres, complete with roaming buffalo and Texas longhorn cattle. The Joseys used their property for recreation and hosted elaborate parties at their Carrollton ranch for their friends. (Courtesy of Linda Sollinger.)

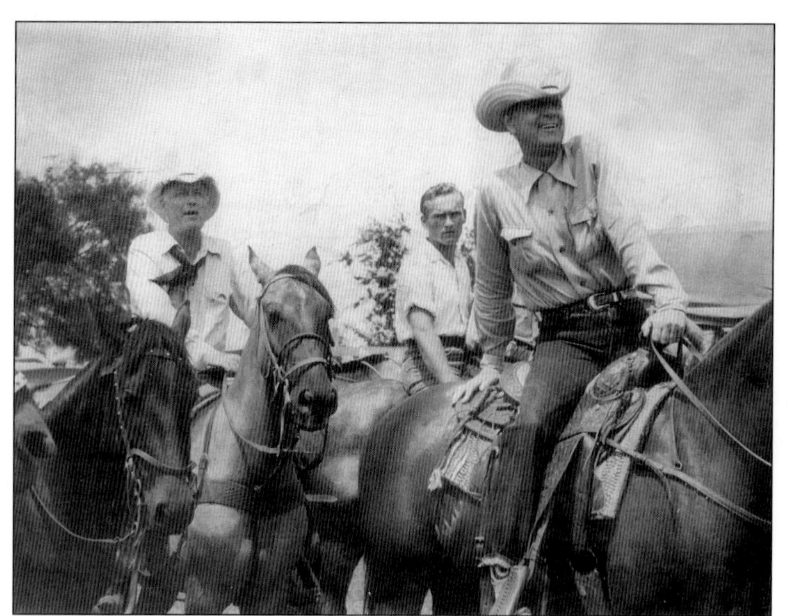

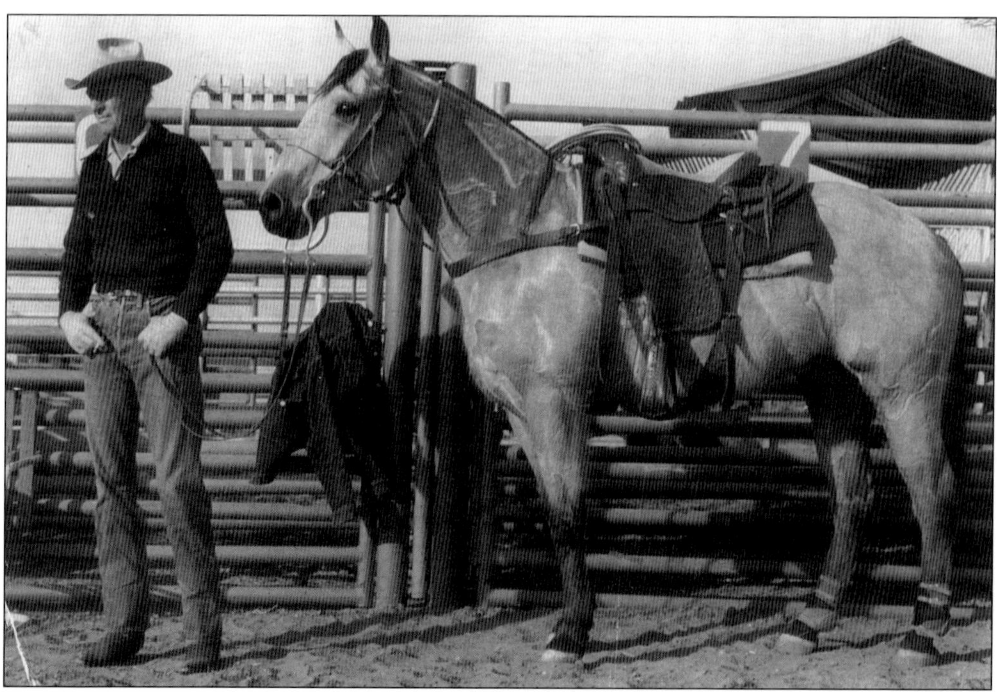

DON JOSEY, 1950S. Don Josey, who also ran Rancho Oil Company, is pictured here with his horse on the ranch. When interviewed in 1984, at the age of 84, Don Josey reminisced about the ranch and how his foreman had taught him how to rope cattle in the corral. (Courtesy of Linda Sollinger.)

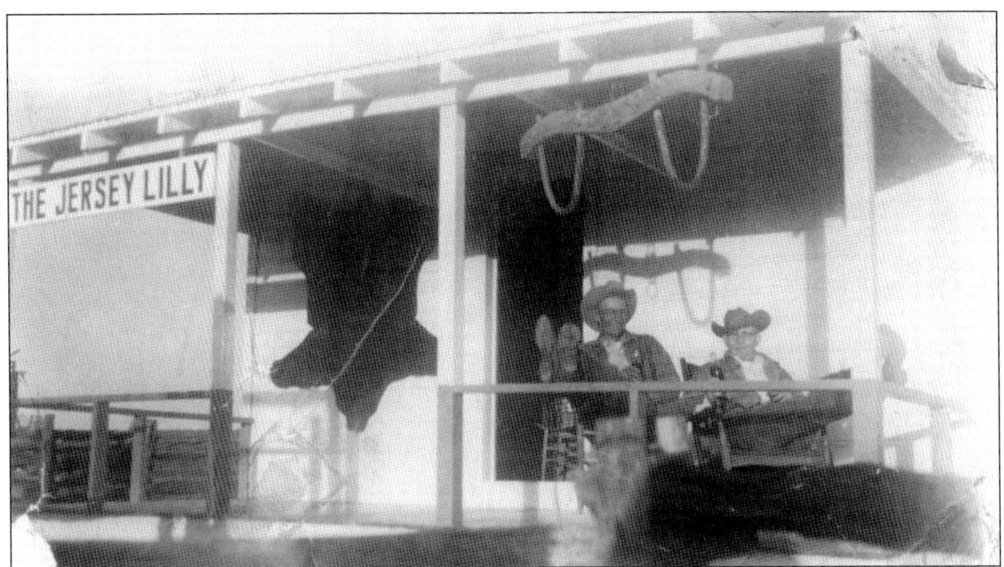

A VISIT TO JOSEY RANCHO, 1950S. The nostalgic Josey Rancho was used as a location backdrop for numerous movies and television series. For example, an episode of *Have Gun Will Travel* was filmed there. It has even been reported that controversial author Forrest Carter named his "Josey Wales" character, which was later portrayed in the film version of the novel by Clint Eastwood, after Don Josey. Carter claimed to have grown up as an orphaned Native American and penned the autobiography *The Education of Little Tree*, which was highly acclaimed but was later proved to be fabricated.

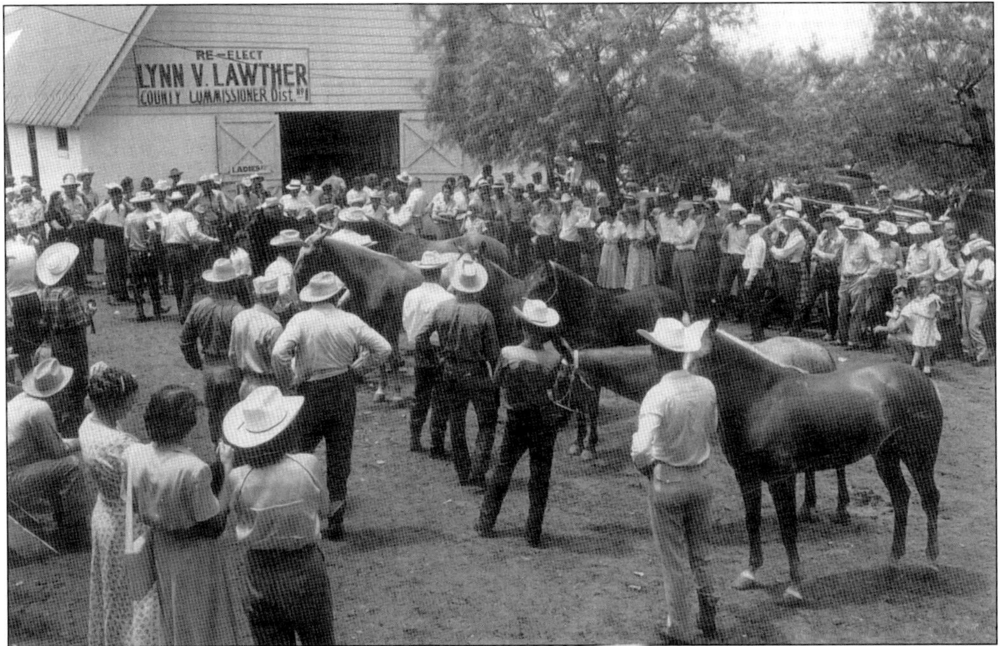

JOSEY BARN, 1950S. A crowd gathers in front of the Josey barn during the annual rodeo. The barn is still on the property and has been converted to modern office space. Two identical reproduction structures have been placed on either side of the converted barn. (Courtesy of Linda Sollinger.)

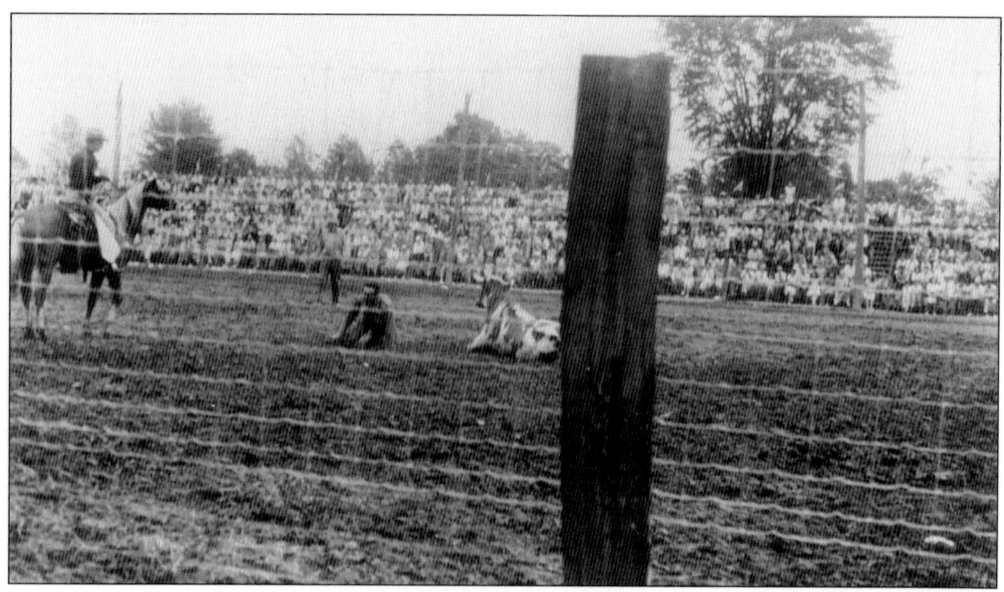

FOURTH OF JULY RODEO, 1950S. Beginning in the 1940s, the Josey sons, Clint and Don, organized an annual free Fourth of July Rodeo that attracted people from across the country. At its height, crowds of 15,000 to 17,000 people attended. Movie stars, foreign dignitaries, and politicians were often in the crowd. The rodeo and surrounding festivities included a Texas-style barbeque the night before for close friends and neighbors. In 1949, the spectacle was documented by *Town North Magazine*, which reported that *Life Magazine* also was in attendance. That year, a special landing strip was constructed for those coming in by air. The event included a visit by a Mexican general and his entire staff, who, along with the rest of the attendees, witnessed trick riders, buffalo, cowboys, and the Sac and Fox Indian tribes from Oklahoma who presented Clint and Don Josey each with a feathered war bonnet. (Courtesy of Linda Sollinger.)

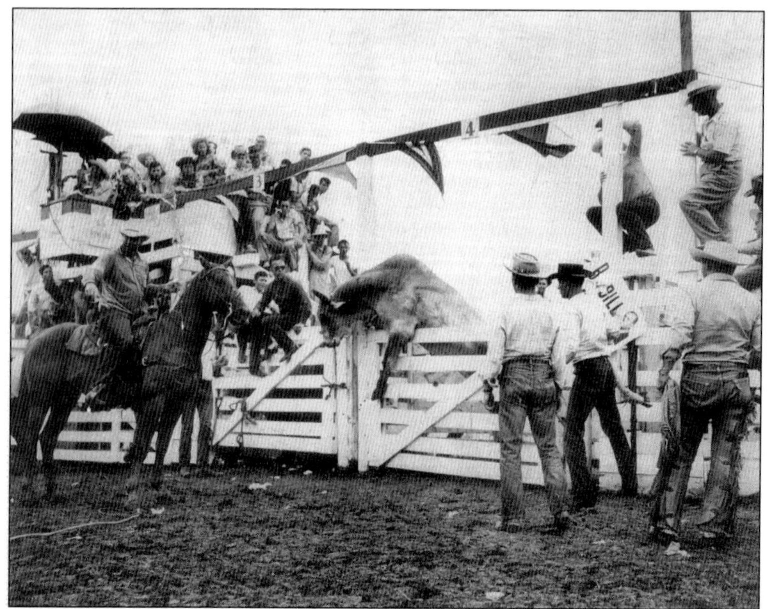

JOSEY RANCHO RODEO BULL, 1950S. In 1951, Dallas County sheriff Bill Decker estimated that there was a crowd of more than 15,000 people in an arena that seated less than 8,500. The crowds got too large, even for the Josey brothers, and the last rodeo on the property took place in the mid-1950s. (Courtesy of Linda Sollinger.)

ARTHUR NEWTON, JOSEY RANCHO FOREMAN, 1950s. Arthur Newton was the first foreman on the ranch and was responsible for managing the vast property, the staff, and the livestock. He served the family until his death in 1977. Ed Johnson, who had worked and lived on the ranch since 1959, took over the foreman's job and continued on until the 1980s. (Courtesy of Linda Sollinger.)

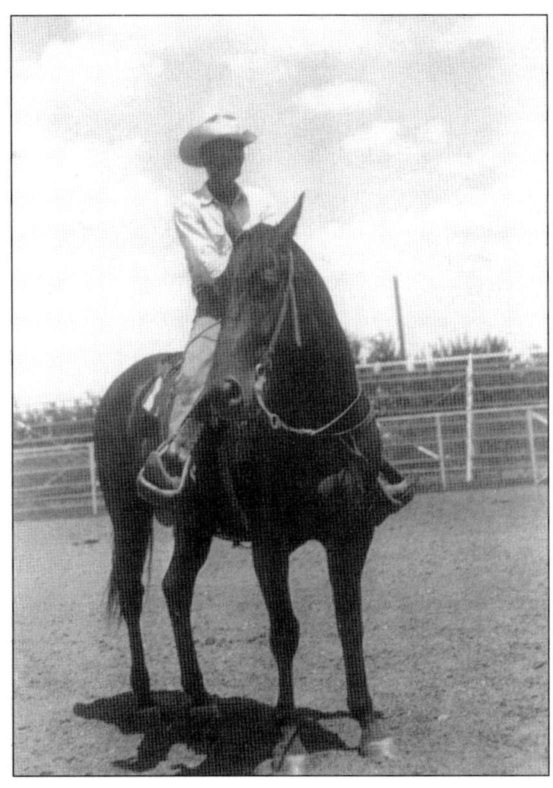

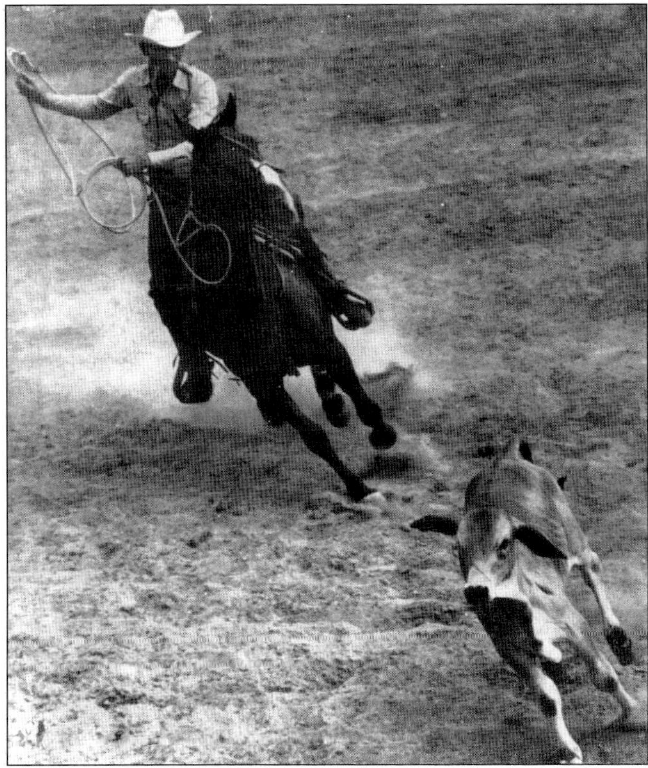

ARTHUR NEWTON AND BOOGER THE HORSE, 1950s. In addition to being the ranch's foreman, Arthur Newton was a championship cattle roper while riding his horse Booger. (Courtesy of Linda Sollinger.)

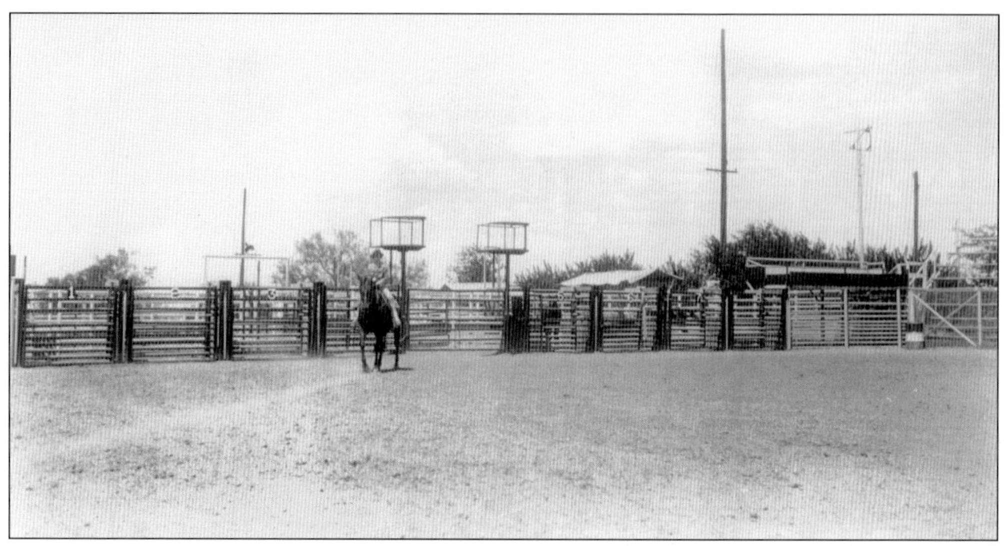

JOSEY RANCHO CORRAL, 1950S. The annual rodeo was held in what was claimed to be the nation's only all-steel arena and billed as the "world's largest single-performance rodeo." The advertisement and high prize amounts attracted top rodeo performers from as far away as California and southern Mexico. (Courtesy of Linda Sollinger.)

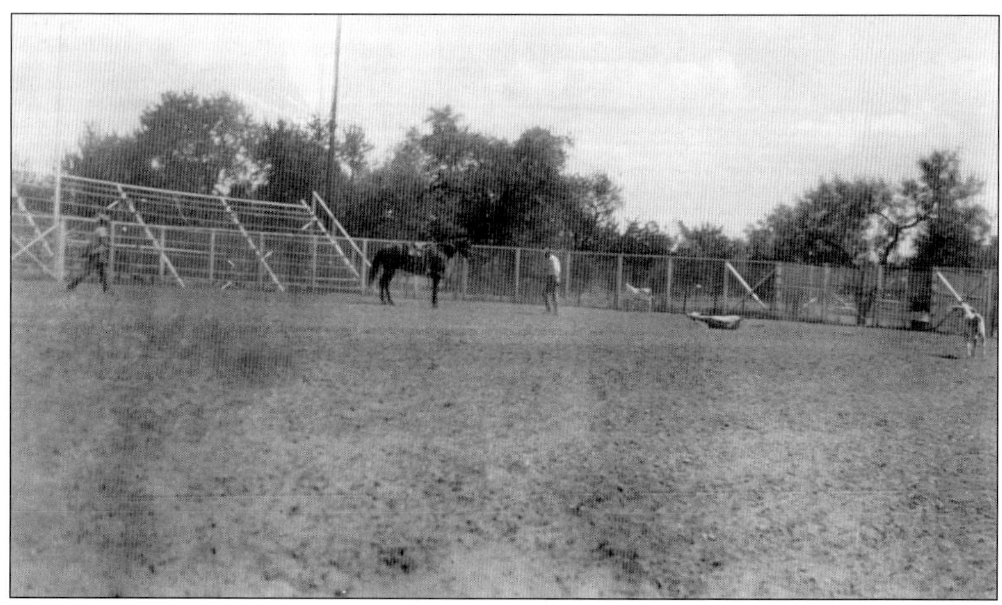

CALF ROPING, 1950S. Cowboys on the ranch practiced roping cattle and other ranching and rodeo skills in the corral. The crown prince of Belgium once asked to visit the Josey Rancho because he wanted to experience riding a Texas cutting horse. (Courtesy of Linda Sollinger.)

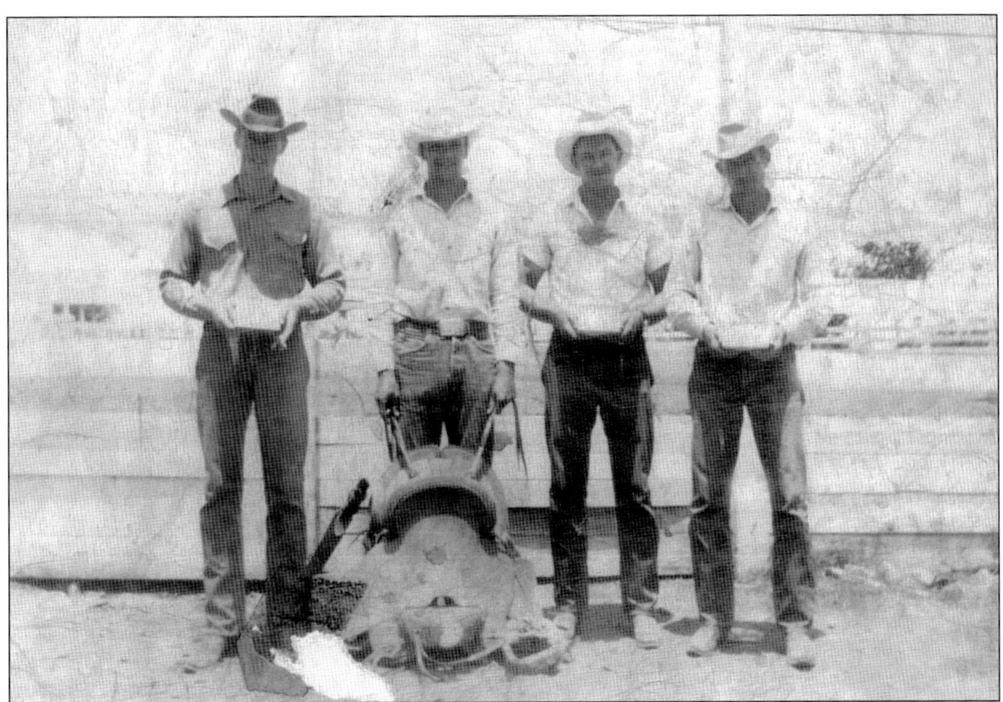

FOURTH OF JULY RODEO WINNERS, 1950S. Because the rodeo was free to those who attended, the Joseys put up the cash prizes for all of the rodeo winners. The prize money awarded was competitive with any rodeo in the country, and because the winnings were so large, champion rodeo performers from across the country were drawn to Carrollton to participate. (Courtesy of Linda Sollinger.)

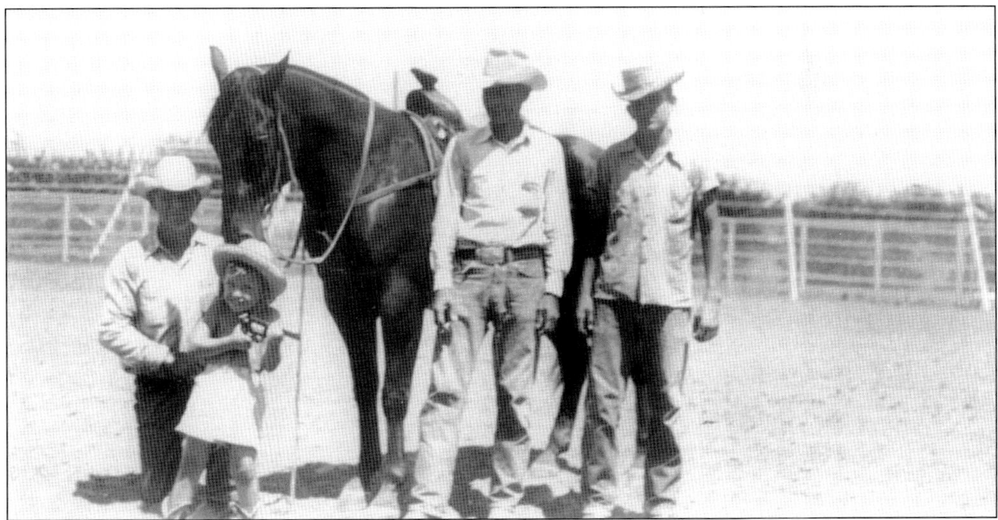

FOREMAN ARTHUR NEWTON AND FRIENDS, 1950S. Fritz and Lucille Hartzel from Oil City, Pennsylvania, made yearly summertime treks to Texas to visit a relative living in Irving. During one of those trips, they were taken to the Josey Rancho. Fritz Hartzel made a lifelong friend in Arthur Newton, the ranch's foreman, and the family continued to visit the ranch each summer. Their daughter Linda Sollinger is pictured second to the left outfitted in classic 1950s Western gear. (Courtesy of Linda Sollinger.)

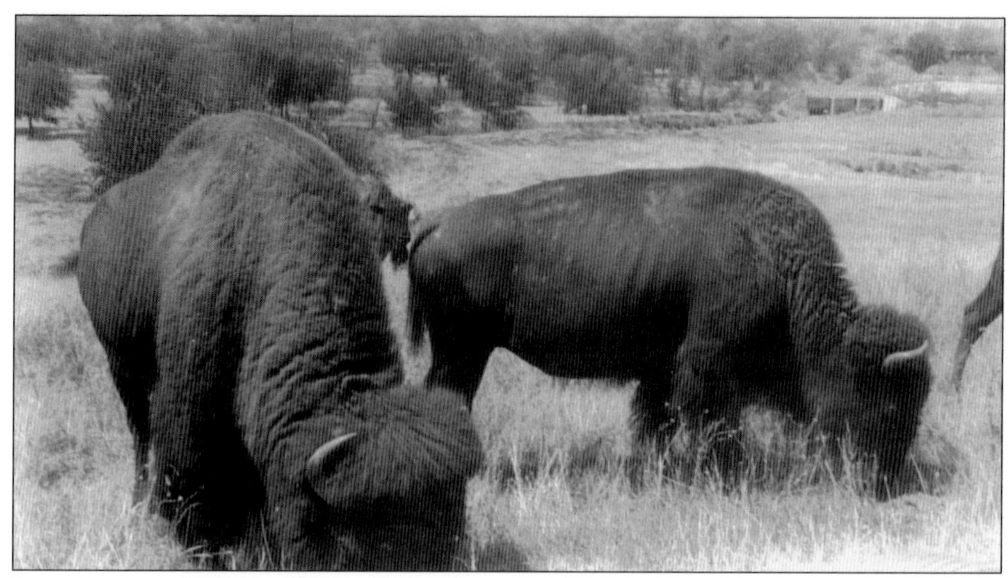

JOSEY RANCHO BUFFALO HERD, 1950S. Don and Clint Josey kept a herd of 40 buffalo on the ranch. Many people visited the ranch to experience Texas traditions. The buffalo added ambiance for the ranch's visitors who were entertained by the feeling that they were truly on the Western frontier. (Courtesy of Linda Sollinger.)

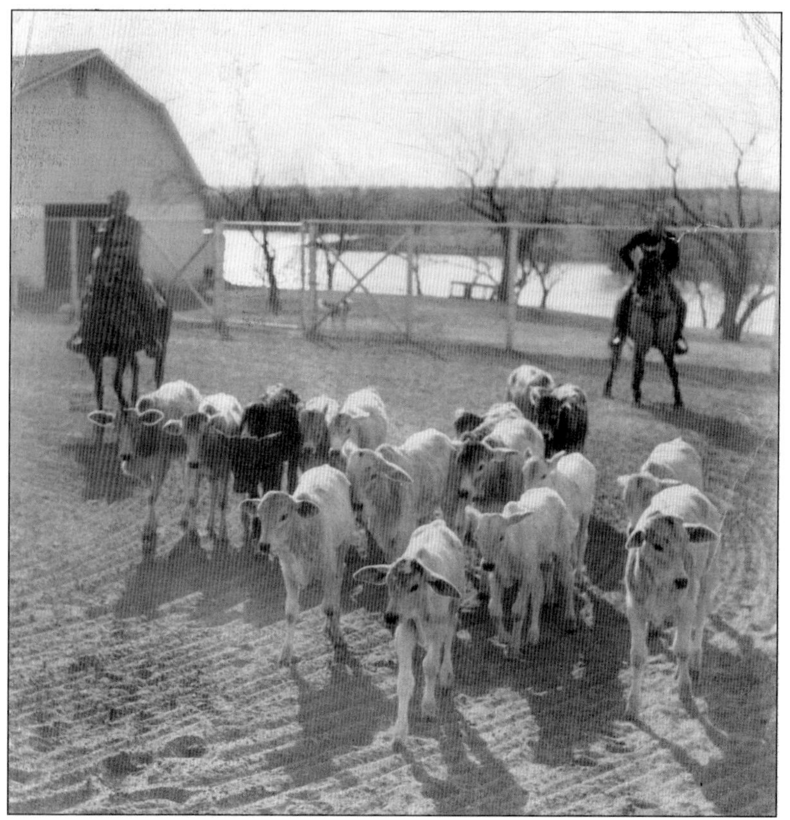

JOSEY RANCHO CATTLE, 1950S. The ranch was the location of movie and television filming. In 1960, the herd of 150 Texas longhorn cattle were sold and used in the John Wayne film *The Alamo.* Buffalo and cattle continued to be kept on the property until its sale to a developer in the 1980s. (Courtesy of Linda Sollinger.)

JOSEY RANCHO
MAIN HOUSE AND
TERRACE, 1950S.
These photographs
show the terrace area
at the back of the 1939
main house, which
overlooked the lake.
The bedrooms were
located down a long
hall, and each had a
set of French doors
that opened up to the
terrace overlooking
the lake. Close friends
and weekend visitors
from Dallas often
stayed in the guest
rooms. (Both courtesy
of Linda Sollinger.)

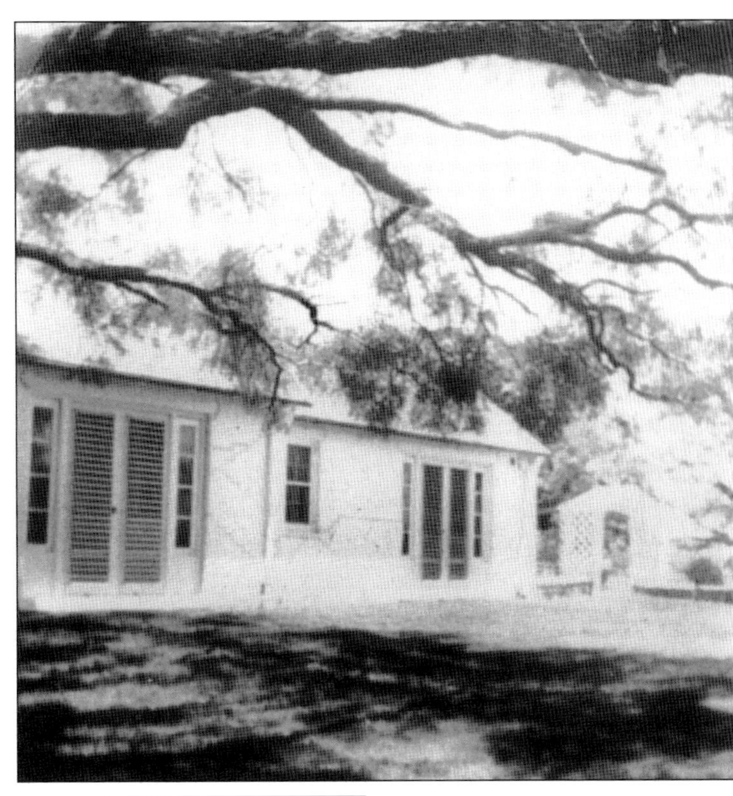

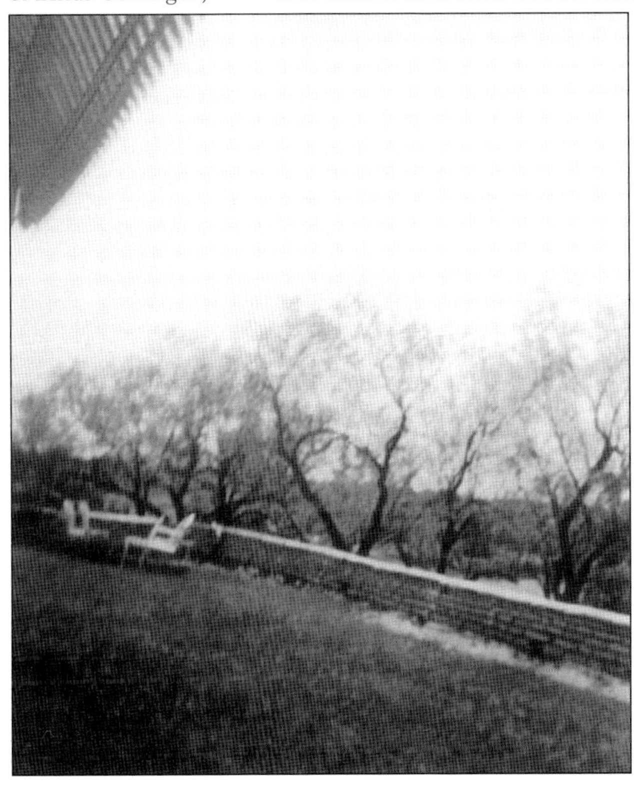

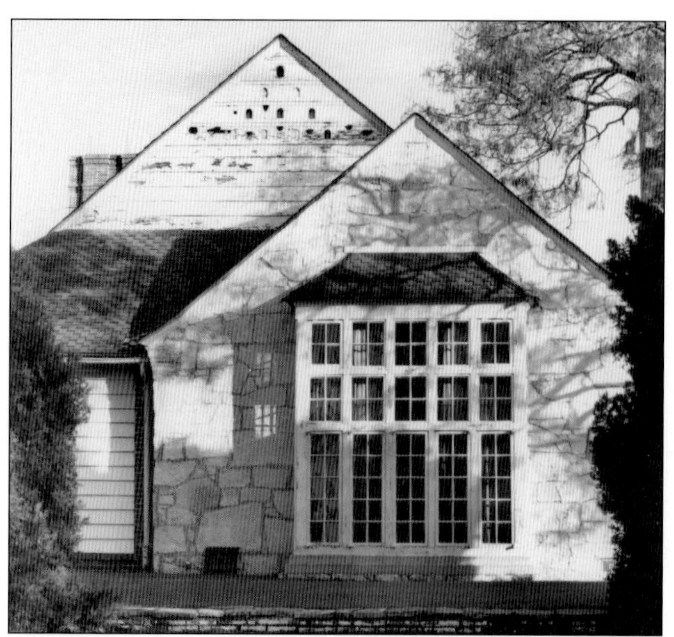

JOSEY RANCHO HOUSE AND LAKE, C. 1990. These photographs show the Josey home, which was completed in 1939. The redbrick structure with white wood trim was positioned to overlook the Josey Lake. The main house was located on top of the hill on the west side of Josey Lane and south of the Josey barn and two smaller homes for staff and the ranch's foreman. The house and outbuildings were torn down in 2008 to make room for new development. (Both courtesy of Carrollton Public Library.)

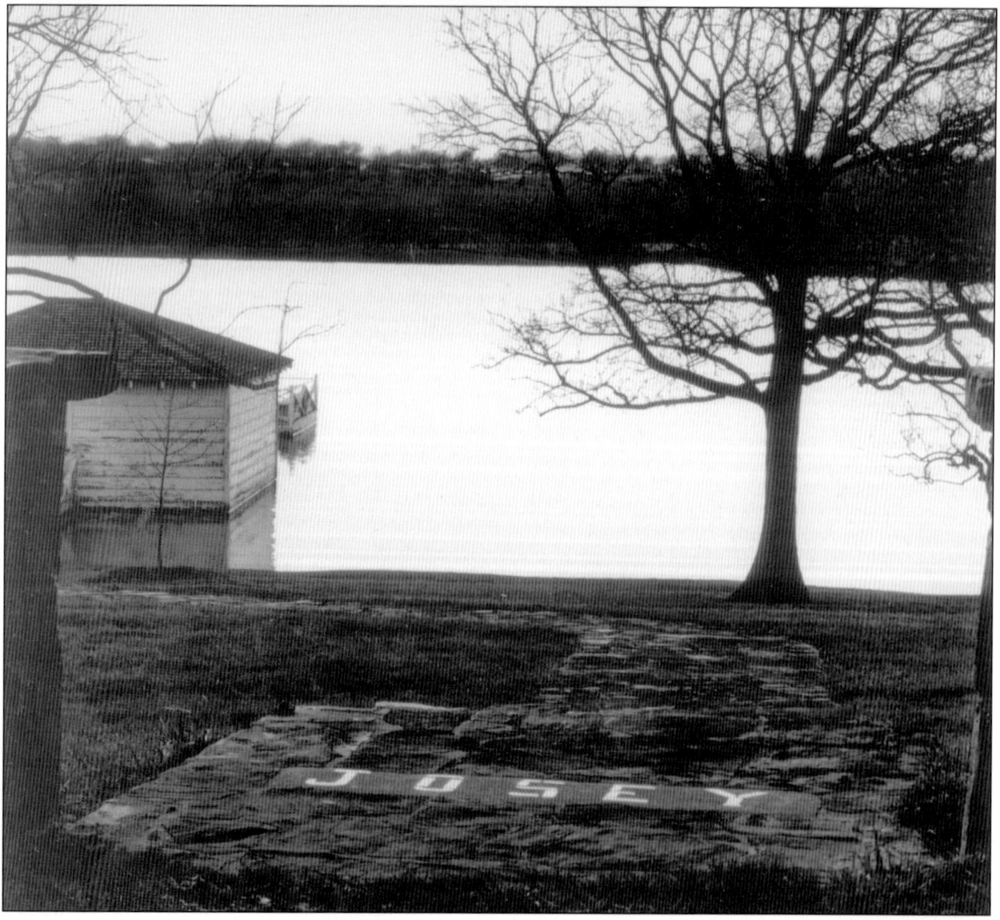

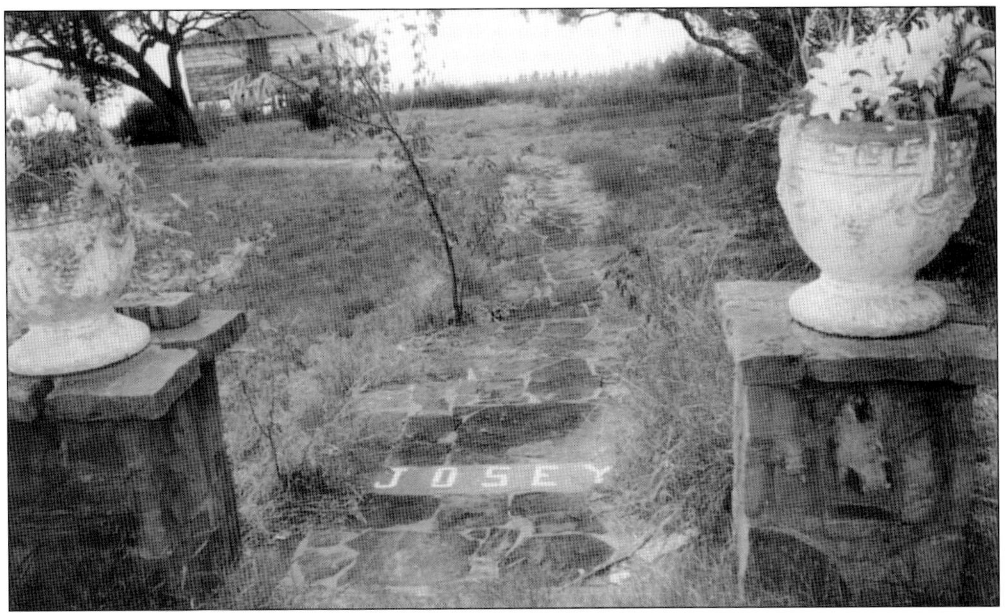

JOSEY RANCHO, 1996. Pictured is the Josey walkway down to the lake and boathouse. There was also a large cook shack on the property. On the eve before their annual Fourth of July Rodeos, the Joseys would serve a huge Western barbeque dinner to friends and neighbors. The offerings included beef, pork, lamb, chicken, and buffalo and all the trimmings. Most of the property can be enjoyed today as a public park and as the sites of the city's senior center and the Josey Ranch Lake Public Library. A walking trail was constructed around Josey Lake. (Both courtesy of Linda Sollinger.)

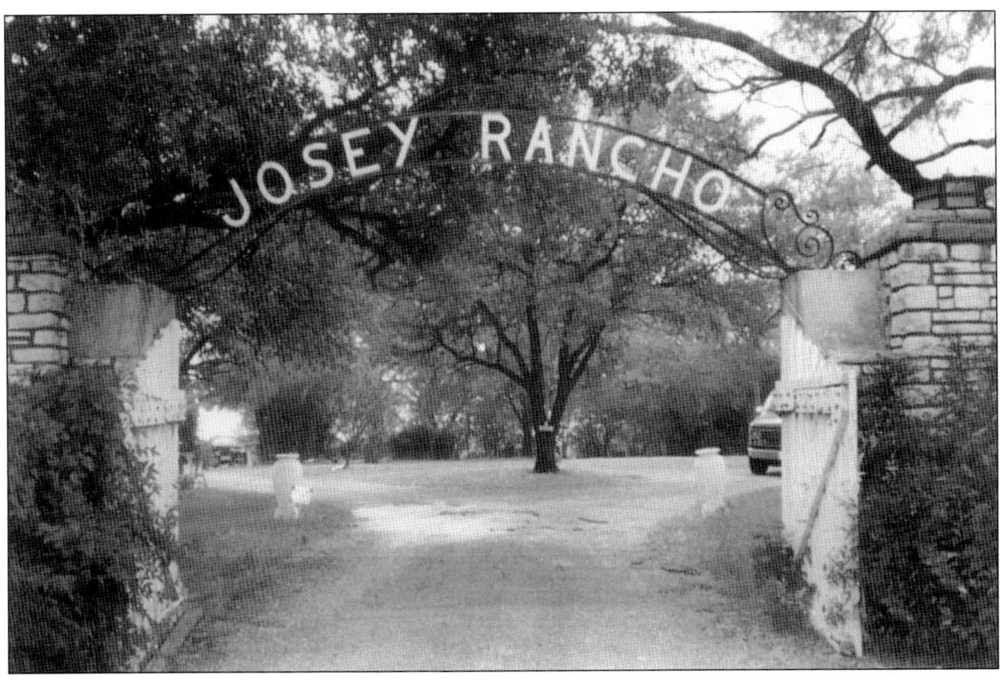

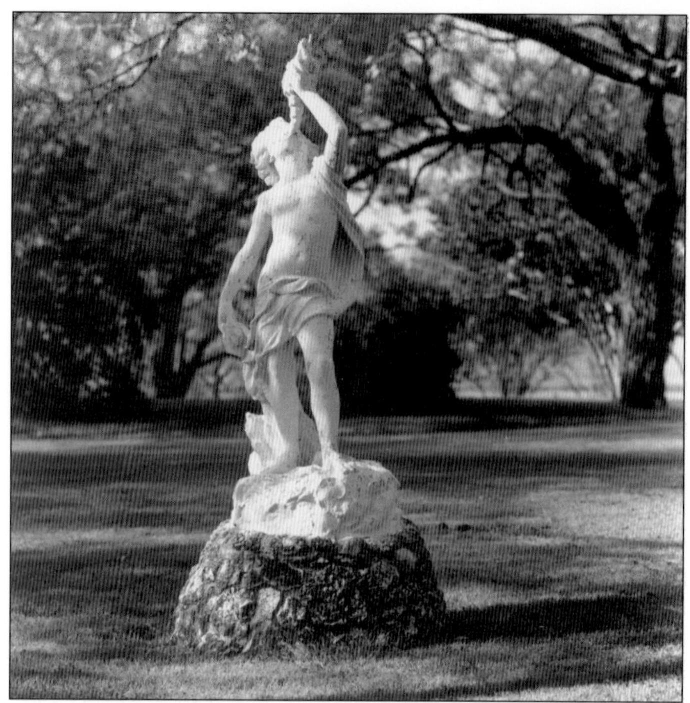

JOSEY RANCHO ENTRANCE STATUE, C. 1990. This statue of a young boy with a conch shell was a fixture of the Josey Rancho entrance in the later days. It was a simple cast concrete garden statue that was placed in the center of the circular drive, which could be seen from Josey Lane. (Courtesy of Carrollton Public Library.)

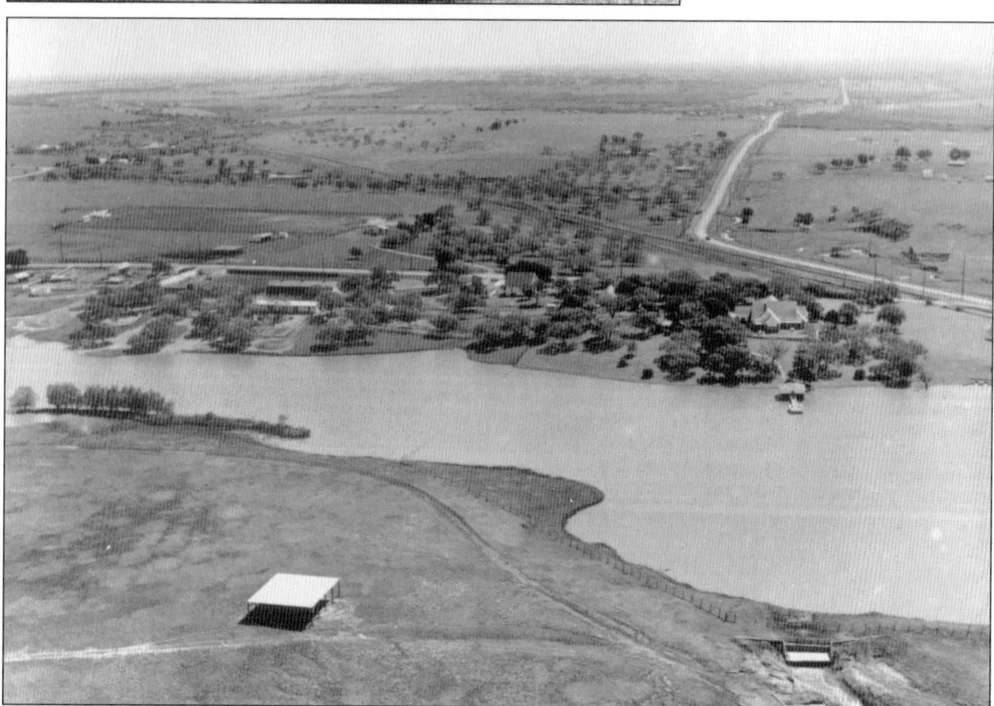

JOSEY RANCHO AERIAL PHOTOGRAPH. Few photographs exist in local museum or library collections of the Josey Rancho. This aerial photograph was recognized and rescued from an antiques store booth in Addison by Lynette Jones, a Carrollton librarian. It was taken back to the library, preserved, and reproduced for background displays throughout the Josey Ranch Lake Library. (Courtesy of Carrollton Public Library.)

Seven

RURAL ROOTS
CITY AND COMMUNITY

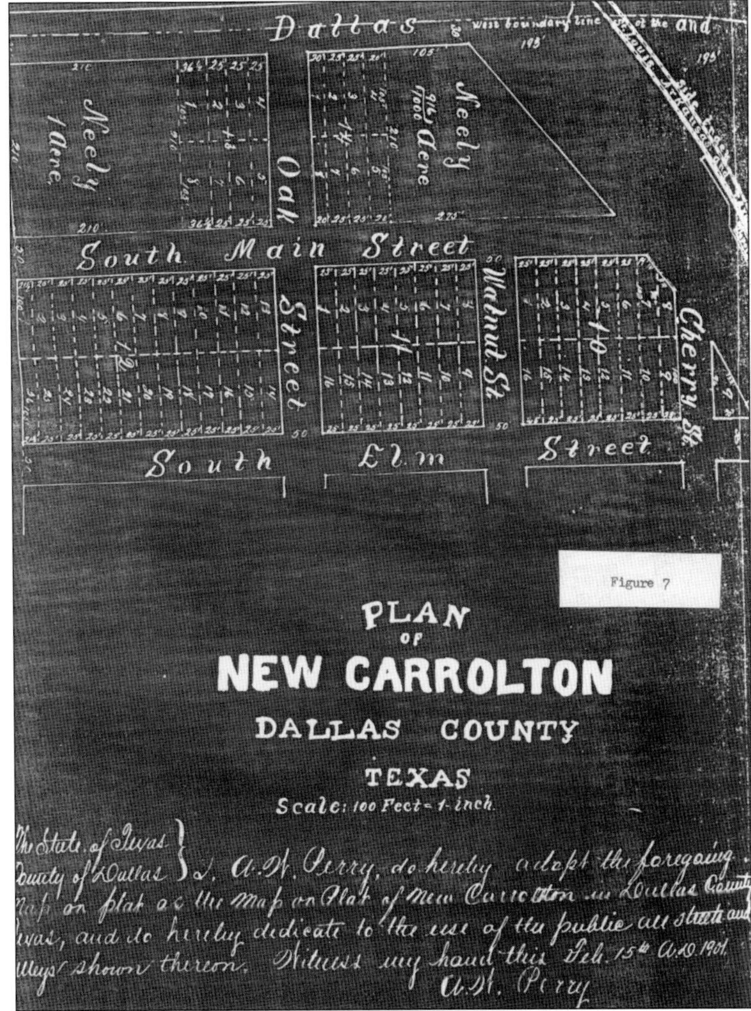

PLAN OF NEW CARROLLTON, 1901. Filed by A. W. Perry, the plat of town lots refers to the city as New Carrollton. Many of the town's early residents emigrated from Carrollton, Illinois, including the Perrys, Myers, and Nix families. (Courtesy of A. W. Perry Homestead Museum, Ogle Collection.)

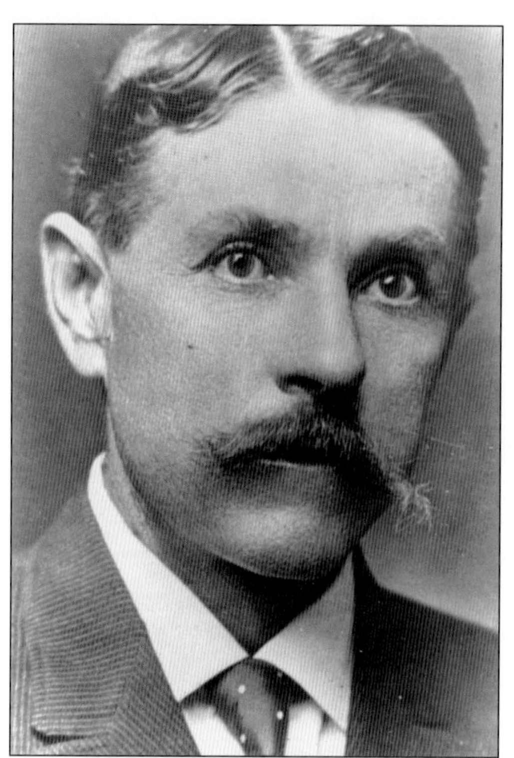

FIRST MAYOR OF CARROLLTON, 1913. The City of Carrollton was incorporated June 14, 1913, by a 52 to 23 vote. The city council was elected in July 1913. William Forest Vinson was elected as mayor but declined the office since he was already serving as the presiding officer over the election, a school board trustee, a precinct chairman, and the Dallas County sheriff. In August 1913, Junius Tribble "J. T." Rhoton took the office of mayor. (Courtesy of A. W. Perry Homestead Museum, Ogle Collection.)

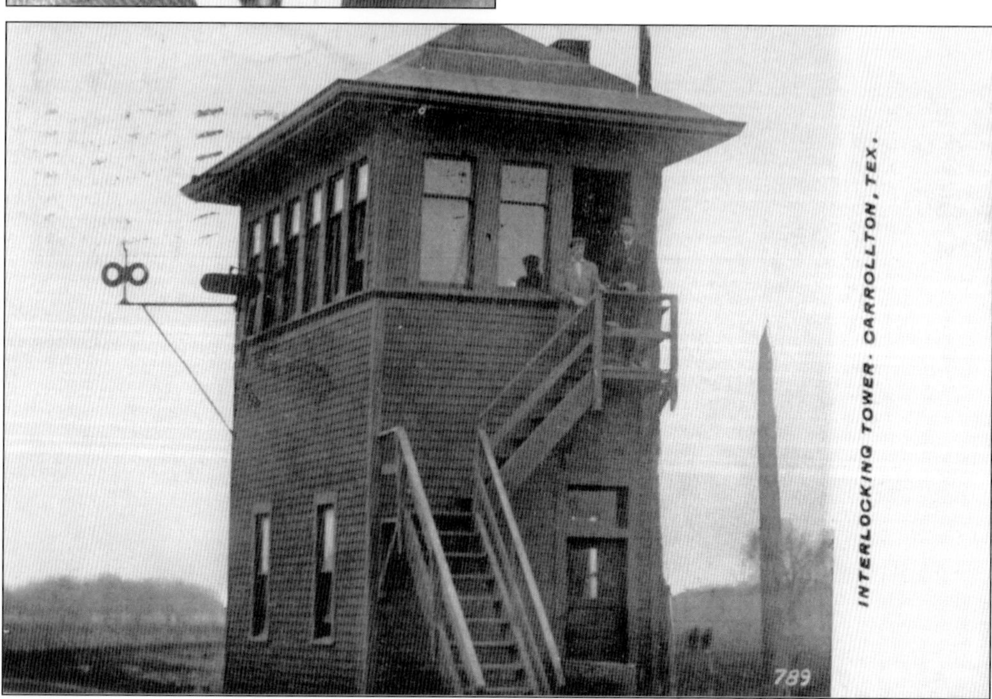

INTERLOCKING TOWER POSTCARD, 1917. An interlocking tower or switching tower was constructed near the depot. The lower portion housed the control equipment for the rail lines' signals and switches. The upper story of the tower provided better visibility of the tracks and incoming and outgoing trains for the operator. (Courtesy of Ed Williams.)

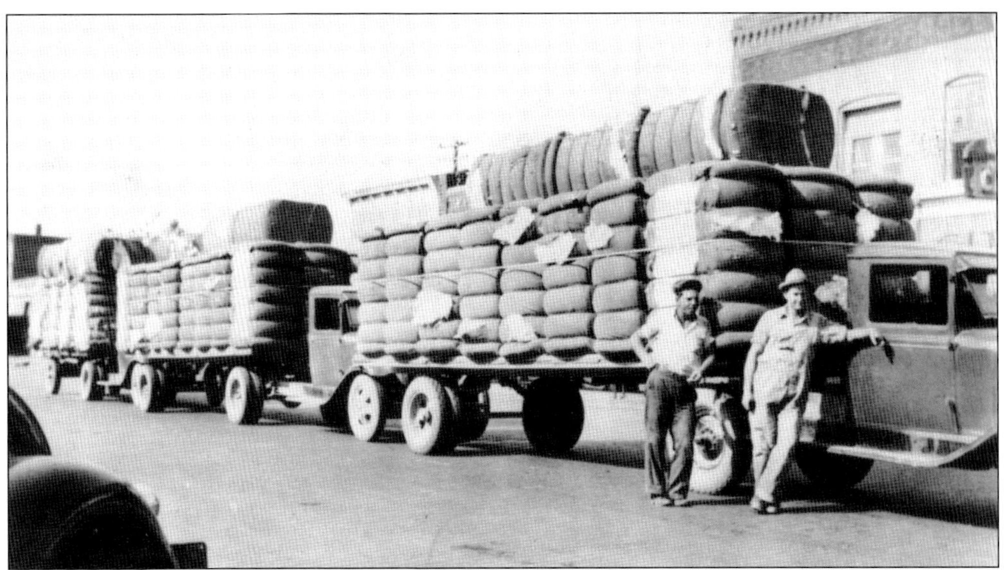

TRUCKS WITH COTTON BALES, 1930s. Will and Clifton Myers stand next to trucks parked on the squares that are full of ginned cotton on their way to the mill. Carrollton was a major grower of cotton and, with the intersection of three railroad lines, was a busy shipping point of the product as well. (Courtesy of City of Carrollton.)

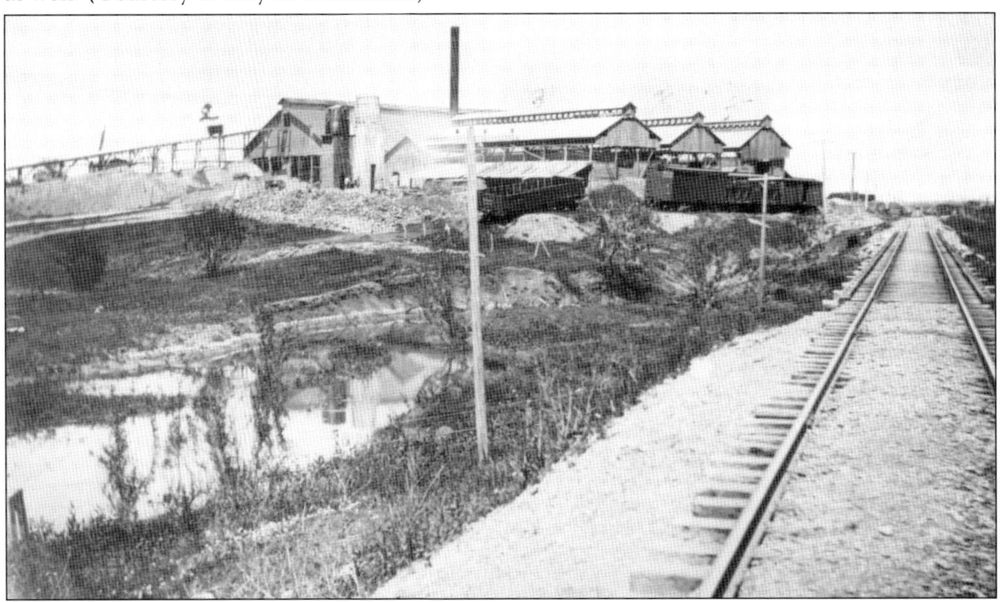

MODEL BRICK PLANT. The Model brick plant was located on the present-day Josey Ranch property, which was originally a part of the Jackson family land grant and whose ownership changed hands numerous times. Removal of clay for manufacturing brick produced the two lakes on the property. The brick plant was located on the north side of the Frisco railroad tracks. The Model Brick Company and the Carrollton Pressed Brick Company were the two businesses producing brick in the area. The photograph shows the Model brick plant. The numbers in the photograph label different parts of the plant: "1" is the powerhouse, "2" is the little car on rails that goes into the pit and hauls out the dirt, and "3" and the barely discernible "4" and "5" are the kilns where the brick was fired. (Courtesy of A. W. Perry Homestead Museum, Ogle Collection.)

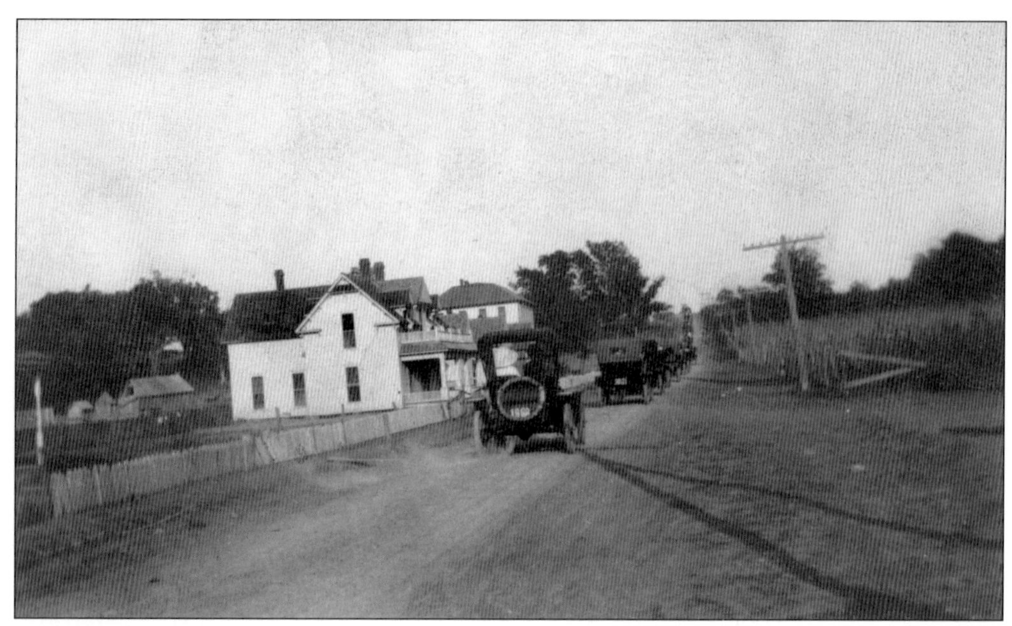

COLLEGE AVENUE/BELT LINE ROAD, C. 1925. These images show how College Avenue, which is now Belt Line Road, appeared in the 1920s. The first photograph documents a funeral procession. The house on College Avenue at the corner of Erie Street was built about 1905 by the Burnett family, and the furthest building from the foreground is the 1902 schoolhouse. The second image shows homes on College Avenue in 1926, now the 1100 block of Belt Line Road. The child is Peggy Perry on the front sidewalk of her grandfather Wade Hampton Perry's home. (Both courtesy of Fancy Oliver Tanner.)

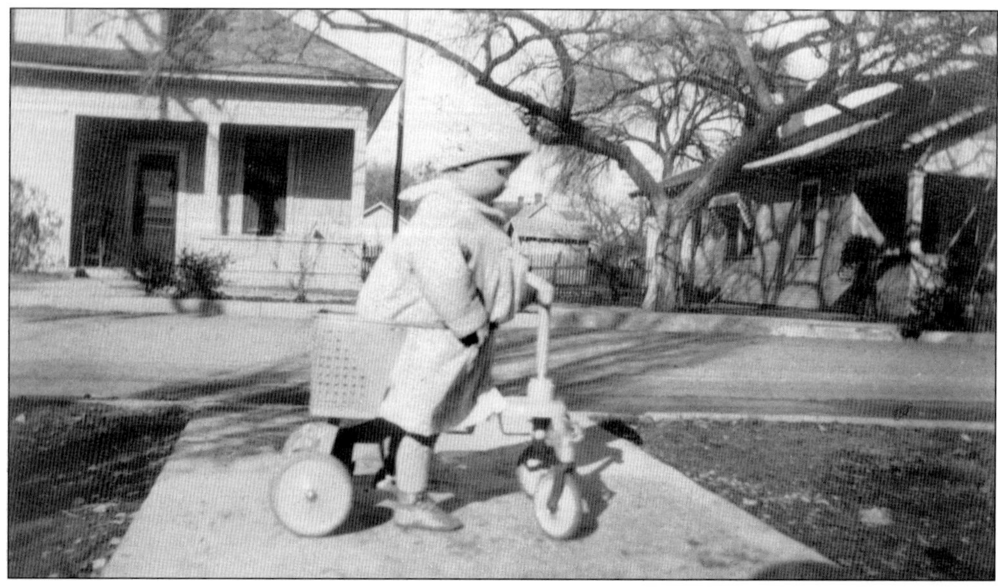

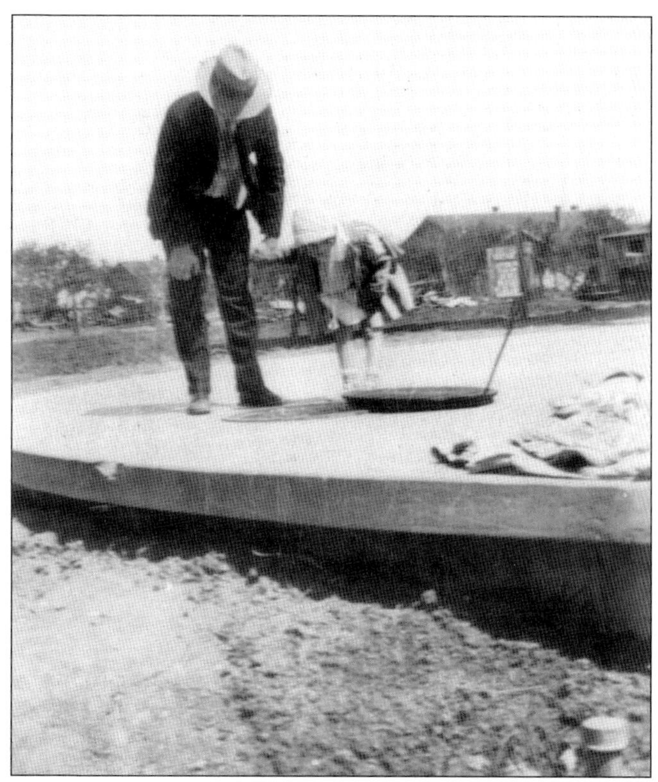

CARROLLTON WATER WELL, 1928. This was the water well on Clint Street just north of Belt Line Road. As the town's mayor, J. T. Rhoton organized the digging of the first well for the town. In 1914, owners of the Carrollton Water Company were E. W. Burnett, J. T. Rhoton, and W. F. Vinson, who sold it to C. J. and H. L. Gulledge for $789. This early system included a pump, windmill, storage tank, and an overhead tower. (Both courtesy of Fancy Oliver Tanner.)

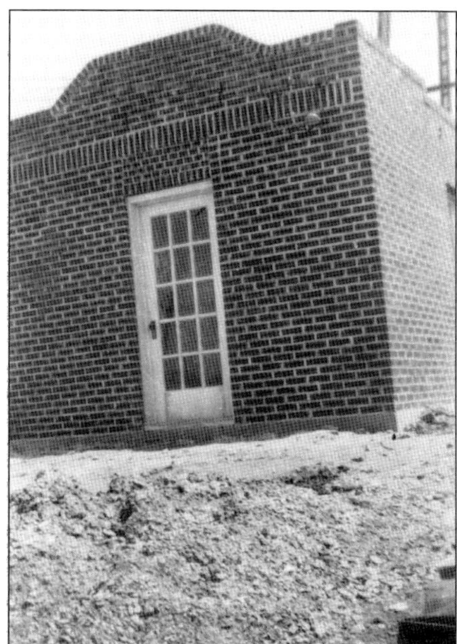

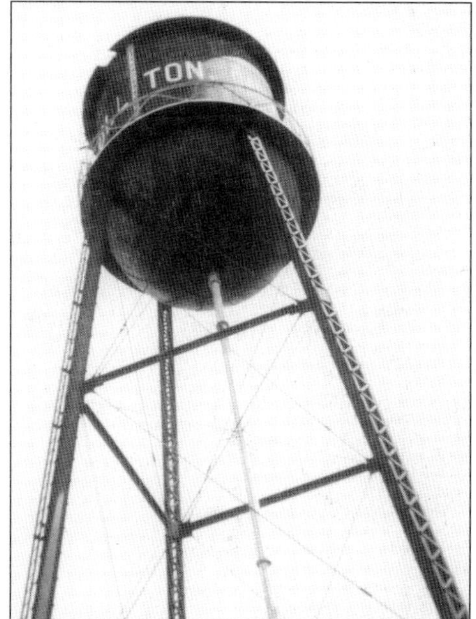

CARROLLTON WELL PUMP HOUSE AND WATER TOWER, 1928. The city hired the C. H. Gardener Company to drill a 325-foot deep, 8-inch well. The pump house stored the equipment that pumped water from the well to the storage tower. It was located next to the well and the water tower on Clint Street just north of Belt Line Road. This artesian well supplied Carrollton's water until mid-1960s. (Courtesy of Fancy Oliver Tanner.)

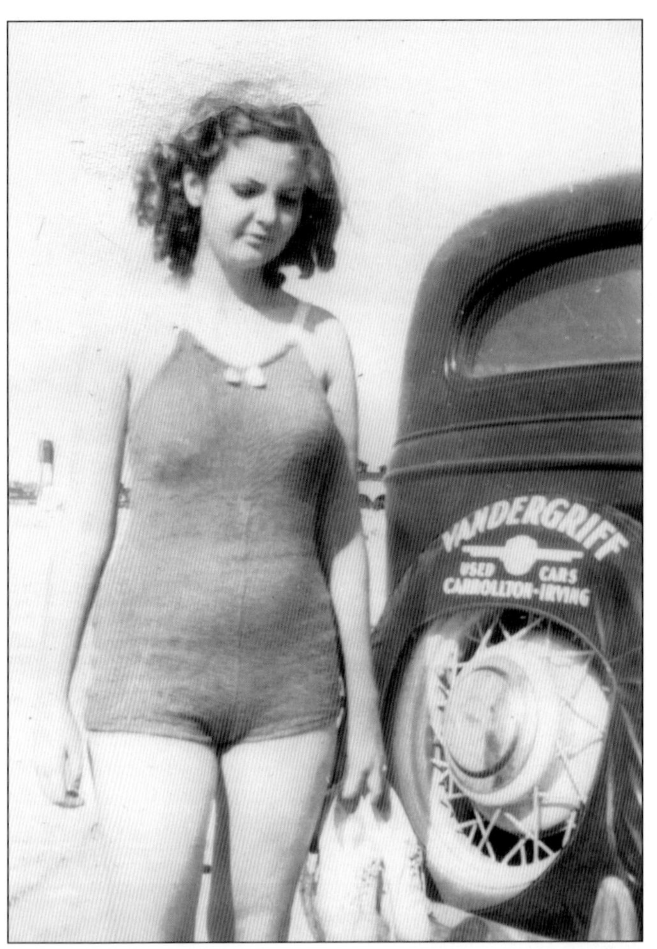

VANDERGRIFF USED CARS, CARROLLTON. Jack Brown was the first blacksmith in town. Later he rented his building and tools to Tom Vandergriff for $5 per month. Vandergriff's blacksmith's shop was located on the south side of the square facing north on Broadway. In 1915, J. C. Davis and Bob Patterson opened the first automobile garage and sold Ford Model Ts for $600. Patterson taught customers how to drive their new machines. Vandergriff eventually added the sale and maintenance of automobiles to the service he offered as well. Galveston became an even more popular destination for families once travel by car was common. A luggage rack was added to the running board for long trips; the example below is from 1928. The photograph to the left shows Burnett Perry's daughter Peggy on a family trip to Galveston in the 1940s. (Both courtesy of Fancy Oliver Tanner.)

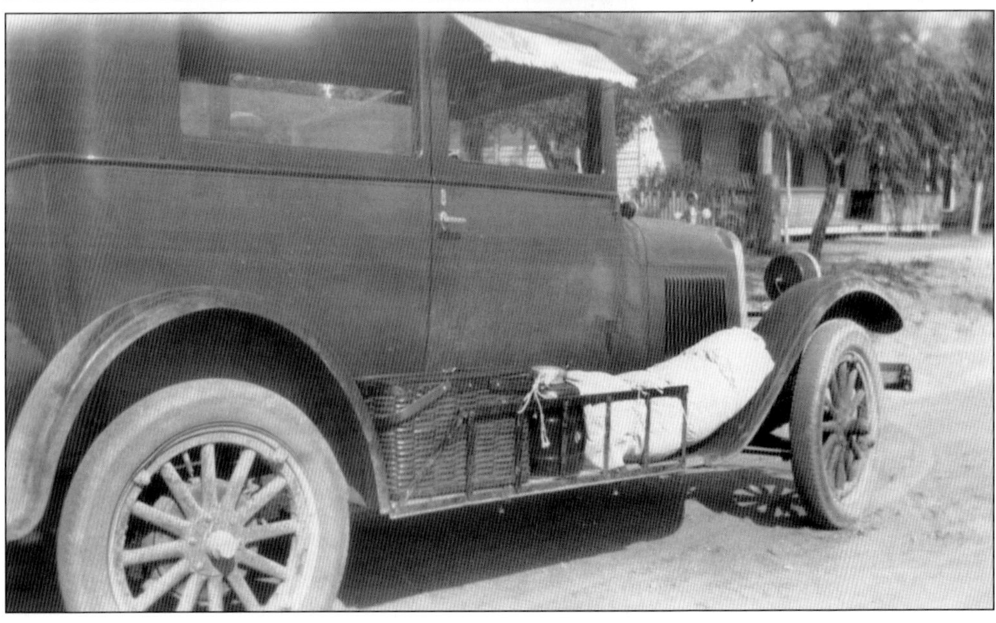

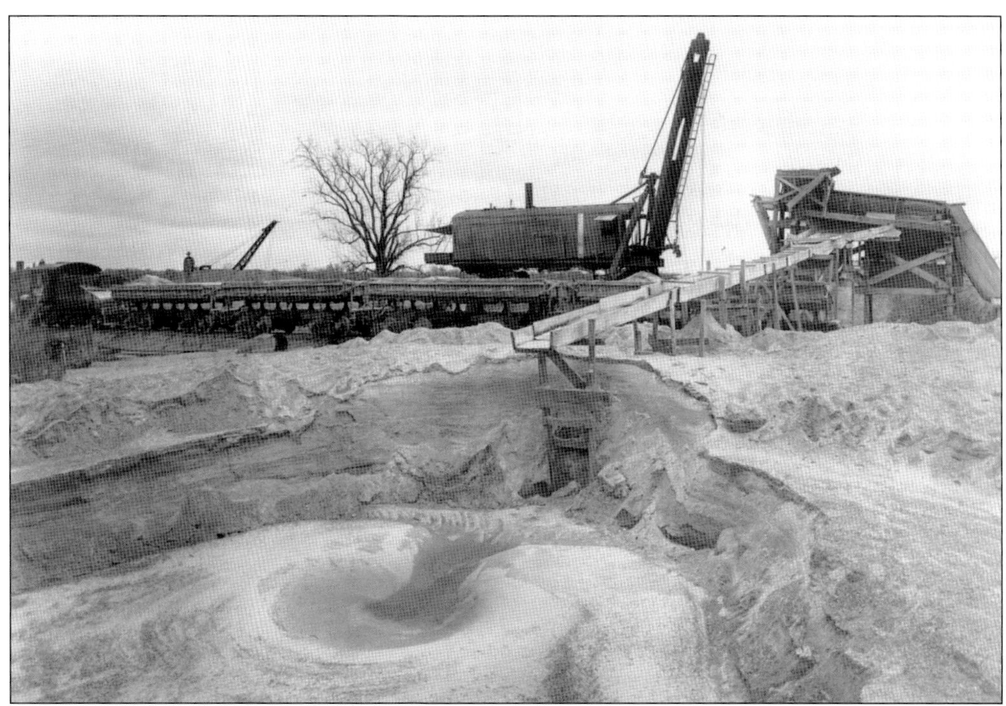

J. FRED SMITH GRAVEL COMPANY, 1912. The J. Fred Smith Gravel Company, Inc., was established in 1912 in the area around Carrollton. The company had a large gravel pit just north of the Sandy Lake Amusement Park property. They shipped large quantities of gravel via the rail lines leading out of Carrollton. (Both courtesy of A. W. Perry Homestead Museum, Ogle Collection.)

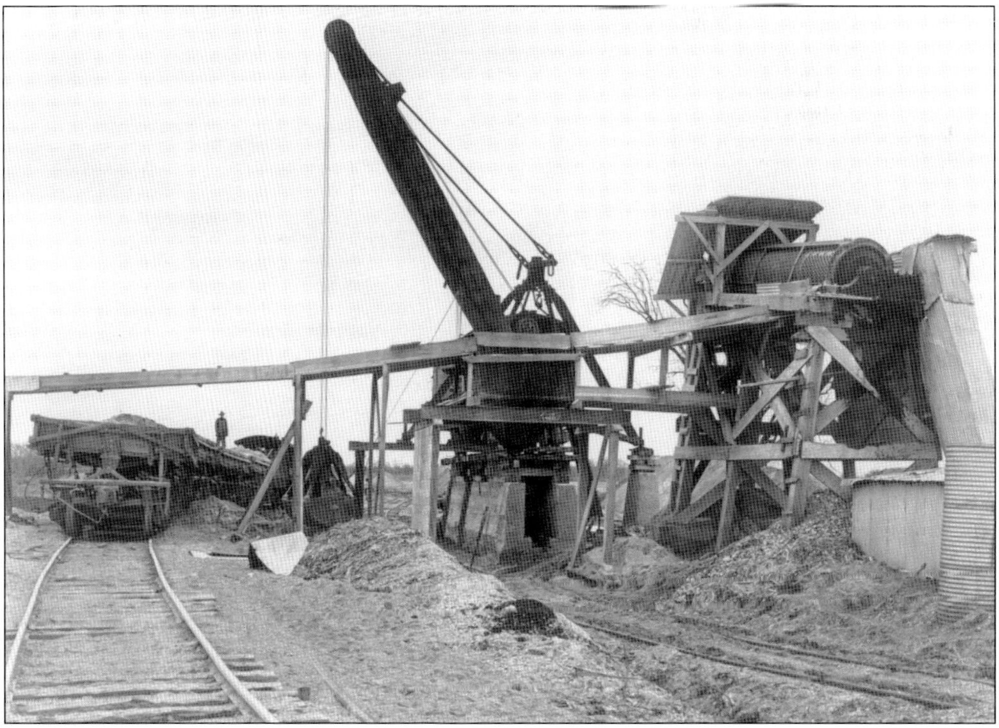

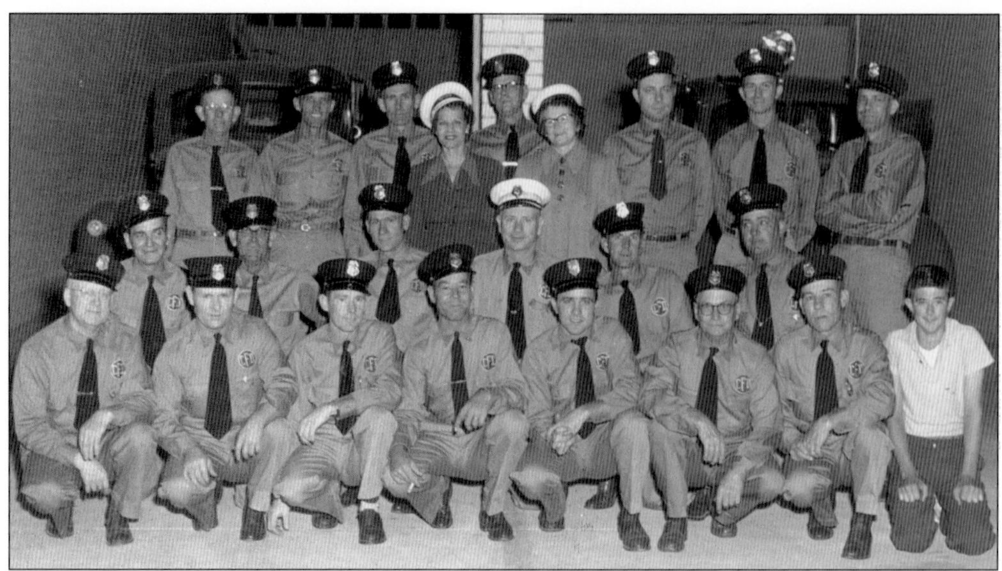

CARROLLTON VOLUNTEER FIRE DEPARTMENT, 1950S. The all-volunteer fire department was started in 1927. After the wives of a couple of the men saw the group fight their first fire without any protective equipment, they raised enough money to buy each member a pair of boots, a helmet, and a slicker. The first fire station was named the Lillie-Ann Hose Company No. 1 in honor of Lillie Patterson and Ann Kennedy, who led the fund-raising effort. A mother and a mascot were chosen each year by the fire department. Lucille Burgess was chosen more years than any other as the mother, and the mascot changed each year and was usually a son of one of the firemen. They constructed their first building in 1939, and in 1951, when the new city hall structure was built on the corner of Denton Drive and Carroll Street, it included a two-story, fireproof structure for the fire department. The first full-time, paid fireman was hired in 1959, and the volunteer service was phased out by the city as more employees were added. (Both courtesy of A. W. Perry Homestead Museum, Ogle Collection.)

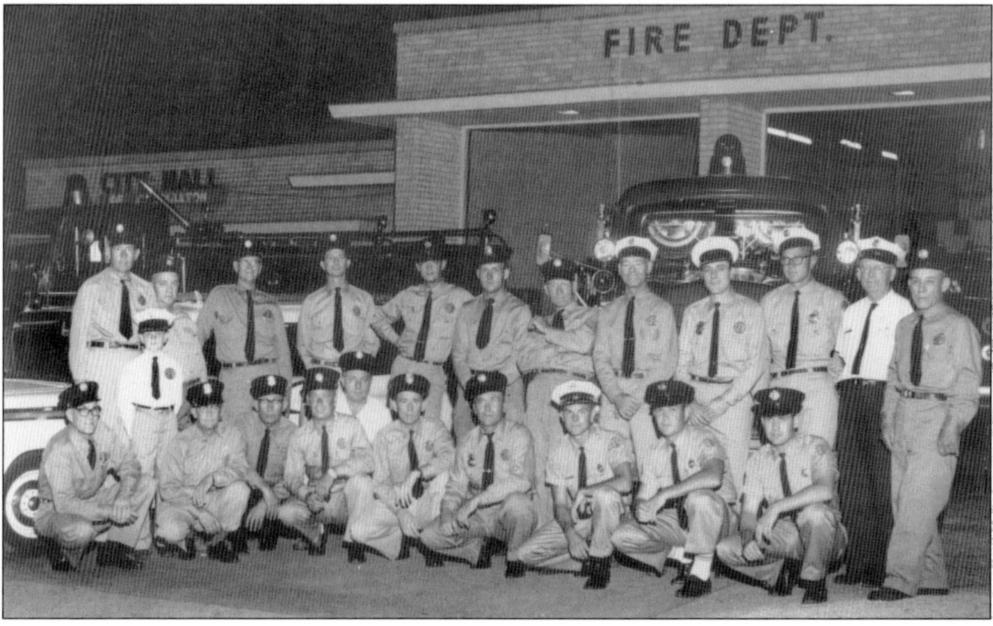

CARROLLTON FIRE DEPARTMENT, 1950S. Volunteer fireman Darrell Myers saved this pig from a well in Addison. Duties of the fire department included rescuing animals, watering the football field, and emptying flooded basements as well as the more serious business of fighting fires, dragging the river and creeks for flood victims, and lecturing in schools about fire prevention. (Courtesy of A. W. Perry Homestead Museum, Ogle Collection.)

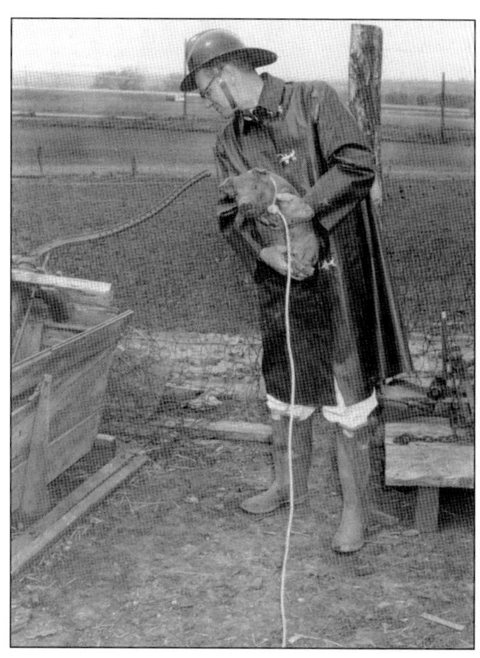

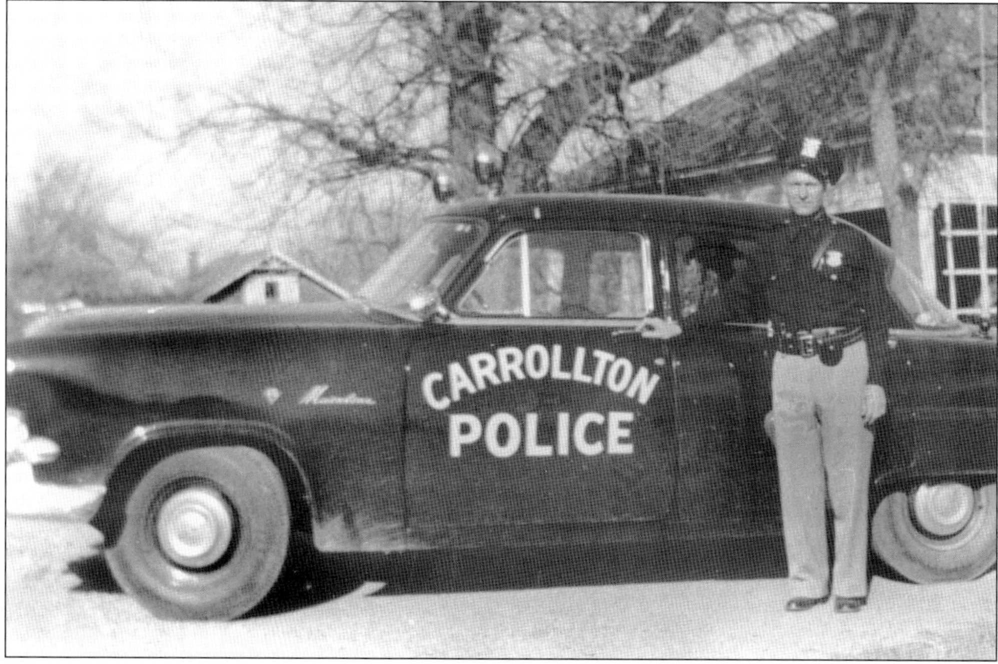

CARROLLTON POLICE DEPARTMENT. H. C. Harrison was appointed the city marshal when the town was incorporated in 1913. The first jail was a 20-foot-by-20-foot wood-frame building along the Katy railroad tracks behind the east side of the square. It was reported that one regular prisoner would get out after dark by prying loose one of the boards, would enjoy a night on the town, and then return to the jail before morning. The first full-time officer was hired in 1947. The office of city marshal was abolished, and the office of police chief was established. Ernest L. "Hobby" James was served as the first police chief until 1950. The first squad car was purchased in 1952. (Courtesy of Carrollton Police Department.)

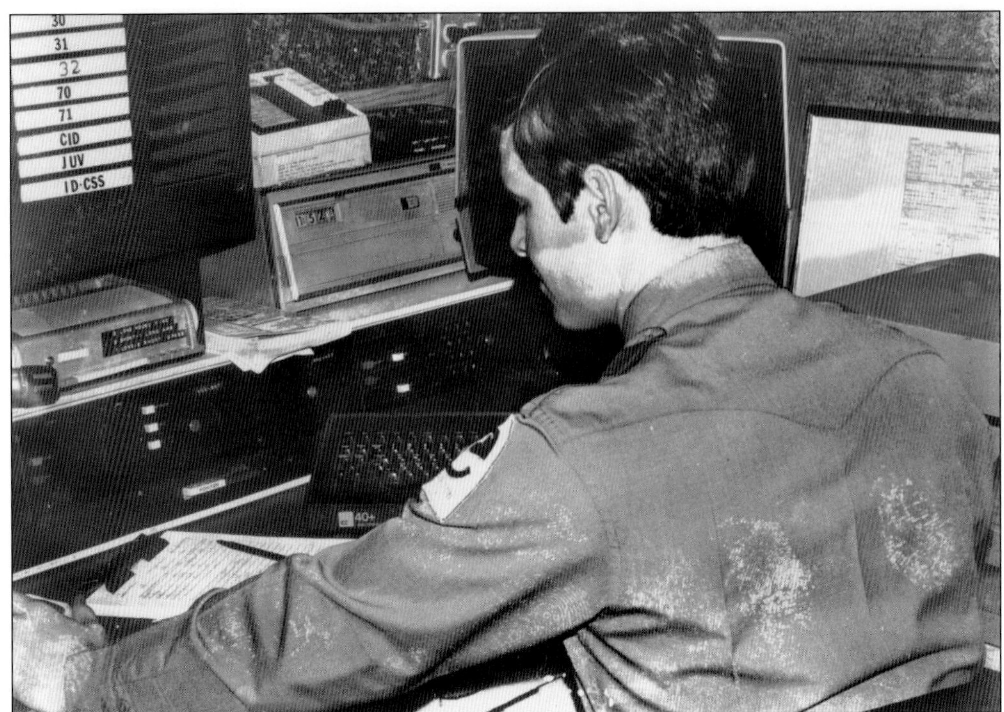

CARROLLTON POLICE DEPARTMENT, RADIO OPERATOR. Two radio-equipped cars were purchased in 1956. There were four full-time officers in 1958 with a population around 4,000 people living within the town's limits. (Courtesy of Carrollton Police Department.)

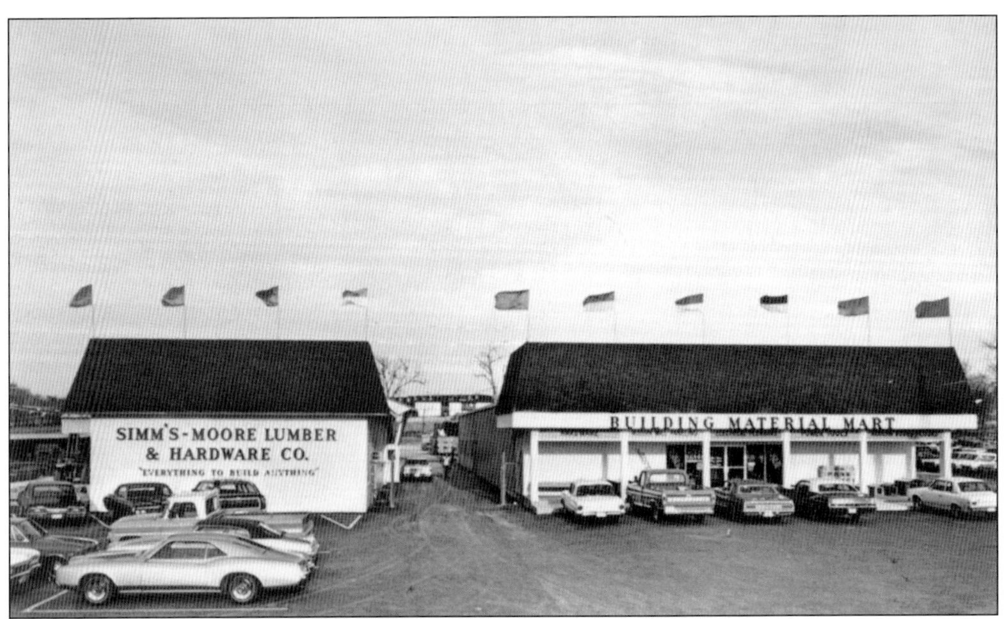

SIMM'S–MOORE LUMBER AND HARDWARE COMPANY, 1974. This postcard is an example of the businesses in Carrollton and the personal service they offered. The lumber company was located on Crosby Road and Stemmons Freeway/Interstate 35. The store manager sent this card to a customer to thank him for his purchase earlier that week. (Courtesy of Ed Williams.)

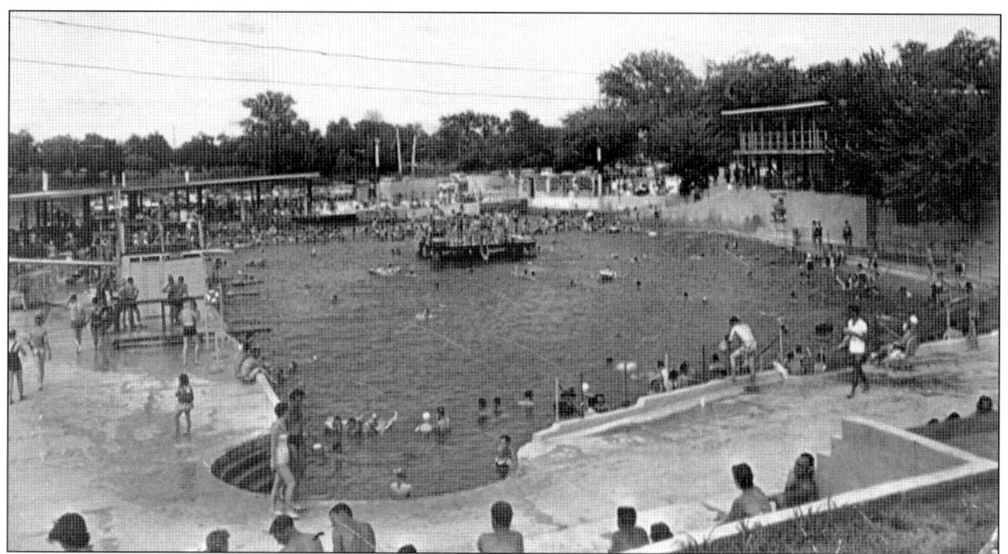

SANDY LAKE POOL, 1961. Advertised as the largest pool in the Southwest, Sandy Lake Pool was a popular destination. The pool boasted a beautiful, spacious picnic area, outdoor fireplaces, and a large dance floor. It could also be rented for private parties. The property would later add amusement park rides and is still open and running as a family business. (Courtesy of Ed Williams.)

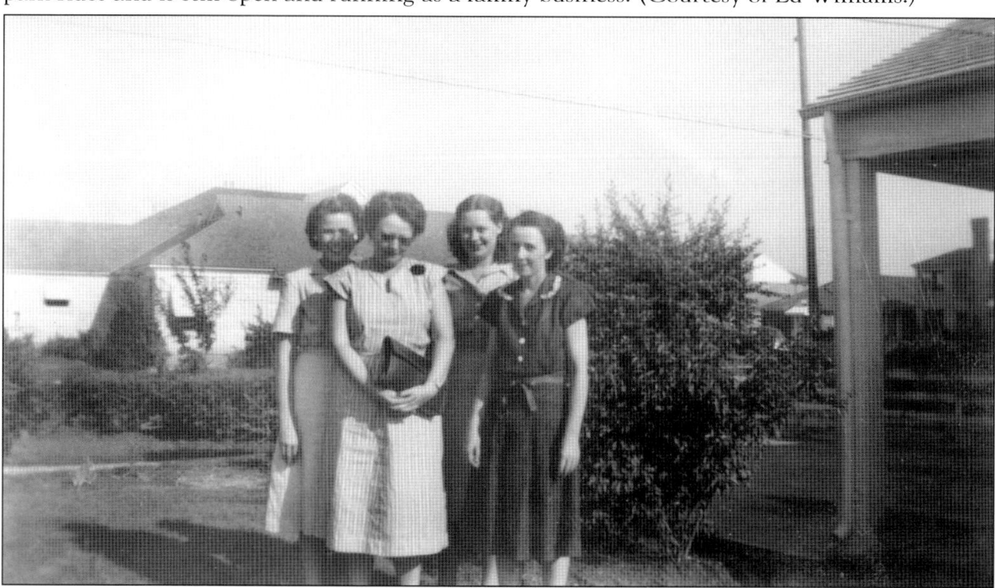

PETERS COLONY HISTORICAL SOCIETY. Georgia Myers Ogle (front left), Olivene Patterson (front right), and two women identified only as McRight and Ogle are pictured here. Ogle and Patterson were two of the charter members of the Peters Colony Historical Society. The idea for the society first took hold during a gathering in the living room of Olivene Patterson, who lived in what is now known as the Carrollton Heights Historic District. The city's 50th anniversary was celebrated in 1963 with a large banquet and a celebration of the city's past, which included residents participating in a show-and-tell by bringing photographs and artifacts from the past. More people began to be interested in preserving Carrollton's history, including Peggy Perry Oliver, who would become a local historian and preservationist and another founding member of the Peters Colony Historical Society. (Courtesy of A. W. Perry Homestead Museum, Ogle Collection.)

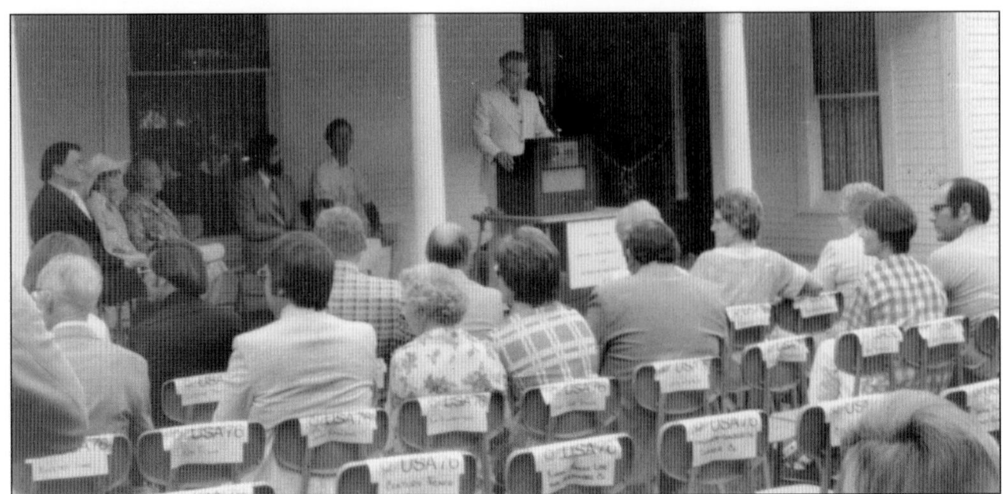

1976 BICENTENNIAL CELEBRATIONS. Carrollton celebrated the U.S. Bicentennial in 1976 with a community project that included the restoration of the 1909 DeWitt Perry home in preparation to open it as a museum dedicated to preserving Carrollton's history. Pearl Perry Gravley donated the home and 10 acres of land to the project, and the city and volunteers worked on it for two years starting in 1974. The opening of the A. W. Perry Homestead Museum took place on Sunday, July 4, 1976. Mayor Ward Steenson spoke at the dedication ceremony. Seated on stage from left to right are Doug Swaringen, museum board chair; Peggy Perry Oliver, historian; Pearl Perry Gravley, donor; Reverend Soper, who gave the invocation; and P. David Smith, chairman of local Bicentennial Commission. (Courtesy of A. W. Perry Homestead Museum, Ogle Collection.)

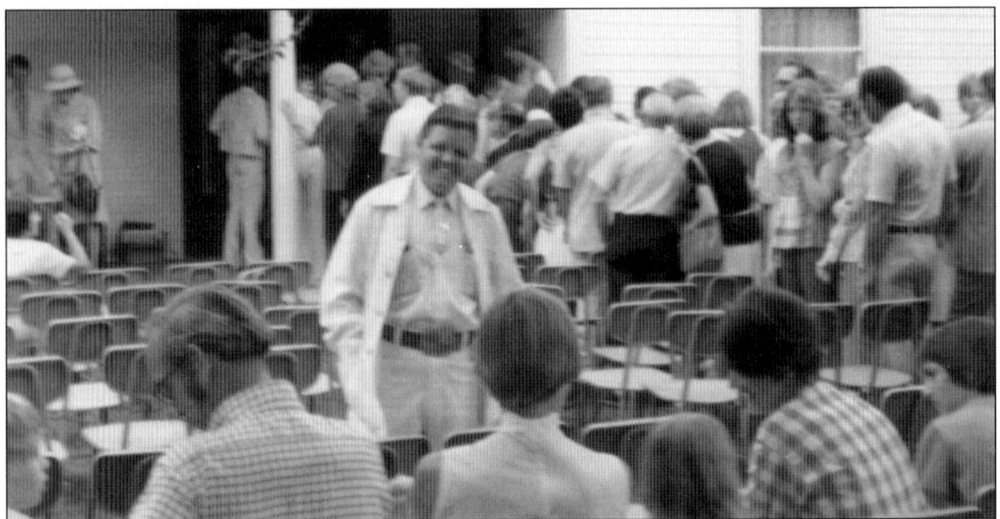

TEXAS JIM COOPER AT THE OPENING OF THE A. W. PERRY HOMESTEAD MUSEUM, 1976. The young man in the center is Texas Jim Cooper. He was a native of Carrollton and wrote for the local newspapers for many years. He was a familiar face at all local events, and he was interested in local history. The bicentennial celebration also included crowning a Miss Bicentennial for Carrollton. The young woman selected was a 16-year-old high school junior named Kathy Grigsby. She listed her hobbies as "riding horses, twirling batons, doing jazz dances, working on her car, and talking on her CB radio as the Midnight Dazzler." There was also a large parade that day and a dance that evening at the Carrollton Civic Center, which is now the Crosby Community Center. (Courtesy of Fancy Oliver Tanner.)

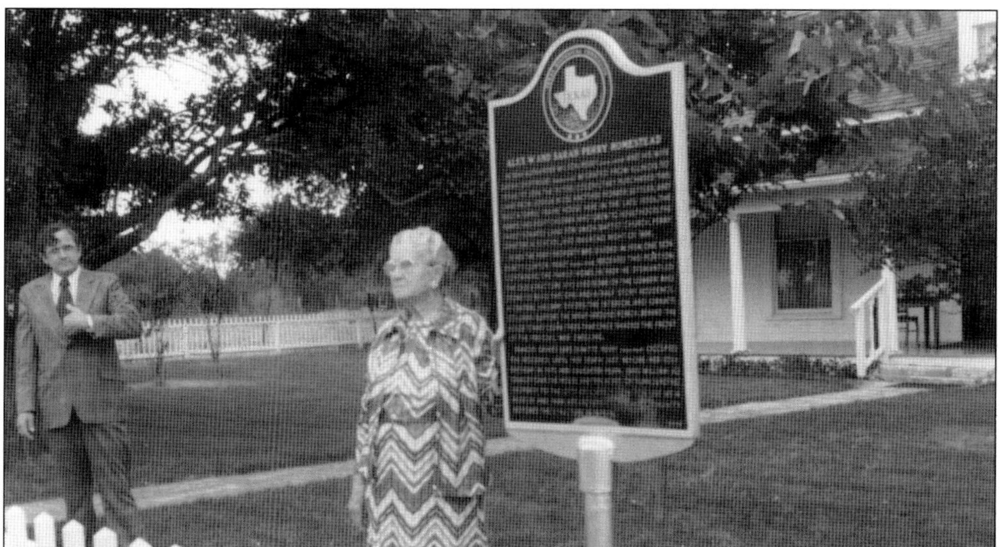

TEXAS STATE HISTORICAL MARKER DEDICATION FOR THE DeWITT AND FRANCIS PERRY HOME, 1977. The Texas Historical Commission recognized the home and property as a historically significant landmark for Texas in 1977. Pearl Perry Gravley, the daughter of DeWitt and Francis and granddaughter of A. W. Perry, stands with her youngest son, Milburn Gravley, at the dedication. Milburn Gravley served on the city council at the time of this photograph and was later elected to the office of mayor several times in the 1980s and 1990s. (Courtesy of A. W. Perry Homestead Museum, Ogle Collection.)

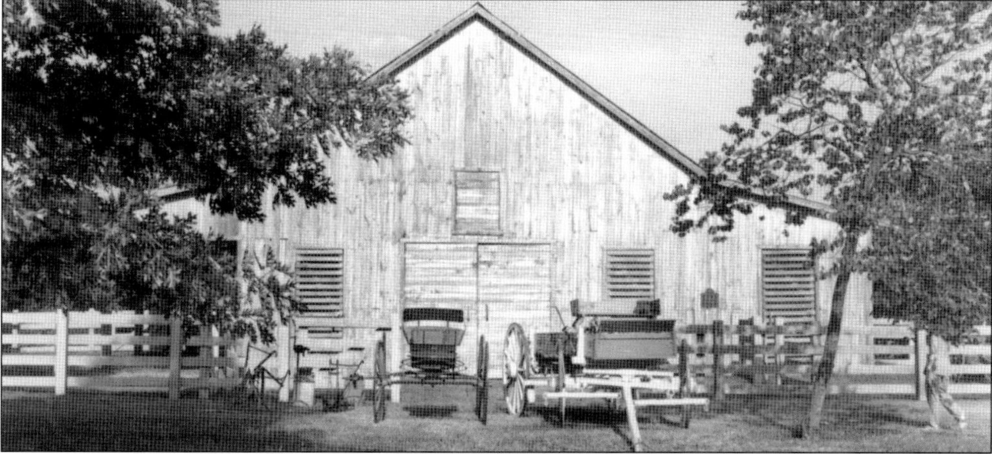

SESQUICENTENNIAL CELEBRATION PROJECT, A. W. PERRY HOMESTEAD MUSEUM BARN, 1986. The City of Carrollton celebrated 150 years of Texas from 1836 to 1986 by building a barn to expand the museum site. Members of the Carrollton Sesquicentennial Committee organized the building of the barn. A driving force behind the research and construction of the barn was Ray Ogle. Ogle was a longtime resident, museum volunteer, charter member of the Peters Colony Historical Society, World War II veteran, and Carrollton's first rural mail carrier. The barn used traditional mortise-and-tenon construction to join the posts, and its construction included salvaged beams from historic barns in the area that were being torn down for development at the time. Ogle shared his knowledge of farm implements and life on a farm with thousands of schoolchildren and other visitors over the years on tours of the barn and home. (Courtesy of A. W. Perry Homestead Museum.)

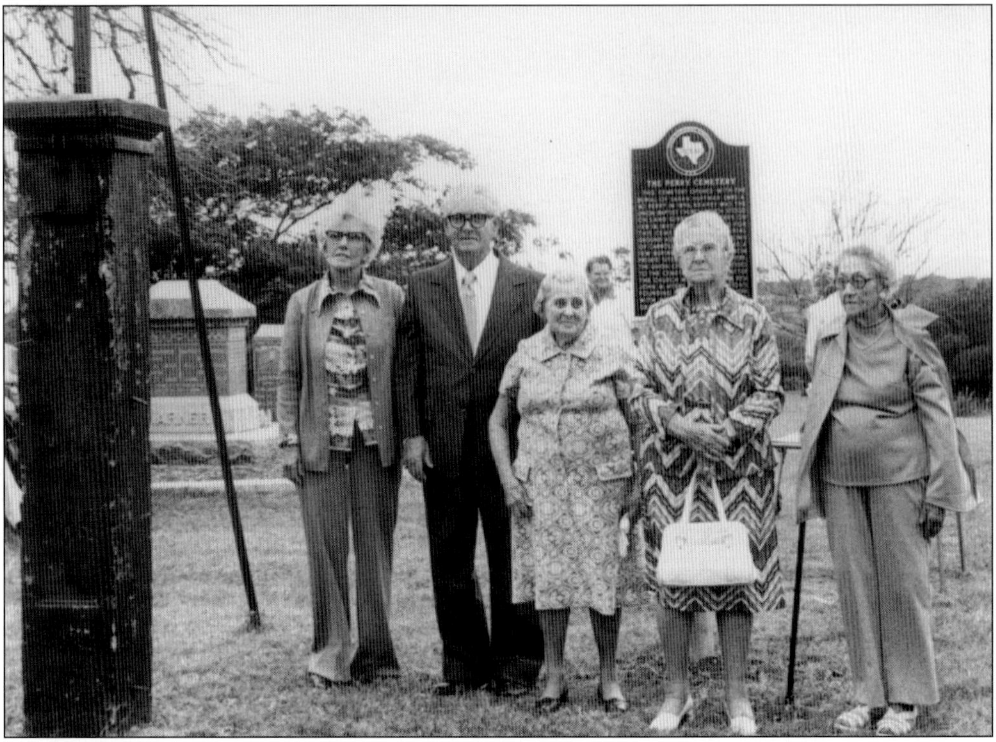

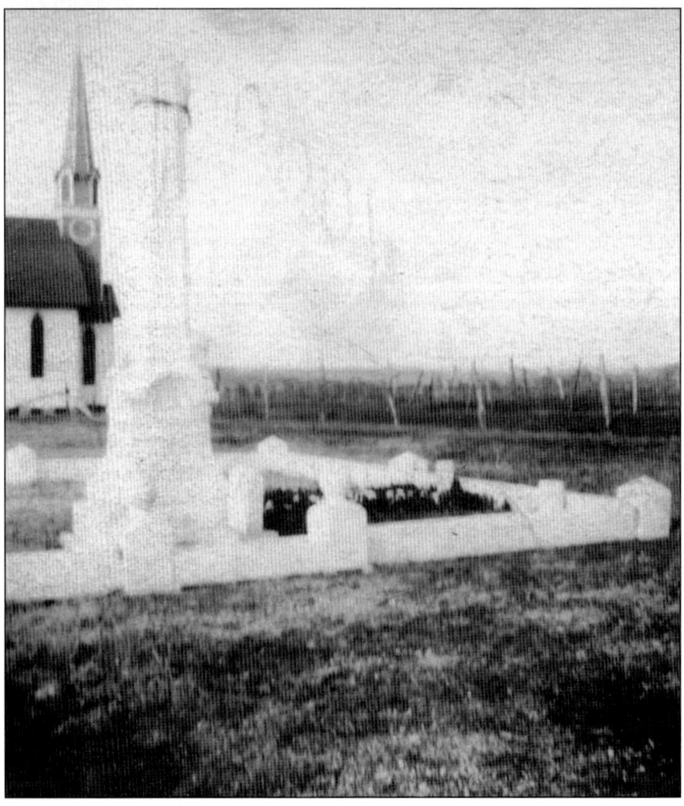

TEXAS STATE HISTORICAL MARKER DEDICATION FOR THE PERRY CEMETERY, 1977. Surviving grandchildren of A. W. Perry gathered for the dedication of the historical marker for Carrollton's first public cemetery. The cemetery opened when A. W. Perry donated land for the cemetery with the burial of his wife, Sarah Huffman Perry, in 1896. The Union Baptist Church was also located on adjacent land also donated by Perry. Pictured from left to right are Alfredda Perry Parkey, Burnett Perry, Sallie Fyke Myers, Pearl Perry Gravley, and Minnie Bell Perry Bailey. (Both courtesy of A. W. Perry Homestead Museum, Ogle Collection.)

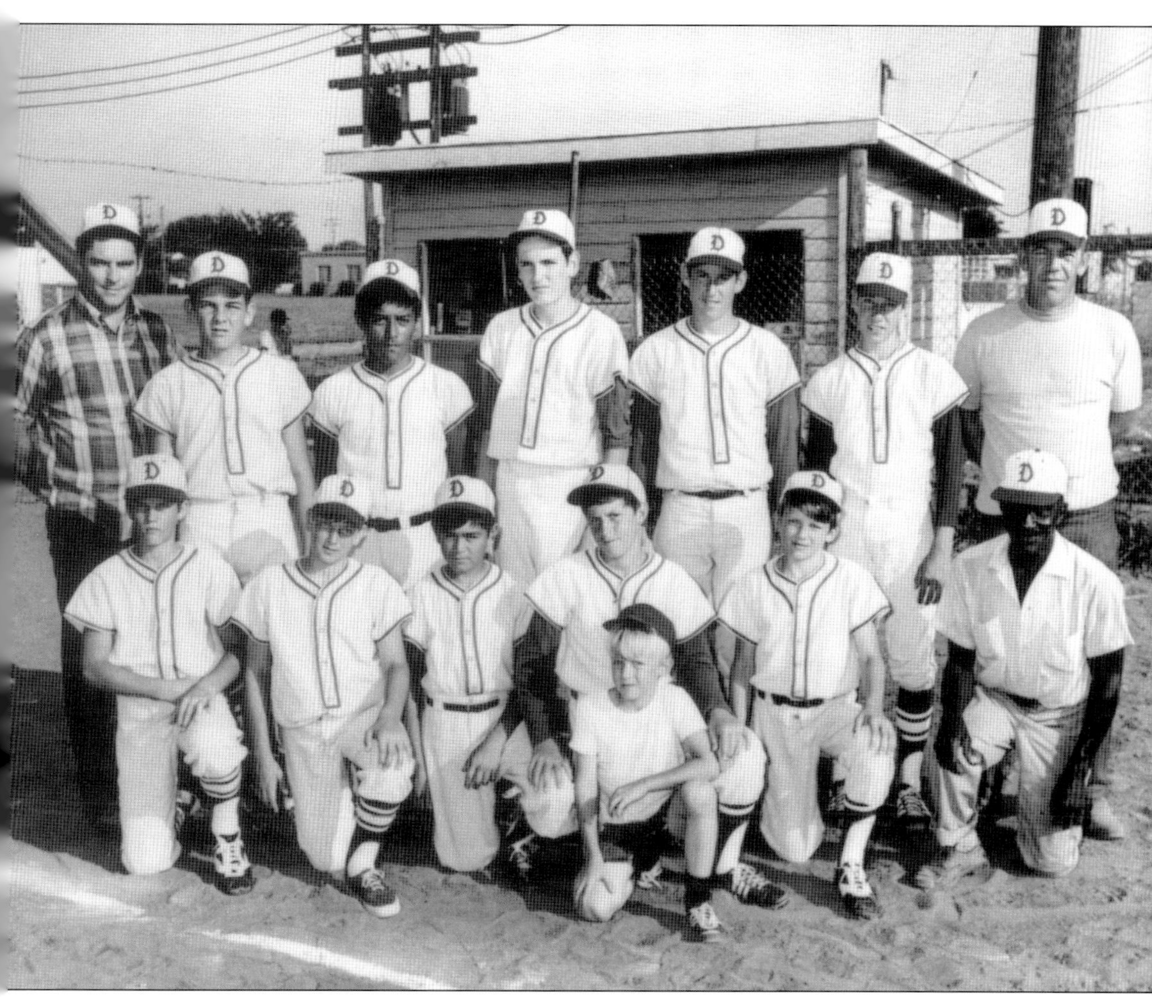

JIMMY PORTER AND JIMMY PORTER PARK. Born in east Texas in 1900, Jimmy Porter moved to Carrollton in 1928 after reportedly spending time playing baseball in the Negro League. Most people in Carrollton knew Jimmy or at least something about him. Porter would walk down the street with his baseball bat and glove slung over his shoulder, and children would follow him to the nearest open field or ballpark for a pick-up game. He taught more than just baseball; he also played horseshoes, football, and instructed children on how to garden, fish, and hunt rabbits. Porter was a man of meager means, and for a time, he lived in a railroad boxcar without electricity or running water. When the land where he lived was developed, the community undertook a fund-raising campaign to build him a small home in the alley of Rosemon Avenue in the Carrollton Heights neighborhood. The community dedicated a Little League baseball park in his name, and he received several other honors during his lifetime, including regional and national press coverage of his story. Jimmy Porter Park is located on the corner of Josey Lane and Sherwood Lane. (Courtesy of A. W. Perry Homestead Museum.)

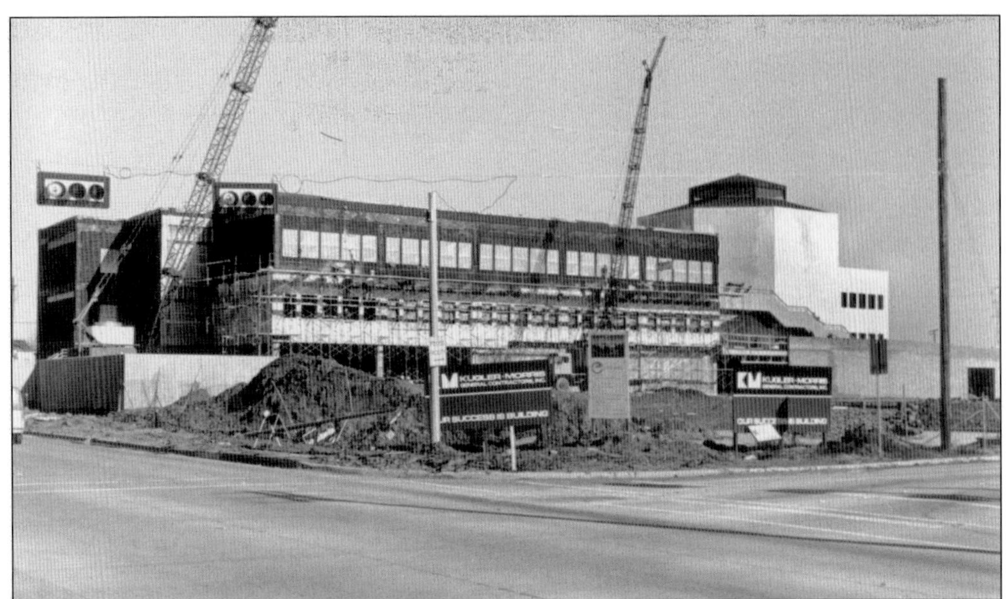

CARROLLTON CITY HALL CONSTRUCTION, 1987. Carrollton's first city hall was constructed in 1933. It was located east of the square on the site of present-day Pioneer Park. It was a two-story, wood-frame structure, which housed the fire truck on the lower level and had offices on the upper level for the city secretary and volunteer fire department and where they held council meetings. A second city hall, which also housed the fire department, was built in 1951 for a cost of $30,000 on land donated by Hooker Vandergriff. (Both courtesy of Carrollton Public Library.)

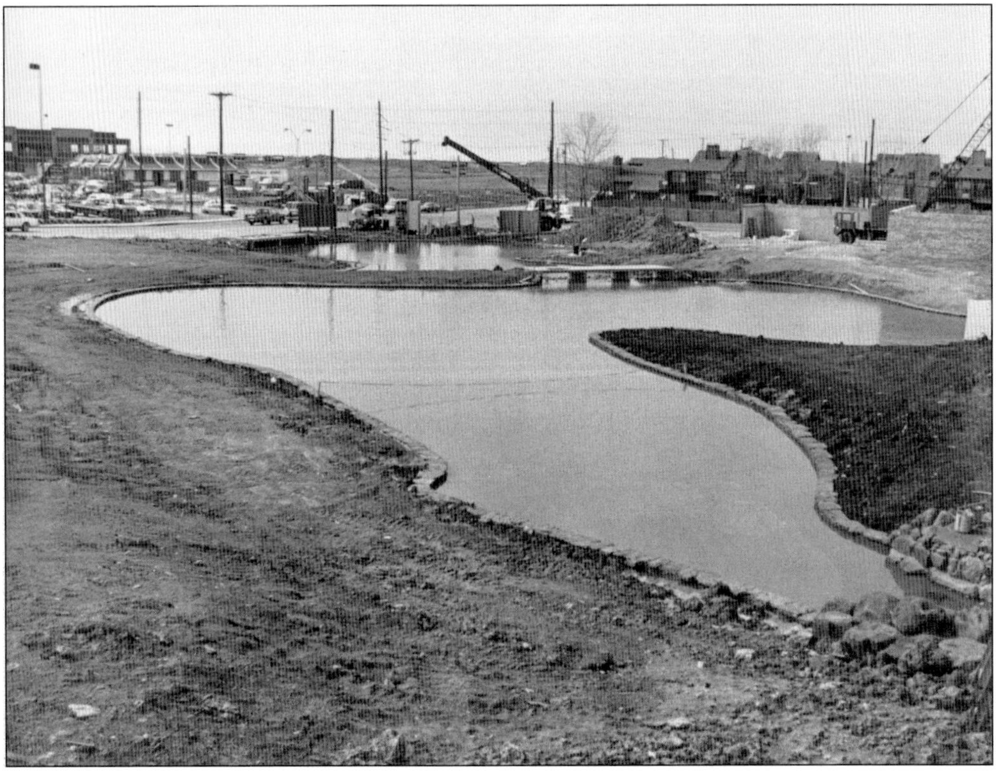

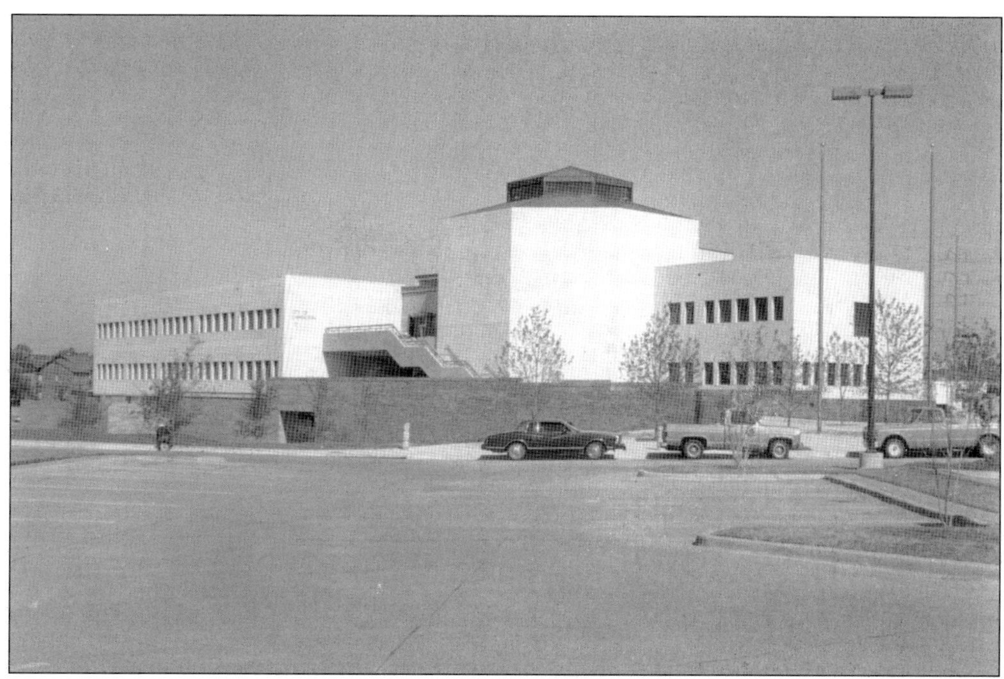

CARROLLTON CITY HALL, 1987. The city hall on Jackson Road and Josey Lane replaced the third city hall at 1002 South Broadway near the square, which opened in 1964. The city's population was growing rapidly and expanding to the north. The population in 1960 was 4,242 people. In 1980, the population had grown to 40,595 people. By the time this structure was completed, the population was close to the 1990 total of 110,000. The new city hall featured Texas limestone and a copper roof for a total cost of $6.4 million. (Courtesy of Carrollton Public Library.)

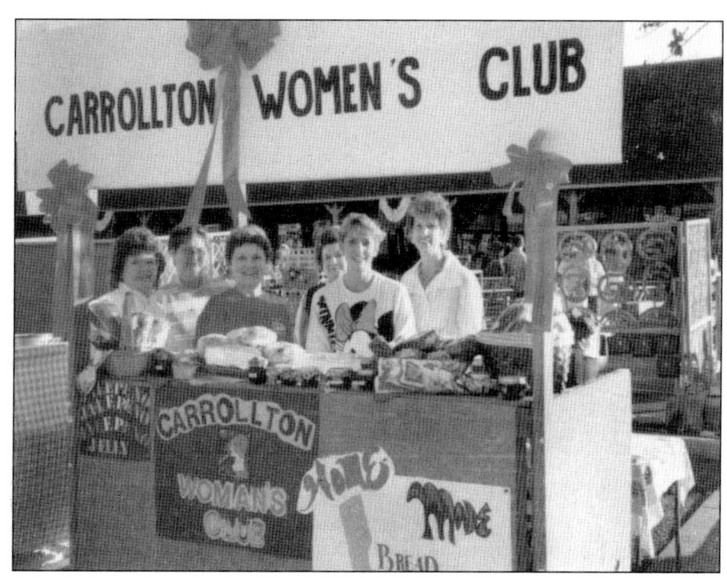

CARROLLTON WOMEN'S CLUB, C. 1985. The Carrollton Country Fair has been held annually from as early as 1921 on the square and features homemade crafts, food, and carnival rides. The Carrollton Women's Club booth from the fair sometime in the mid-1980s featured homemade jams, jellies, and breads. (Courtesy of Carrollton Public Library.)

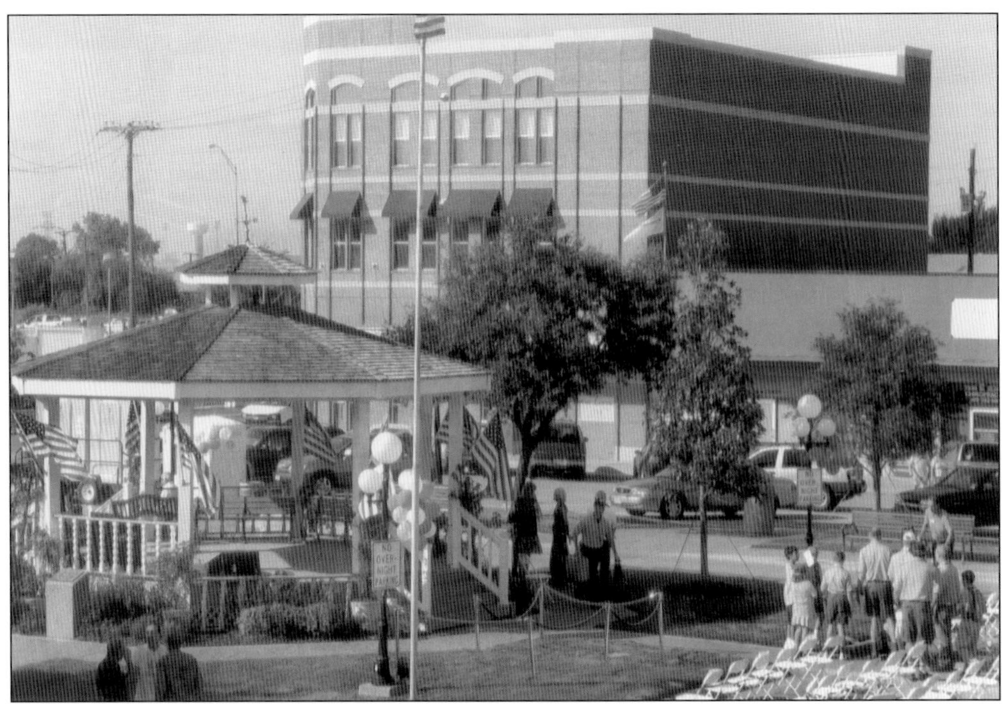

OLD DOWNTOWN CARROLLTON DART STATION GROUND-BREAKING CEREMONY, 2007. Three light-rail stations are planned to begin serving commuters in 2011: the Old Downtown Carrollton station, the Trinity Mills station, and the Frankford station. The ground-breaking ceremony attracted citizens and local and state dignitaries. The station in Old Downtown Carrollton will be a rail hub that connects Carrollton to Dallas by rail for passenger service for the first time since the 1920s Texas Interurban Railway. Future east and west service is planned on the Cotton Belt line. (Courtesy of City of Carrollton.)

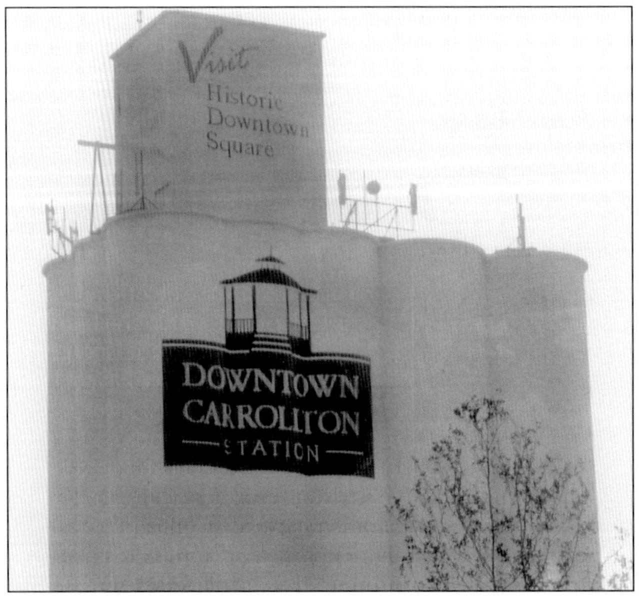

CARROLLTON GRAIN TOWERS, 2007. The historic grain storage towers near the square now house one of the world's tallest indoor climbing gyms. At the ground-breaking ceremony for the Old Downtown Carrollton DART station, the newly painted towers were unveiled along with their new slogan "Visit Historic Downtown Square, Downtown Carrollton Station" painted across the top of the towers, which can be seen by thousands of drivers passing by on Interstate 35 each day. (Courtesy of City of Carrollton.)

BIBLIOGRAPHY

Connor, Seymour. *The Peters Colony of Texas*. Austin, TX: Texas State Historical Association, 1959.

Hogan, William Ransom. *Texas Republic. A Social and Economic History*. Norman, OK: University of Oklahoma Press, 1946.

Jackson, George. *Sixty Years in Texas*. Quanah, TX: Nortex Press, 1975.

Ogle, Georgia Myers. *Elm Fork Settlements. Farmers Branch and Carrollton*. Quanah, TX: Nortex Press, 1977.

Rainwater, Willie. *Annie Heads Rainwater. A Torchbearer for Justice and Freedom. How one woman stood up for justice and equality*. Dallas: Great Impressions, 2001.

Rogers, John William. *The Lusty Texans of Dallas*. New York: Dutton, 1951.